From Revolution to Reunion

From Revolution to Reunion

The Reintegration of the South Carolina Loyalists

Rebecca Brannon

THE UNIVERSITY OF SOUTH CAROLINA PRESS

© 2016 University of South Carolina

Published by the University of South Carolina Press
Columbia, South Carolina 29208

www.sc.edu/uscpress

Manufactured in the United States of America

24 23 22 21 20 19 18 17 16   10 9 8 7 6 5 4 3 2 1

Library of Congress Cataloging-in-Publication Data
can be found at http://catalog.loc.gov/.

ISBN: 978-1-61117-668-1 (hardcover)
ISBN: 978-1-61117-669-8 (ebook)

For my parents and Joan, with thanks from the very bottom of my heart

Contents

Illustrations

Acknowledgments

Years of research inevitably leads to the desire to graciously thank all of the people and institutions that make extended projects such as archive-intensive books possible. And just like the Loyalists I study, sincere apologies are often in order.

I would like to thank my fellow faculty at both James Madison University and the University of South Carolina Aiken for their collegiality. The Interlibrary Loan departments at both institutions were also valuable all along the way. Reference staffers at the South Carolina Department of Archives and History, the South Caroliniana Library, and the South Carolina Historical Society were very helpful. In particular I owe Charles Lesser, Steven Tuttle, and the overworked and harried staff at the South Carolina Department of Archives and History, who have been unfailingly pleasant in the face of constant budget cuts and layoffs. Along the way, I have received valuable research support from the David Library of the American Revolution, the University of Michigan Rackham Graduate School, the Sweetland Writing Center of the University of Michigan, and the graduate fellowships endowment at Amherst College.

Susan Juster shepherded this book through many drafts with her usual insight into what a writer is trying to say, rather than what she would herself do with the material. Thank you so much for your tradition of intellectual generosity. David Hancock provided close reading and analytic comments on multiple drafts. He also reminded me at a crucial moment that the best first book is the done book. Both also generously provided the seemingly constant infusion of recommendation letters that a career in academia requires. The University of Michigan history department was an incredible place to study history. My additional mentors J. Mills Thornton and Susan Scott Parrish were also instrumental in helping shape this project. Of course, I would never have become the historian I am today without the influence of Kevin M. Sweeney, David Blight, and Margaret Hunt, who guided me into the study of history as an intellectual endeavor while at Amherst College.

I certainly owe thanks to the following people, who all read and commented on at least one chapter of the work in progress, for their carefully marshaled thoughts. I owe Skip Stout and the participants in the 2010 NEH and Calvin College seminar on Religion, War, and the Meaning of America, Linda K. Kerber and the participants of the 2009 NEH and New York Historical Society seminar on constitutional history, and the participants in the history department reading group of the University of Mississippi, the American History Workshop at the University of Michigan, and the history department brownbag colloquium at James Madison University. All of these forums provided a chance to get thoughtful and candid feedback on earlier drafts. Tamar Carroll, Kevin Hardwick, Jeffrey Kosoriek, and Marc Lerner read sections of the manuscript as it moved to completion. Robert M. Calhoon, Sheila Skemp, and the anonymous readers for the University of South Carolina Press generously read the entire manuscript and made pointed comments that vastly improved the project. In some cases I did not understand how wise the suggestions were until I was almost done with the manuscript. I owe Alex Moore at the University of South Carolina Press and David Gleeson for recognizing the promise of the manuscript even when it was still a little rough at the edges.

Over the years friends and colleagues in Ann Arbor, Oxford, Aiken, and Harrisonburg have been invaluable. Thanks to Natalia Bowdoin, Tamar Carroll, David Dillard, Chris Dodsworth, Kevin Hardwick, Kaetrena Davis Kendrick, Jeffery Kosoriek, Marc Lerner, Amanda Moniz, Maggie Morehouse, Jeremy Peirce, Alison Sandman, Lars Schumann, Deborah Solomon, Kari and Dulaney Weaver—tech support, astute readers, drinking buddies, conversationalists, and so much more.

Thanks to my parents, who provided me with the wonderful Amherst education that has allowed me to flourish. Thanks too for the supportive calls, and good company. Joan and Anthony Brannon encouraged my joy in intellectual pursuits for a long time, and both enjoy history themselves. My father would probably say I study the wrong war, but I have never doubted that they are always in my corner. My sister, Hillary Brannon, was a history major herself and is always supportive.

And thanks so much to Joan Anderson, for making it possible and for making it worthwhile. She has moved twice with me as I pursue the academic life. She was even willing to move to Aiken without ever seeing it, which seems the very definition of love. Her good humor always makes our days enjoyable, and her warm smile always brings joy. Seth Anderson-Brannon arrived as I finally saw the light at the end of the tunnel with this book. He too makes life sweeter and more intense—l'chaim, sweet Seth. Mommy can play choo-choo now.

A Note on Terms

Throughout this work I use the term *Loyalist* in preference to *Tory* to refer to people who were associated with the British cause during the American Revolution. I maintain the use of the word *Tory* in quotations to render the strong hatreds of the time intact. I further use *Loyalist* even though many of the people I talk about were probably not motivated by ideology at all. On the other side, unlike many recent historians, I have chosen to use *Patriot* to refer to those who supported the cause of American independence during the war. Many recent writers have used *Whig* instead so as to avoid suggesting that Loyalists were not themselves patriotic. While I agree that many Loyalists were brave, patriotic people, I have maintained the older use of *Patriot* in the service of clearly delineating the differences between the two sides without unduly emphasizing any specific political ideology such as the Whig cause might suggest. In fact strongly ideological South Carolinians were rare.

I use *Loyalist* and *Patriot* to mean white Loyalists and Patriots exclusively throughout most of this book. I am well aware that thousands of Africans and African Americans supported the Loyalist cause and are usually identified as the black Loyalists. In addition several southern Native American tribes supported the Loyalist cause as well. However the majority of this book deals with the intertwining fates of white Patriots and Loyalists after the war. White Patriots and Loyalists united in ignoring black and Native American participation and interests in the fate of South Carolina. Therefore in the interests of clarity and concision, I have simply avoided racial and ethnic identifiers when the context makes it clear I mean white folks. In places where such identities might be in doubt, such as discussions of the war itself, I use *white Loyalist* and *black Loyalist*. Given that black South Carolinians did not consider the Patriot side to be a source of freedom, and therefore never chose that side, you will not read anything about black Patriots in this book.

Finally Charleston was usually identified as Charles Town in documents of the eighteenth century. I have maintained that designation in quotations but have used Charleston consistently in the text.

* Introduction

This is certain, that a man that studieth revenge keeps his own wounds green, which otherwise would heal and do well.

Francis Bacon, "On Revenge," 1625

He that forgets and forgives most . . . is the best citizen.

Christopher Gadsden to General Francis Marion, Nov. 17, 1782

Elite and ordinary, enslaved and free—when civil war came to South Carolina in the American Revolution, no one was spared. The elite Ball family of low-country South Carolina was split by the Revolution. While one Ball brother fought in the Patriot militia from 1775 on, his brother Elias Ball (of Comingtee) and cousin Elias Ball (of Wambaw) ultimately ended up espousing Loyalism. (The family began to call family members by the name of the plantations they owned so as to clearly separate so many relatives proudly carrying the same name.) Prominent Patriot leader Henry Laurens had married a Ball sister, keeping his side of the family firmly ensconced in the Patriot cause. Yet most of the family, like many others around them, instead became Loyalists out of self-interest. They accepted British protection and later took positions in the Loyalist militias in an effort to maintain their lives, their status, and their fortunes. In so doing they represent the majority of South Carolina Loyalists in that they all became Loyalists for pragmatic reasons. Elias Ball of Comingtee had an undistinguished military career in which, like many others, he avoided actually fighting and molesting local Patriots. Elias Ball of Wambaw may or may not have been a more ideologically convinced Loyalist, but he was a better military leader and rose to colonel in the Loyalist forces. When the Revolution ended, this military prowess backfired on Wambaw Elias Ball, and he joined the minority of white Loyalists who actually left the country and established new lives in the Loyalist diaspora. Unfortunately he also tried to take his (and others') slaves with him, and he was even willing to starve his slaves to try to force them into being captured and transported. In the end he used his considerable investment in human beings to fund both his establishment in

England and his eventual settlement with the British government for £12,700 and a lifetime pension.

Yet the story does not end there. What about all those other Loyalist relatives? Elias Ball of Comingtee was typical of the wide swath of South Carolina Loyalists (as was the rest of his family) in not leaving South Carolina with the last of the British troops in December 1782. The South Carolina legislature had confiscated his property and banished him from the colony along with 166 other local Loyalists (out of many thousands). Wisely Ball ignored this and instead began to look for ways to apologize and reconcile with his neighbors and the wider community. He turned to his uncle by marriage, Henry Laurens, who was at the time not simply a well-off Patriot but one of the American negotiators for the eventual peace treaty. Like most Patriot South Carolinians, Laurens was willing to extend the olive branch to Loyalist relatives and friends who put themselves out there to apologize and seek to renew those ties of neighborliness. Laurens was willing to offer Ball a position as his plantation overseer on his Georgia lands and hoped that "the time is coming when I shall take [him] again into my arms as a friend." Laurens's offer was generous but not entirely without self-interest, as Ball could serve as his Georgia overseer and would cultivate all the land with his own slaves, making profits for both men. Laurens was willing to do this despite the fact that he found his nephew's first attempt at an apology unsatisfactory.

Victorious Patriots found it vital, for their own emotional healing and willingness to reintegrate Loyalists, that those Loyalists apologized and made personal efforts to reconnect with their neighbors. In the case of the Laurens/Ball family, Laurens warmed considerably toward his nephew when Ball finally offered him a personal apology (or at least an apology that Laurens found satisfactory). He responded to Ball's 1783 overtures with pleasure that he had "discuss[ed] the matter of [his] political conduct & the part [he] took in the late cruel and unjust persecution of your Country" with "reflection." It was that reflection, or rather the emotional tenor of the letter, and the frankness of the apology that finally moved Laurens to see Ball as a figure deserving of mutual efforts at reconciliation. Still he could not resist the chance to chasten Ball a little, chiding him for not having enough "resolution to persevere in a cause which you had engaged in & knew to be righteous." In the end Laurens accepted his nephew's attempt to apologize and reintegrate himself in family and neighborly connections—so much so that he was willing to help Ball in his efforts to escape South Carolina's decree of confiscation and banishment. Undoubtedly Ball, like others, reached out to other family and friends just as he did to Laurens. In the end it worked. Like a majority of white Loyalists who faced confiscation, he was relieved of the penalty of confiscation and banishment in 1784. His gamble, and his willingness to suffer the temporary discomforts of a little personal embarrassment as he apologized and was gently chided by others, paid off with a comfortable reestablishment for himself and his children and grandchildren.[1]

The family saga did not end there. Even now-absent Wambaw Elias Ball continued to have cordial, even close, relationships with his South Carolina family for years after leaving for England. This was true even though he sometimes complained about American independence in his letters to them. He was also able to use his personal connections with South Carolinians to build a new business in England as a merchant specializing in the importation of rice—in other words, he used his former neighbors as his clients. His family, like so many other South Carolinians, worked to put the war behind them. They practiced a careful selective memory publicly and privately. At first loyalism was the elephant in the room. Yet with the passing of time, and the astute manipulation of memory within families, social circles, and public events, South Carolinians came genuinely to forget about their Loyalist past. As the Revolutionary generation died, the South Carolina–born family lost touch with their relatives on the other side of the Atlantic. It was only at that point, when South Carolinians had healed the wounds of revolutionary civil war, that "Wambaw Elias Ball" became a figure used to scare children. The "Wambaw Elias" was a "mean fella" who captured his own runaway slaves and sold them before departing for England (which was true). His portrayal as the family Tory lived on, coming to match the later nineteenth-century portrayal of Loyalists as especially cruel, hard people.[2]

Noted historian John Shy once questioned "how a national polity so successful, and a society so relatively peaceful, could emerge from a war so full of bad behavior, including perhaps a fifth of the population actively treasonous (that is, loyal to Crown)."[3] This work provides an answer. Both vengeance and forgiveness are cross-cultural human behaviors. The whys are historically specific, but the instincts are deeply human. Therefore the right question is not why South Carolinians considered and acted on both instincts after the American Revolution, but why the more unusual option of forgiveness became the dominant way South Carolinians and their state government ultimately responded to the plight of Loyalists.

It was certainly not foreordained. South Carolinians had experienced a brutal civil war that swept the entire state in the last few years of the American Revolution. Despite their historic differences, the lowcountry and the backcountry were united in suffering from 1780 through 1782. The American Patriot victory at Yorktown did not clearly end the war from the vantage point of southerners, who found their major port cities still occupied by British and Loyalist troops, Loyalist militias still conducting raids on their farms, and their people still imprisoned or huddled on their properties wondering when the next raid would come. In fact some of the worst atrocities of the war in South Carolina came after Yorktown, as frustrated Loyalist militiamen took out their anger on Patriot militiamen who tried to surrender after otherwise routine small engagements. Tales of frenzied atrocity filled the ears of Loyalist and Patriot alike. It is true that these tales were almost always exaggerated, but they set the mood for each side to be unforgiving. And yet in reality most South Carolinians brushed these off and dealt generously with the majority of Loyalists.

All Americans pursued official governmental sanctions and punishments for Loyalists during and after the American Revolution. South Carolina was in the mainstream of American states in choosing to pursue harsh punishments for at least a few, making some Loyalists public figures of derision and schadenfreude for frightened, angry, and shaken Patriots. South Carolinians joined with the citizens of all other American states in enacting official, government-sanctioned confiscation and banishment for some male Loyalists. Yet this fact obscures how few Loyalists ultimately faced this ultimate postwar punishment. The 1782 legislative assembly (which South Carolina histories refer to as the Jacksonborough Assembly) looked like hostile ground for Loyalists, since it was dominated by Patriot military officers and governmental leaders who until recently had been imprisoned or were fugitives. Further this was a legislature that had more backcountry representation than ever before. To the extent that the backcountry had suffered unrestrained, chaotic violence more than the lowcountry, this meant that a sizable number of legislators had suffered deeply for the Patriot cause and had reason to hate and fear Loyalists. This boded ill for the cause of Loyalist clemency from the government and reintegration into society.

Victorious Patriots gave vent to great rhetorical steam, yet in the end restrained themselves from acting on it. They literally chose the strategy of talking out their rage. Historians who have considered the matter have long enjoyed quoting the always fiery, often earthy Aedanus Burke on his fellow South Carolinians' unholy lust for revenge. "The inveterate hatred & spirit of Vengeance wch. they have excited in the breasts of our Citizens is such as you can form no idea of. The very females talk as familiarly of shedding blood & destroying the Tories as the men do." Burke was horrified that people might even admit to wanting revenge and used the specter of women openly advocating for executing Loyalists to animate his horrified vision of a society spinning out of control as the lust for revenge overcame the self-control and refinement required to make any society, let alone a democratic republic, function. Yet this flurry of spoken and epistolary conversation rehearsing the pleasure of revenge turned out to be just that—revenge talk. When the actual time came to exact punishment, again and again South Carolina Patriots turned out to be generous and mild in their treatment of Loyalists. While Burke condemned the loose talk of vengeance he claimed to hear in every parlor he visited, he seems to have misunderstood his fellow citizens. Up to a point, endlessly rehearsing vengeance served as an escapist fantasy that allowed South Carolina Patriots to release their anger rather than wreak the vengeance they spoke of so frequently. Recent research in evolutionary psychology shows that human brains (at least the parts of the brain related to reward and pleasure) receive stimulation in the anticipation of watching someone receive just punishment. All that parlor talk was actually stimulating pleasure centers in the brain—a powerful incentive to continue talking about vengeance. Yet research also shows that the anticipation of watching someone get justly punished is more pleasurable than actually seeing the punishment. The reality of watching punishment, even when the observer believes it to be deserved, is not satisfying. Instead of wiping the slate clean, it simply encourages the person who felt wronged to dwell on the injustices they faced and their anger about their treatment. In fact evolutionary psychology supports what people have long suspected: it is better to forgive than to nurse anger, however justified.[4]

Generations of literary and religious thinkers have incessantly preached about the virtues of forgiveness. And generations of people have cheerfully ignored these nagging voices—because forgiving and forgetting is very hard. So what is remarkable about South Carolinians' behavior in the years after the American Revolution is the way in which they embraced reintegration of the Loyalists, which required them at least to extend governmental forgiveness at a time when they could have chosen to punish Loyalists harshly instead. Why did they choose to turn the other cheek? Perhaps all Americans were more generous to vanquished Loyalists than we have believed.

Historians of American Loyalism have long favored those who left (and were forced into diaspora) over those who stayed. In part this is because the Loyalists who did leave included many articulate, committed, and elite individuals. Wealthy Loyalists who relocated to London wrote witty letters complaining about the cost of living and the difficulties of diasporic living. Even better they left large caches of these letters that are now held in major archives—which are understandably very attractive to historians. White Loyalists who fled to Nova Scotia are of especial interest to Canadian historians because their anger bled into nineteenth-century Canadian politics for generations. And the Loyalist diaspora has also commanded historical attention due to what Maya Jasanoff has termed the "social diversity of Loyalism." Tavern keepers and bakers joined merchants and planters on British-provided transport ships that took them to new lives across the British Empire. The social diversity of Loyalism encompassed black Loyalists as well. Across the South, and certainly in South Carolina, some 20 percent of the prewar slave population sought freedom by joining the British cause. These black Loyalists had to join the Loyalist diaspora, since if they stayed in the South they would either be summarily executed or sent back into lifetime bondage. This social diversity is also of great interest to historians, as it makes Loyalism and the resulting Loyalist diaspora a moment of transatlantic linkages of ideology mixed with an incredible array of people of widely varying experiences.[5]

Nevertheless some Loyalists faced real devastation. The sad advertisements that the British would arrange final transportation for Loyalists stranded in Charleston were chilling to those trying to decide what to do. While some huddled in Charleston waiting for the ships, others wrote letters and otherwise tried to feel out the lay of the land with their former communities. Many found a lukewarm acceptance and chose to slip out of occupied Charleston and return to their lands or stay in the city and await the arrival of Patriot troops as the British withdrew. Comingtee Elias Ball suggested to a relative that he had approached Patriot neighbors and tried to reconcile with them. At first he was harshly rebuffed, even threatened with a public whipping or lynching. Yet no one acted on the threat, and then the possibility of revenge faded from his life. Certainly almost four thousand people, white and black, found themselves compelled to board those ships in the chilly harbor in December 1782. Perhaps they told their children they were going on an adventure—but the adults knew better.[6]

Still those sad, lonely Loyalists who joined the diaspora were the minority of white Loyalists. The majority of white Loyalists stayed and helped build the new United States. They were able to convince victorious Patriots that they too would help build a strong nation despite their wartime conduct (or more accurately their wartime lack of principles). They did this by convincing others that they possessed the character traits and neighborly qualities necessary to maintain a stable society. Further they convinced their Patriot neighbors that forgiveness and reintegration would create a stronger, more generous understanding of citizenship and belonging that would ultimately redound favorably on all Americans.

Loyalist reintegration depended on local community ties that were strong enough to survive the intense chaos and anger of South Carolina's civil war in the American Revolution. The white Loyalists who were successful in negotiating reintegration depended on rebuilding and strengthening their ties to their neighbors and greater community. When they were able to demonstrate convincingly their solid immersion in the flexible yet tensile bonds that held eighteenth-century communities together, they were able to avoid or evade governmental punishment as well as shape social, political, and economic reintegration into the postwar state. Finally these ongoing robust ties allowed Loyalists and Patriots alike to shape a culture that made forgetting seem effortless—so much so that the reality of South Carolina's legacy of sizable, armed Loyalist efforts slipped out of public conversation and eventually out of public memory. By the nineteenth century, Loyalists who had feared the "stigma to the rising generation" found that their children and grandchildren faced no stigma at all.[7] Loyalist families gave rise to grandchildren who even helped promulgate a burnished view of the Patriot cause for themselves, their communities, and future generations. Ann Pamela Cunningham, the woman who did more than anyone to preserve Mount Vernon as a hagiographic shrine to George Washington, was the granddaughter of a Loyalist commander— and knew it.

Every step in the process of reconciliation depended on these community ties and the ability of local people to make decisions about each individual. Even at a time when Enlightenment values of universality and individualism were reshaping both politics and culture, in practice these values rested on a much older network of community ties. Grand ideals about individualism depended on more traditional mores to restrain and shape those individualistic impulses. Further victorious Patriots had the need to feel a sense of control over their own circumstances. One outlet for that need for some control was the ability to decide on the fates of individual Loyalists. So what the state got in practice was a halting, messy process of Loyalist reintegration that ultimately turned out to be generous at each stage along the way and overall added up to a mass reintegration of a sizable majority of white Loyalists.

So when the state legislature met to consider the individual names of Loyalists who might be subjects of official punishment, those individual names were read out and debated by a legislature that claimed to know the reputation and character of each man. Spirited discussions broke out over some individuals—about both what they had actually done during the war and how much money their estate would bring in for the state if it was confiscated and sold. Legislators also were moved to help individuals they knew, at least if they felt their local communities would welcome them back. A cynic might say they helped their own friends only, and there might be something to that. But what stands out from the process of choosing these Loyalists who avoided legislative punishment from the beginning is that they had already approached their neighbors and friends either at the safe distance of epistolary conversation or at the considerably more risky and emotionally immediate level of standing in front of them and engaging in personal conversation. Loyalists apologized and worked to rebuild their connections. It was this humbling process of solidifying preexisting relationships that allowed Patriots to support former Loyalists in their efforts to evade official punishment. And it worked.

South Carolinians were generous in extending legislative clemency to the vast majority of Loyalists. The legislature ultimately chose to single out fewer than 300 white male Loyalists who had used their elite positions in society to help the British cause at high levels. Of those 277 men found themselves suffering the harshest punishment the legislature levied—complete confiscation of their estates and banishment from the state. While this was a very harsh punishment that set out to make those men and their families poor and dependent on the generosity (or, usually, lack of generosity) of the British government, it was kinder than the summary executions some soldiers faced during the war. Another 62 Loyalists were forced to pay a one-time levy on the total value of their estates (including land and property in slaves) ranging from 12 to 25 percent. Everyone else—thousands of people—escaped official legislative notice.

At the time the legislature considered and constructed a larger system of governmental Loyalist punishment, although it is not clear that it was ever expected to be effective at actually driving out and punishing Loyalists. Certainly South Carolina's legislators recognized that confiscation created a schema that meant that only elite South Carolinians (such as doctors and planters) and a handful of prominent artisans would be punished—and yet the brutality of the war and the chaotic nature of the guerrilla warfare ensured that ordinary Loyalist militiamen were accused of atrocities. The legislature solved both problems in a way that highlighted the ultimate emphasis on local community decision-making on the fate of every individual. First it provided a way to confiscate the estates of Loyalists who fled the state even when they were not named by legislative act. In practice this meant that Loyalists who were not successful at approaching and negotiating reintegration with their former communities would have to leave and that their leaving would be profitable for the state. Further the legislature also imagined that local communities would use both the civil and criminal court system to prosecute a handful of individual Loyalists who misread the social signals their communities were giving them—people who stayed when they should have left. Courts could also work to facilitate reintegration by serving the needs of Patriots who were willing to embrace Loyalist community members so long as they felt justice was served. Justice could be served in these cases by civil lawsuits intended to reclaim financial damages from the war. In practice other states did use the court system as a method of reintegration for Loyalists, but South Carolinians turned away from using the courts. They did so because litigation and criminal prosecution did not (and does not) serve the interests of forgiveness and reintegration. South Carolinians moved away from punishing even a nominal cast of elite, well-known Loyalists after 1782, and they ultimately abandoned efforts at continuing punishment.

The sizable majority of Loyalists resisted even limited efforts to punish a select few of them. They worked to convince their neighbors and former friends to reconnect. Even Loyalists who faced confiscation often ignored the legal requirement to leave the state, just like Elias Ball. Instead they worked their connections to receive military passes protecting them or simply dispensed with even that formality and stayed on their own plantations. Overwhelmingly this worked. While a few Loyalists faced the threat of physical violence or actually suffered a humiliating public whipping, only a handful who physically remained in the state after the British withdrawal of 1782 later had to leave. Instead more than 70 percent of those Loyalists subject to confiscation and banishment petitioned the General Assembly for clemency—and got it in 1784, a short two years after the legislature punished them in the first place.

How did these white male Loyalists convince their neighbors and the South Carolina legislature to be so generous? They wrote petitions that argued for their own strong character. Any wartime behavior that could possibly exculpate them was pulled out in petition after petition. This person gave money to the orphans of Patriot soldiers, while another risked his health by visiting Patriots on board the filthy, disease-ridden prisoner ships stationed in Charleston's harbor. While they rarely outright apologized for choosing the wrong side, they sometimes went out of their way to abase and humiliate themselves through excuses that made the petitioners seem unlikeable—or frail and aged. They walked a thin line between making it possible to excuse their behavior and making themselves seem like undependable people whose character failings made them useless (or dangerous) neighbors and worthless citizens. And for the most part, their varied strategies in composing their petitions effectively played out these tensions. The victorious Patriots who composed the 1784 legislature were already amenable to considering these appeals, given that in practice most of these petitioning Loyalists were already living among other South Carolinians. Further the successful petitions were marked by the ultimate seal of approval from community members—supporting petitions (with almost identical language, indicating the Loyalist or his lawyer had drafted both) with anywhere from thirteen signatories to more than fifty drawn from the surrounding community. It was these testaments to local acceptance and successful reintegration of Loyalists that convinced the legislature to put their official stamp of approval on these already-codified local decisions. In the end the result was a generous reintegration of the majority of Loyalists by early 1784.

Even then Loyalists who had received clemency continued to press for greater social acceptance and governmental forgiveness from any remaining restrictions. And they were increasingly successful in gaining freedom from any and all restraints by the end of the 1780s. The rewriting of the state constitution by 1790 led to the end of even limited restraints on the franchise for former Loyalists. Those who were still supposed to pay an amercement (or tax) increasingly evaded paying these debts, and the state turned a blind eye and then absolved them of the obligation. And Loyalists were able to reintegrate themselves into social networks across the state. William Rees had suffered the (unusual) indignity of a public whipping at the hands of an angry Charleston crowd in 1784 for his wartime allegiance. Yet by 1788 his generous pledge to a local church building fund earned him a well-placed pew right at the front.

South Carolinians were astute about human nature. They knew that it was important not only to reintegrate the Loyalists in the immediate aftermath of the Revolution, but also to follow through resolutely in genuinely reconciling with them in the decades after the war. At first they found their way by avoiding any public conversation about Loyalists and the reality of their military support of the Crown. Even families monitored their conversations at home in front of younger people. For every story such as William Gilmore Simms's, who later remembered his grandmother's vibrant and chilling stories of wartime atrocities at the hands of the Tories, the more common experience was the Ball family's, where both Patriot and Loyalist family members avoided mentioning anything at all about Loyalists—especially those in the family. South Carolinians did not stop at avoiding acknowledging unpleasant realities at home. They carefully shaped a public culture of commemoration to strengthen their national attachments to the infant Republic while avoiding stirring up any embers of the late civil war. And it worked very well—perhaps too well. By the time South Carolinians again contemplated civil war, they had done such a good job of forgetting about their predecessors' anguish that they even used what they thought was the legacy of the Revolution to talk themselves into another conflict.

South Carolinians offered the most generous reconciliation to Loyalists across the new United States despite suffering the worst extremes of violent civil war. While they were the most generous, all Americans were more open to Loyalist reintegration than historians accept. The few historians who have considered the question of what they have variously termed the fate of the Loyalist returnees or the question of amnesty have had no problem finding numerous examples of Loyalists who successfully reintegrated into their local communities and their states after the Revolution. The details change from study to study, but even these other limited studies make it clear that Loyalist reintegration was ultimately successful and worked without bloodshed. The reconciliation was rapid. Americans absorbed former Loyalists into the body politic and the culture so successfully that the true history of the Revolution as a civil war was excised from public memory. American self-understanding came to see the United States as the light to all nations. Americans in the early Republic recoiled from the violent extremes of the French Revolution with remarkably little self-knowledge or introspection about the revolution they had just lived through. This suggests that South Carolina's experience was not dissimilar from that of the rest of the nation. It also suggests that their savvy use of public memory as a way to heal the wounds of war may have been widely shared by other Americans. If so that would be a particularly American way to approach the problem of reconciling after civil war. Europeans have long accused Americans of being future-obsessed, and Americans have long marveled at how Europeans seem surrounded by, and occasionally oppressed by, their history. Americans have cultivated this focus on the future and the deliberate ignorance of the past for good reasons. They should be thanked posthumously for their recognition of what prominent Patriot advocate Christopher Gadsden made explicit: "He that forgets and forgives most ... is the best citizen."[8]

ONE ✳ *The American Revolution*

South Carolina's First Civil War

Patriot Thomas Robertson was using a tree for cover during the Battle of Kings Mountain when a Loyalist neighbor spied him and called out his name. Robertson instantly responded to the well-known voice from his childhood, whose familiarity overcame his careful, guarded soldier instincts. That familiarity pierced into his subconscious memory, leading him to the foolhardy step of poking his head out from behind his shelter. In that instant his Loyalist neighbor shot at him. Luckily for Robertson, the shot missed him. He used the opportunity to pay his former Loyalist neighbor back by killing him—and of course bragging about it to later generations. The Loyalist soldier, whose voice was so familiar as to pierce the consciousness of a hardened soldier, lay on the ground cursing the Patriot neighbor who had delivered the fatal blow. All Robertson could find it in his heart for this man was the contemptuous advice that "the devil help you." He felt nothing that someone he had once known well was dying at his feet, and by his hand. South Carolina's first civil war was brutal.[1]

Popular memory paints the American Revolution as a uniquely nonviolent war. In the popular imagination, a few triumphant battles such as Lexington and Concord, Saratoga, and Yorktown are leavened with the image of the Continental Army stoically starving to death at Valley Forge. Americans are not simply being ignorant. By believing that the nation's founding was uniquely nonviolent, they can feel that the Revolution was purer and more consensual than independence movements in other countries. Americans who know nothing about the French Revolution but the guillotines are reassured that they somehow managed to revolt better than anyone else in the world. Our popular memory of the American Revolution is therefore simply one more episode in the long history of American exceptionalism. Historians have long abetted this understanding of the Revolution as a learned dispute about political ideals—despite the fact that it depended on an eight-year war fought across thousands of miles by militias and regular armies filled with real people. Those real people stole property, went hungry, took out their frustration and rage on civilians in their path, and generally behaved in ways that military commanders far away might predict but could not control. Our historical understanding of the effects of widespread violence in the American Revolution is further obliterated in our dominant narrative of the period as our historical writings and general education surveys skip blithely from the surrender at Yorktown to the difficulties of national governance under the Articles of Confederation to the Constitutional Convention. We know better, and yet we often fail to incorporate the difficult realities that Americans faced in creating an independent republic from the shattered unity, and in many places shattered physical environment, left after the Revolutionary War.

Civil war was an American experience of the Revolution, but South Carolinians experienced the extreme vicissitudes of guerrilla warfare by residents on both sides—and therefore the haunting consequences. New York was the only other place in America where an extended period of civil war was fueled by organized combatants on both sides. In New York the British invaded in 1776 and were able to hold the city and much of the hinterlands for the rest of the war. Raiding parties went back and forth across military lines, using local knowledge to wreak havoc. In the city military rule meant that both quiet Patriots and outspoken Loyalists chafed under the heavy hand of quartered troops and restraints on the food resources of the city. Angry Loyalist New Yorkers complained about the ravages of the troops who regarded all civilian property as prey to be harvested regardless of whether the property supported Loyalists or Patriots. Yet the secure military occupation meant that the war simmered instead of exploding. Judith Van Buskirk has compellingly called Loyalist and Patriot New Yorkers "generous enemies." No one has ever used that phrase to describe what happened in the Carolinas. Instead military historians of the war in the Carolinas have emphasized the brutality and hatred between Loyalists and Patriots, who were all locals.[2]

South Carolina's uncivil war exploded in part because South Carolina society was already strained by the time the war started.[3] This instability before the Revolution helped fuel both the armed Regulator movement in the 1760s and the civil war in the 1770s and 1780s. South Carolina politics had long been dominated by the problems of ensuring a white majority statewide in the face of a sizable black majority in the lowcountry and a restive, large, and well-organized Native American population to the west. Charleston's aristocratic elite controlled the state's politics, often giving scant regard to the needs of the backcountry.

As one travels into the interior from the sunlit harbors and beaches of the lowcountry, the landscape changes from the sand, swamps, and dreamy, huge oak trees draped in overhanging Spanish moss to large stands of tall pine trees. As the landscape gives way to pines, the rivers become unnavigable due to repeated falls. This geographic change also marked a dramatic change in the culture and economy of the state. While South Carolina was the wealthiest

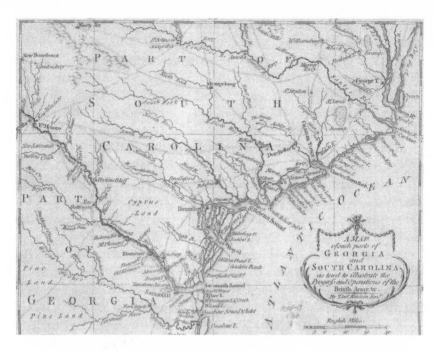

A map of South Carolina and Georgia by Thomas Kitchen, 1780. Courtesy of the South Caroliniana Library, University of South Carolina, Columbia.

colony on the eve of the American Revolution, that wealth and sophistication was concentrated entirely in the rice-growing region of the lowcountry. European visitors to the area commented favorably on the architecture and tasteful manners of Charleston, which was often the only American city they found attractive by European standards. Yet the built environment and the realities of life in the backcountry were very different, offering a much grittier experience. The government was headquartered in Charleston, and the interior regions had no court system or other access to state government unless they were willing to travel there. Some people liked it just fine this way, since it meant that the government paid vanishingly little attention to them. But for many the backcountry's lack of governmental resources and investment was a problem and a sign of disrespect.

The backcountry itself had only been settled for a generation on the eve of the Revolution, and some areas had gained population only in the last decade. These areas were often predominantly Scots-Irish (and Presbyterian), although religious and ethnic minorities of all sorts settled in the Carolina backcountry. Isolated geographically and culturally from Charleston, the men and women who lived in the backcountry hated (or at least distrusted) the lowcountry ruling elite far more than the British imperial administration, and many initially viewed the Revolution through that prism of distrust. South Carolina's rising interior elite used the War of the Regulation in the 1760s as a chance to demonstrate their fitness for power and their shared political and social priorities with the Charleston elite. Some disgruntled Regulators became Loyalists during the Revolution precisely because they identified the Patriot cause with the hated Charleston elite. And always hovering over everything in eighteenth-century South Carolina was the distorting nature of the reality of an enslaved black majority in the lowcountry.[4]

South Carolina's beauty overlay a society already fractured, with sizable discontent from those outside the narrow ruling elite from the lowcountry. The British would seek to capitalize on these discontents in an explicit strategy to foment civil war.

✳ *The Making of a South Carolina Loyalist*

Southern loyalism never wore a single face. Loyalism in South Carolina turns out to have little to do with class tension, political ideologies, or even social relations. The Loyalists were a varied bunch, made up of white, black, and Native American civilians and soldiers. Perhaps the most surprising thing is how little ideology had to do with who became a Loyalist. Historians have focused on the most learned and outspoken Loyalists, who were inevitably the most ideological. If you read the writings of southern Loyalists, they seem curiously apolitical as well as nonideological. Even the few Loyalists who rose in support of the British cause in the initial campaigns of 1775–76 did not frame their decisions in terms of an ideological commitment to the principles New England Loyalists often spouted. Instead they understood loyalty viscerally.

For white Loyalists there were many paths that led to Loyalist affiliation. Certainly a handful of South Carolina Loyalists supported the king early and remained committed to the Loyalist cause consistently throughout the war. In return Patriot authorities repeatedly singled them out to be controlled and punished. The foremost example is the Cunningham family from the Ninety Six district of the backcountry. These brothers and cousins gave rise to the well-respected militia commander Robert Cunningham and the infamous William "Bloody Bill" Cunningham. James Brisbane, a lowcountry Loyalist, was also later singled out for having "taken the most early opportunity to evince his attachment to the British cause" and being rewarded by the British for his longtime loyalty.[5] These valuable Loyalists were rare, however. The majority of South Carolinians were disaffected, but they did not want to stick their necks out for anyone.

Social historians have tried to identify characteristics that led people to Loyalism. These historians suggested that in South Carolina the backcountry disproportionately produced Loyalists because Loyalism tended to attract people from ethnic and religious minorities who feared their colonies' ruling elites more than they feared the (faraway) British authorities. There certainly were pockets of this in South Carolina. The legislature feared widespread disaffection in the backcountry and reacted accordingly. In 1775 it sent a delegation of Baptist and Methodist ministers on a Patriot oratorical tour of the most restive districts of the backcountry. The mission had limited success. In areas without powerful Loyalist leaders, William Henry Drayton, a respected Patriot-identified jurist, managed to persuade many men to sign lists promising support to the Patriot cause and even to take up arms when called. Of course later in the war, men on all sides became used to signing documents that, when push came to shove, they had no intention of honoring. They were probably not so cynical in 1775, however. In other areas backcountry residents made it clear that they just wanted to be left alone. But in areas with strong Loyalist leaders such as the Cunninghams, the effort to persuade failed. One of these Patriot missionaries was intimidated at a meeting at Fairforest Baptist Church by the Loyalists, who proclaimed they were hoping "1,000 Bostonians might be kill'd in Battle." If this was not bad enough, a local man warned him that there was the "greatest appearance of a Civil War," which perhaps only "Providence" could spare.[6] This Patriot member of the delegation became so concerned for his personal safety while traveling in these Loyalist strongholds that he began to keep his journal in code. There was Loyalist support in the backcountry, but it was not easily predicted by religious beliefs, ethnicity, or class. White Loyalists were drawn from all ranks of society. It was the British —not the Americans—who believed you could easily predict who was a Patriot or a Loyalist by their religious beliefs. British officials in South Carolina identified Patriots with Scotch-Irish Presbyterian "agitators"—so much so that British major James Wemyss specialized in burning down Presbyterian churches, decrying them as "sedition shops."[7]

If anything Loyalism could be predicted by the choices of the local community patriarchs. The decisions of those local patriarchs do not follow some easy formula, but once they were made, South Carolina's long history of paternal political practices took over. After the Cunninghams decided to support the king, the lesser men of the district elected to follow them politically—and eventually into battle after battle.

Most white South Carolina Loyalists were situational Loyalists who were motivated by practical concerns. They chose the strongest side when forced to choose and avoided choosing whenever possible. A majority of all Americans at that time were disaffected, and most wanted to maintain neutrality. In South Carolina many people actually changed public allegiances during the war. They were Patriots until the British successfully invaded the state in 1780 and secured Charleston and the lowcountry. When faced with the reality that the Patriot government could no longer protect them, they made their best deal with the British and became Loyalists publicly. Unfortunately for them, this meant they were identified with loyalism when the war unexpectedly turned against the British at Yorktown. In the end many men of dubious commitment to either Patriotism or Loyalism found themselves forced to negotiate for their position in the postwar state with the much smaller number of strongly committed Patriots who had reason to resent and distrust these wavering men.

Charleston, and with it seemingly all of South Carolina, fell to the British invasion in May 1780. The Patriots had mustered sizable forces to defend Charleston, but in the end it was not enough. In the aftermath of the reduction of Charleston, each man in those Patriot forces had to decide whether to accept the terms of surrender and parole that the British offered. Those parole terms were actually quite generous—at least initially. Men who chose to accept the parole simply promised to return home and not take up arms against the British. Crucially they were promised that they could sit out the rest of the war as neutrals. They would not have to fight for the British. Given these terms, the majority of combatants took the parole and returned to their homes. Even such famous (and hotheaded) partisan leaders as Andrew Pickens and Andrew Williamson accepted paroles and headed back home. South Carolinians accepted British protection since they had no other attractive option and the British were in fact offering generous parole terms. Thousands of South Carolinians were sure they could accept paroles and sit out the rest of the war and were happy to do so with as much honor as they could scrape together.[8]

The British decision to offer paroles of neutrality made no sense in the light of British war aims. They had invaded the South precisely because they believed that a majority of the white population were Loyalists. They intended to use these men as additional and much-needed forces to march north and bring the rest of America under British control. Therefore it made little sense to release expressly so many men from any military obligation to the British. Further many observers on the British side worried about the consequences of allowing men whose own political instincts were certainly not solidly Loyalist to scatter across the state without any oversight. Capt. Johann Ewald was "convinced that most of these people will have guns in their hands again within a short time."[9] As it turned out, he was correct—but not for the reasons he supposed.

The British retroactively changed the terms of the paroles, and in response anxious South Carolinians were obliged to reconsider their choices once again. Sir Henry Clinton, the British commander, summarily changed the rules of the paroles as he was leaving the Carolinas for New York a month after Charleston's surrender. In so doing he dumped the problem of what to do with thousands of South Carolinians who had accepted paroles under one set of rules but were suddenly expected to honor very different terms to his understandably annoyed successor, Lord Cornwallis. The new set of rules, delivered by official proclamation on June 3, 1780, required all paroled prisoners to take up arms against their fellow Americans in support of the king because "it is fit and proper that all persons should take an active part in Settling and Securing his Majesty's government." Unfortunately for the British, many paroled Patriots embraced neutrality but not armed defense of the king against their own neighbors. One astute British commander quickly complained that "that unfortunate Proclamation of the 3rd of June has had very unfavorable consequences. The majority of the Inhabitants in the Frontier Districts, tho' ill disposed to us, from circumstances were not actually up in arms against us." After the proclamation "nine out of ten of them are now embodied on the part of the Rebels."[10] That number may have been an exaggeration, but the reality was that the change in terms presented people with yet another choice. The retroactive change to the parole terms led plenty of paroled Patriot soldiers to reject their vow and take up arms again. Yet others weighed the situation carefully and took the opposite tack—to continue under British protection. Often they tried to equivocate as long as possible. Men might serve in the Loyalist militias that were organized to enforce the new parole terms, but they did what they could to avoid actual military service. These were the men who made sure their units arrived a day late to the battle. Others made sure their militia units avoided enforcing British punishments on their openly Patriot neighbors. These men were motivated not by ideology but by the need to protect themselves and their families.

Commanders tried to recruit white South Carolinians to the Loyalist militia. Maj. Patrick Ferguson was put in charge of recruiting Loyalist officers and enlisted men under six-month terms. He believed that a militia willing to serve at least half the year could be shaped into an effective fighting force that would relieve pressure on the British regular forces. (Cynics might point out that there was nothing to date in the American Revolutionary experience that supported this conclusion, and they would be right.) While Ferguson was able to find willing volunteers in the backcountry who were "very fit . . . being all excellent woodsmen," he quickly discovered that they were both spectacularly unused to military discipline and resentful of such discipline (like most Americans). Further many of them thought they were agreeing to only one six-month term. When the rules were clarified to indicate that in fact the militia was expected to serve at least six months of every year, many Loyalists felt the British had performed a bait and switch on them—just as they had on the paroled Patriots. They resented what they saw as an imposition after the fact. South Carolina's Loyalist militias gained a reputation outside the state as unreliable and uncommitted despite the fervor of some of the officer corps. A Pennsylvania Loyalist remarked that the South Carolina militia was "in general faithless." Despite the militia's general lack of military utility, commanders on both sides of the southern theater turned to them due to their otherwise limited manpower.[11]

Rawlins Lowndes was like many of these men who suddenly became Loyalists due to nothing more than a desire to protect their lives and property. He had served in the Patriot state government in the initial war years when the Patriots controlled the state, but he chose to take the initially generous British parole offer days after Charleston fell. Lowndes explained, after complaining of his losses from plunder at British and Patriot hands during the campaign for Charleston, that a man "used hitherto to all the Comforts and Conveniences of Life, and now . . . in the most necessary Exigency," would simply have to continue to live under the rules for British protection.[12] He could not risk his property and his comfortable life. Lowndes may at first seem too honest for his own good, but in fact he is typical of South Carolina Loyalists. Self-interested? Yes. Romantic? No, not really. But this behavior is human and understandable. This is not the loyalism of ideological motivations or strong ideas about empire and the king. This is not even the temporal loyalism of a conservative psychology concerned about lightly overthrowing lasting political and societal bonds. And it is also not the loyalism of ethnic and social minorities. This is the loyalism of pragmatism. And it is what defines most white men who became known as South Carolina Loyalists. South Carolina Patriots would bitterly term them "trimmers," suggesting they tacked with the prevailing winds as a sailboat might. And as long as the war continued, the British rewarded these wavering Loyalists even as it became clear that many of them gave the British cause only halfhearted support. One longtime Loyalist bitterly noted that "having been steadily Loyal" was no advantage, because the British treated men who had "shed their fellow Subjects blood" on an equal footing with men who had long suffered for their open avowal of loyalism when it was not convenient.[13] Loyalism among South Carolina whites was born of pragmatism and caution—and because of that it was widespread. Yet there was nothing ideological about this choice, which meant that when the war finally ended, thousands of men who had taken British protection as a means of self-preservation faced the question of how to reintegrate themselves into a community they fit into well. These shirking "trimmers" now had to persuade the few who had stuck their necks out in dangerous times that they were worth the effort of reintegration.

The British recruited allies wherever they could find them, working to attract the loyalties of African Americans as well as whites. Black Loyalists made choices born of reality as well, and those decisions reverberated into physic and economic losses for white Patriots and Loyalists alike. Historians have calculated that somewhere in the neighborhood of twenty to twenty-five thousand South Carolina slaves, or some 20 percent of the enslaved population, fled to British lines seeking freedom during the war. From the moment Virginia's last royal governor offered freedom to enslaved men who were willing to fight for the British cause, the war became a war for freedom for slaves. While a handful of northern slaves were offered freedom in return for fighting for the Patriot cause, southern slaves never received any such offer. Therefore they saw the British as potential liberators. As Gary Nash and other historians have noted, the American Revolution was "the largest slave uprising" in American history—and a substantial portion of those slaves were South Carolinians.[14]

British officials were conflicted about offering slaves freedom, because they saw it as a dangerous strategy. The vast majority of South Carolina Patriots were adamantly opposed to including slaves in any way. John Laurens, the son of prominent Patriot Henry Laurens, did once propose offering slaves freedom in return for taking up arms in defense of America. His fellow southern slaveholders adamantly shunned the proposal. For the British and Loyalist side, the dilemma was twofold. If they encouraged mainland North American slaves to consider supporting the British as a surefire way to claim freedom, they risked undermining slavery in the valuable Caribbean sugar-planting colonies—colonies that were heavily dependent on African slave labor and had chosen to remain in the British fold. Secondly Loyalist southerners were vigorously opposed to anything that equated black freedom with British service. They were slaveholders too, and they did not want the British to encourage their valuable property to dream of liberation. Southern planters understood that once slaves began to run to the British military camps, there would be no practical way to differentiate between the slaves of Patriots and the slaves of Loyalists. British promises of freedom could destroy the slaveholding regime on which all white South Carolinians depended for their profit. As John Adams of Massachusetts noted while discussing the state of affairs in the lowcountry, "all the Kings Friends and Tools of Government have large Plantations and Property in Negroes. So That the Slaves of the Tories would be lost as well as those of the Whigs." The British did try to protect white Loyalist property in slaves during the Revolution and in the chaos of the final withdrawal, but it did not work very well. Fleeing ex-slaves had every reason to lie in the effort to secure their own freedom. Both the British and the Patriots used the chaos of war to seize additional property in slaves at the same time that those "properties" were busy liberating themselves. As one British commander noted, "all the friends of Government have been plundered of their Negroes" by the Patriots, despite attempts to preserve this profitable property in people. In the aftermath of the war, white Loyalist planters tried desperately to lay claim to their former slaves during British preparations for withdrawal, but they were frustrated time and time again in their efforts.[15]

British efforts to temporize with the question of how to treat black Loyalists led them to continuing chaos while failing to pacify Loyalists or Patriots. British commanders were conflicted on how to use escaped slaves as labor during the war. While many of them saw it as a way to free up their troops, they still resisted using slave labor for fear of encouraging slaves to run away. They kept the vast majority of escaped slaves working as menial laborers rather than using them as troops or using skilled slaves in specific roles. British commanders did pump escaping slaves for military information. Occasionally former slaves with maritime experiences were allowed to contribute their particular expertise in the service of the Royal Navy. British officials often assigned fugitive slaves to sequestered Patriot plantations and forced them to perform agricultural work. While the British saw this as a practical solution (use slaves to perform agriculture on plantations and use the resulting crops to support the war effort), former slaves resented being shoved back into the world they had risked so much to leave. Southern Patriots were no better. They insisted throughout the war on the inferiority of slaves and sought to keep them enslaved. Gen. Thomas Sumter even pioneered a new approach to the use of captured slaves. When he caught fugitive slaves or captured British- or Loyalist-owned slaves, he used them as reenlistment bounties to his own militia troops. Given that the South Carolina Patriot government had perpetual problems paying soldiers, this was an effective inducement. Of course it also encouraged Sumter's militia to spend more time plundering Loyalist properties in order to feed their desire for slave bounties.[16]

South Carolinians had always been nervous about the possibility of a slave uprising, and they were well aware that the American Revolution made it more likely. While in fact most slaves chose individual solutions (running away alone or in small groups) over mass rebellion, the constant threat unnerved South Carolina Patriots. They were afraid that slaves would rise ahead of or with British troops when they successfully invaded Charleston in 1780. Errant bells ringing in a church steeple led panicked Charlestonians to conclude that a slave rebellion had begun, although all they found in the tower was a drunk black man sleeping off a good night. The mass slave defections, coupled with the terror of slave uprisings, created traumatic memories for both white Loyalists and Patriots.[17]

Native Americans also were crucial British allies in the Revolution. Eighteenth-century South Carolinians strove to maintain a large, unified white population to neutralize both the threat of Native American war on the western side of the state and a slave uprising in the eastern part of the state.

Traditionally the white population of the backcountry was an essential part of this delicate balancing act—and this act required white South Carolinians to tamp down open conflicts between whites in order to discourage armed conflict on the borders. The Revolution shattered efforts to maintain white solidarity in the face of threats from both slaves and Native Americans. Patriots were afraid this might invite the British to inspire dangerous Native American revolts. In other words the British might capitalize on South Carolina's greatest strategic weakness. As Henry Laurens put it, the regular British army might attack while "the Indians are to make inroads on our backs—Tories & Negro Slaves to rise in our Bowels." In 1776 the Cherokee took advantage of ever-halting Loyalist and British efforts to bring the war to South Carolina. They attacked the southern frontier days after the British made an effort to invade Charleston Harbor. Nervous Patriots whispered that the Cherokee were using secret signs to spare white Loyalists, but in practice there is no evidence this actually happened. The fact that Patriots believed this certainly speaks to the perception of both the British and the Patriots that Native Americans were likely to be British allies. The British turned to these allies again when they finally got serious about invading the South in 1778, yet blunder after blunder and hesitation after hesitation meant that they largely squandered the Native Americans' contributions. Lord Cornwallis, commander of the Charleston invasion, preferred not to use Native American forces at all. Jim Piecuch has concluded that the British refusal to use Native Americans hampered British military efforts in the South. Loyalism may have worn many faces and been chosen by people of different skin colors, but British and white Loyalist blindness to the contributions their allies could make meant that they helped seal their own fate.[18]

✳ The American Revolution as Civil War

The American Revolution was a true civil war. In South Carolina more brothers fought brothers in the Revolution than in the Civil War. South Carolina's civil war revolved around people who often knew each other, and they used that local knowledge as a weapon. Judith Van Buskirk opens her book on the civil war of the American Revolution in New York with the story of Patriot raiders who used their intimate knowledge of the geography of Cow Bay on Long Island to raid it in the middle of a December night in 1778. The raiders not only took a prominent Loyalist hostage and plundered for valuables, but they also stopped to socialize with their Loyalist family members. While similar local scenes can be found in the annals of the civil war in South Carolina, they were not touching stories of "generous enemies." The night before the Battle of Huck's Defeat (a telling name in and of itself), Patriot Edward

Lacey led his men to his own homestead. He planned to launch a surprise attack in the morning. But while he was a committed Patriot, his aged father was an ardent Loyalist—so ardent that he tried to sneak out in the middle of the night to go warn the nearby Loyalist militia of the entire plan. The senior Lacey was willing to consign his own son to death in order to aid the Loyalist cause. Luckily for him, his son showed his aged father more mercy than his father had been willing to show him. Lacey tied his father to a bedstead and posted a guard over him. Of course if the son had caught a Loyalist spy who was not his own flesh and blood, he would have put him to instant death. Such was family affection in South Carolina's first civil war.[19]

The British tried to bring the war to the South twice. In the initial campaigns of 1775–76, they made a few halfhearted attempts to take the Carolinas. The end result of these efforts was to discourage deeply those Loyalists who had risen to the king's standard. In South Carolina regular British forces tried to invade Charleston. In a battle for Sullivan's Island (which was a fort protecting the harbor), the British relied on naval power too much and were quickly rebuffed by otherwise inexperienced Patriot forces. British bullets glanced off of the fort, which was built with logs from palmetto trees. The Patriots were so jubilant at their victory that they created a state holiday, Palmetto Day, to commemorate it. To this day the palmetto is the state symbol. North Carolina Loyalists had an even worse experience—one that was instructive for South Carolinians as well. They answered the royal governor's call for troops and fought a bloody engagement at Moore's Creek Bridge in February 1776. In the aftermath of the Loyalist loss, Flora MacDonald, the unofficial ceremonial mascot of the North Carolina Scots, wrote that she was "dayly oppressed with straggling partys of plunderers … and night robbers." After the Highland Scots were defeated, many spent years hiding in the swamps, unable to return to their homes safely—certainly not a precedent South Carolina Loyalists, a largely nonideological bunch, wanted to follow. All in all Britain's first efforts to bring the war to the South destroyed the hopes of the small number of committed white Loyalists who had put themselves in danger to help the cause.[20]

Men who had stuck their neck out for the Loyalist cause were marked for persecution. In concert with other American states, South Carolinians moved to enforce political conformity and suppress dissent through militia force with the occasional covering of anti-Loyalist legislation. In 1776 South Carolina's General Assembly passed an act to "prevent sedition" in an effort to avoid "civil dissensions and animosities." Virginia, North Carolina, and Georgia passed similar acts, all intended to pressure wavering Loyalists into assimilating into the Patriot population. In South Carolina the Committee of Safety ensured Charleston stayed in Patriot hands through an intimidation campaign against suspected Loyalists. One observer warned that Loyalists were "expecting every moment to be drove from their Occupations, and Homes, and plundered of all they have earned." A 1775 expedition into the backcountry tried both to shore up Patriot support and to dissuade potential Loyalist supporters from declaring themselves and offering military support to the British cause. Across the state the Patriots made sure to use every tool at their disposal to suppress Loyalist opposition. One poor Loyalist received a "decent tarring and feathering, for one insolent speech he had made." He was paraded from house to house, the mob pointedly tarrying in front of the houses of other suspected Loyalists. The Patriot message was clear—you were next if you dared speak publicly against the Patriot takeover of the state government. The crowd forced the abused Loyalist to embrace publically the Patriot cause by swallowing a painful toast to the success of the Patriots. The victorious Patriot crowd offered to "charge the grog to the account of Lord North." The author commented with satisfaction that the action had worked very well in suppressing dissent since there was "scarce a [suspected Loyalist] who did not tremble." In the name of maintaining control, the Revolutionaries cheapened the very guarantees of individual liberty that they proclaimed they were fighting to preserve.[21]

Loyalists hunkered down, kept their mouths shut, and hoped that their luck would change. For five years the Patriots dominated the state and seemed to have the upper hand. But when the British finally put substantial military resources on the ground in the South, this multiyear history of abuse ignited a cycle of revenge. In the meantime the Patriot militias found new and inventive ways to pressure wavering people into outward conformity—or else.

The Patriot government of South Carolina, like the governments of other states, was well aware of what is sometimes forgotten—the majority of the population was disaffected. The people who wanted to remain neutral, those who simply did not care, those who wished a pox on both sides, and those who were genuinely loyal to the king and to a vision of a monarchial empire of free Englishmen made up most of the population. Accordingly the Patriot minority did everything they could to preempt open dissent and push dissenters into silence. In 1777 the legislature required all adult men to take an oath of allegiance to the new state and reaffirmed this decision again in 1778. The oath of allegiance was meant to force men out of neutrality. Men who took the oath were furnished with certificates of proof, which local officials and their supporting Patriot militias could and did demand when they randomly arrived on their doorsteps. Local sheriffs were sent lists of oath takers and oath refusers each Independence Day—a not so subtle reminder to the local sheriff and militia to harass those who had not taken it. Despite this pressure there was rampant disregard for the oath. In both October 1778 and February 1779, the General Assembly passed acts to extend the time limit for taking it, a sure sign that only a minority of adult men had bothered to comply.[22]

There were other ways to use oaths as a tool of political enforcement. Both sides ultimately used these tactics against each other. Moses Hall, a Patriot militiaman, recalled his unit going to break up such an effort by Loyalists. "Hearing that a number of persons were going through the country administering oaths of allegiance to [the] British cause," he and other volunteers pursued them for miles.[23] Oaths became a way to reinforce political allegiances and in so doing visibly separate families and communities. Political and military strategies went arm in arm in creating a terrifying experience of civil war in the American Revolution.

Both Loyalist and Patriot militias used plunder and willful destruction of property as a weapon to enforce political conformity. Throughout the entire war, commanders of regular forces on both sides condemned plunder and property destruction, yet they never stopped it and often were forced to turn a blind eye. Sir Henry Clinton, the commander of the British invasion forces, was firmly against plunder and sought to avoid such traditional depredations of war. He did not want to give the civilian population any incentive to turn against him. However there was a limit to what he could do and how far he was willing to antagonize his own troops in order to maintain stability. One astute British captain noted that Patriots "hated us from the bottom of their hearts because we carried off" their belongings. Gen. Francis Marion, the Swamp Fox, controlled his troops carefully (especially in comparison to Thomas Sumter), but even he used his troops as messengers of social control, terrorizing the Loyalists as a way to ensure relative quiet. Marion bragged in October 1780 that his militia's efforts in northeastern South Carolina made "the Toreys . . . so Affrighted with my Little Excursions, that many is moving off to Georgia with their Effects." What his militia's campaign of intimidation through plunder and destruction had ensured was that frightened families would flee with what few possessions they could carry with them. Plunder was an expected part of eighteenth-century war, but in the southern theater militias on both sides made sure to use it as a weapon of fear. Militias had become accustomed to entering houses, harshly questioning people, and otherwise pursuing individuals, not armies. Unsurprisingly they brought these habits with them to partisan warfare, targeting the homes and families of the disaffected.[24]

Observers on all sides did note the particular ferocity of Loyalist regiments, no matter what American state they were actually from. In the northern theater, Maj. John Andre wrote especially disapprovingly of the kind of soldier who would plunder for the "wanton pleasure of Spoil" only to "throw [it] aside an hour" later. He might have disapproved, but his comment suggests how common it was in the context of civil war. In South Carolina, Loyalists who had chafed under Patriot armed harassment for five years took obvious satisfaction in the opportunity for personal revenge. One lieutenant commented that

in order to "do his King and country justice," his Loyalist troops were "destroying furniture, breaking windows, etc." Loyalist troops willingly participated
in retribution against Patriot leaders and ordinary people, thereby escalating
a culture of retaliation. John Lewis Gervais warned Henry Laurens that the
"Ennemy certainly behaved very ill at Mepkin [Laurens's plantation]," breaking open "every trunk" and carrying off "every thing they could carry without a Cart." Further his overseer was stripped of his watch, shirt, and even
his stockings, left half-naked by the troops. The hostile troops undoubtedly
understood the humiliation of the man's nakedness in front of the slaves he
normally controlled. In case the overseer's family did not understand the insult
intended, the Loyalist militia took his wife's shoes as well, despite the lack of
obvious utility. It seems clear that both sides understood the power of plunder
to humiliate and frighten the opponent. Ubiquitous plunder made the rest of
the overheated propaganda mill seem valid, and the wild rhetoric served only
to amplify each side's bad feelings.[25]

Since destruction was a political tool, troops were supposed be choosy
about who they terrorized. But the reality of war was that militias on both
sides became increasingly unconcerned about identifying the allegiances of civilian families, especially when they were in areas outside their own local community. George Park complained to his cousin that even after taking British
protection, their Loyalist neighbors "set to Rob us taking all our living, horses,
Cows, Sheep, Clothing, of all Sorts, money, pewter, tins, knives, in fine Everything that sooted them. Untill we were Stript Naked." A lowcountry man who
had refused to serve as a pilot for the British navy was plundered in revenge
and his plantation "laid waste." In the wake of the Battle of Guilford's Courthouse, when the tide began to turn against the British and Loyalist efforts, Patriot militias pressed home their advantage by turning up the heat on Loyalists
and their families. James Collins's militia stepped up the search for Loyalist
targets. His men set to "ferreting out the Tories, and such as had been in the
habit of plundering, burning and murdering." While Collins insisted his men
differentiated between those who had been neutral ("pet Tories") and those
who had acted against their Patriot neighbors, in fact most Loyalists found
themselves living in fear. When Patriot militias targeted Loyalists, they pulled
down their roofs and dismantled their houses and other buildings. Frightened
"fellows, perhaps expecting instant death, would beg hard for life" and were
promised their lives in return if "they would leave the country, within a speci-
fied time, and never return." Collins felt this was the merciful and just response
and reflected happily that he did not know of any Loyalist who promised
to leave under these circumstances and "failed to comply," although many of
these Loyalists ultimately returned. The militia lost no time in clearing the
country of ideological opposition.[26]

What the militias left in their wake was a scarred people and landscape. As one Patriot commander noted, "Ninety-Six is now a frontier. Plantations lie desolate, and hopeful crops are going to ruin." Without relief "famine will overspread our beautiful country." The motley human toll of this civil war weighed on the leaders and the participants. The inhumanity of the war in the backcountry, and the chaos of militia warfare, gave all sides pause for good reason. Gen. Nathaniel Greene, commander of the Continentals in the southern theater, despaired that the "Whigs and Tories pursue each other with as much relentless fury as beasts of prey." He further opined repeatedly that whichever side could bring order and end bloodshed would have the blessing and allegiance of civilians of all sides. He understood all too well that what had begun with organized militias had spread to the entire populace. The example of widespread plunder and destruction "so corrupted the Principles of the People that they think of nothing but plundering one another."[27] The ensuing destruction devastated the Carolina countryside and embittered civilians and soldiers alike.

✳ The Brutal Reality of Civil War

What was supposed to be a clean victory and peaceful occupation turned into a maelstrom of brutal guerrilla civil war. How did such high hopes on the British side go so wrong so quickly? When the British decided to invade the South, they did it with the expectation that the majority of southerners were Loyalist sympathizers who would be willing to supplement regular British forces in the struggle to subdue the rest of America. While the British always overestimated the degree of Loyalist support they had, they also based their war strategy on a brief investigation into Loyalist support in Georgia and the Carolinas. In 1779 James Simpson, a former royal attorney general for South Carolina, was sent into the backcountry to assess the degree of Loyalist support. His report became the basis for overly optimistic estimates of Loyalist troop strength, even from officers such as Gen. Henry Clinton who were otherwise skeptical of Loyalist support. Simpson's report found that there was considerable, heated support for the king among the "people from the Back Country of Carolina" because they had been so mistreated by the Patriots and wanted revenge. After touring the backcountry, Simpson was convinced that "there is such general resentment raised against most of the individuals who have composed the Congresses and Committees in the different Governments, and those who have been active in enforcing their Tyrianical Edicts," that a large number would gladly rise against the Patriot government given half a chance.[28] The British used this research to support their war planning, essentially because Simpson told them what they wanted to hear.

Simpson's report was actually describing the desire for revenge that would ignite a gruesome militia war across the Carolinas. He was sensitive to the degree to which resentments drove Loyalist feelings, but the British planners who read his report seem to have missed this vital understanding. Five years of relentless militia intimidation and plundering had not made all South Carolinians Patriots. What it had done was left these oppressed people eager for the chance at payback. It was these men who eagerly told Simpson of their glee for revenge. Simpson dryly noted that the backcountry residents had become "most violent in their enmity to those by whom they had been oppressed." He was certainly reassured by the level and enthusiasm of the support he saw, as well as by the fact that so many openly welcomed him and his men, even though such aid was not "consistent with prudence," since "several are now Confined in Gaol and Prison ships at Charles Town" and others were plundered after he left. Desperate for any new way to win the war, the British ignored the warning in Simpson's report about the "sanguine disposition" of the Loyalists anxious for revenge.[29]

The war in the South, and especially in South Carolina, rapidly turned into the militia war for revenge. The very militias that had been so effective in suppressing open dissent over the previous five years had turned with new vigor upon the populace as well as on each other. The militias continued to fulfill their now traditional role as the enforcers of political orthodoxy through routine harassment of civilian populations. In fact they now did it with a thoroughness and fury that was new. Patriot William Gipson bitterly remembered returning home from one campaign in which he fought to discover with horror that the local Loyalist militia had targeted his mother for pain and humiliation in order to send the son a message. His "mother, a widow woman, was tied up and whipped by the Tories, her house burned, and property all destroyed."[30] Further inflaming both sides (and those few souls who clung to neutrality) were roving gangs of bandits, loosely identified with the Loyalist side but actually interested only in personal plunder. Civilians were rightly terrified. The best they could hope for was the destruction of their property—their home, their food, and their source of future income. And lurking in every encounter was the possibility of real violence.

Militia warfare also gave rise to repeated violations of the conventions of eighteenth-century war—violations that each side termed atrocities when committed by the enemy but considered understandable and excusable when committed by friends. The war in South Carolina's backcountry was a "war of the militias," where Patriot and Loyalist militias drawn from local volunteers engaged each other in a series of guerrilla fights. Each side's battle plans relied on organized militias who were willing to take to the field for at least half the year under such legendary commanders as Sumter (whose nickname, "the

Gamecock," provided the University of South Carolina with its sports mascot) and Marion. As historian Wayne Lee has pointed out, the militias depended on a style of warfare that had developed on the frontier, privileging dawn or dusk raids dependent on surprise. With limited visibility, small troop numbers, and the dependence on ambush, it was almost inevitable that death tolls would rise and that taking prisoners, or even seeing white surrender flags, would be difficult. The militias did rely on norms of violence and wartime behavior that restricted what they could honorably do on the field of battle, but with increasing rage and pressure, those norms were superseded by another tradition: retribution. Threatening retribution had long been an acceptable way to control unwanted behavior, but the pressures of civil war toppled Americans into applying what one historian has dubbed the "law of retaliation": compulsory and expected retaliation, such that each side justified all actions and routinely expected to violate the rules of war because the other side did it first.[31]

Both sides used a mix of recent history and propaganda to support their own inhumane behavior. British forces set the tone early with the May 29, 1780, battle that Patriots soon termed Buford's Massacre. The British sent Col. Banastre Tarleton and his legion to overtake the last regular Continentals in the state. When they did they rapidly overwhelmed the Patriot forces. The fighting was mostly hand-to-hand combat, leading one officer to assess that the Loyalist dead and wounded had an "average" of sixteen wounds "to each man." Within a few minutes, at least part of the American line tried to surrender, raising a white flag. At about the same time, at least according to his later (self-serving) memoir, Tarleton had his horse shot out from beneath him. The legion could no longer see him, so they panicked and continued firing on the American forces despite several Patriot attempts to raise the white flag of surrender. American Patriots believed the legion had deliberately refused to allow them to surrender. In later accounts even one British writer felt that "the virtue of humanity was totally forgot." Tarleton reported to Cornwallis that he had "cut 170 Off'rs and Men to pieces," and the American losses were sizable: 113 killed, 150 wounded, and 53 prisoners, or about 80 percent of the Americans engaged in the battle.[32]

Americans referred to the battle as Buford's Massacre to emphasize their picture of Tarleton, and by extension all British and Loyalist soldiers, as wanton destroyers of human life who were willing to commit a massacre against men trying to surrender honorably. Such heated rhetoric helped Patriot militia recruitment and encouraged Patriots to show little mercy to Loyalists. "Give 'em Buford's Quarter" or "Give 'em Buford's Play" became the rallying cry in the militia war that swept both the backcountry and the lowcountry. "Remember Buford," another version of the catchphrase, also worked to stir up strong hatreds in order to motivate Patriot soldiers. Once the militias became used to not taking quarter in some settings, they tended to stop accepting it in almost all circumstances. William Davie justified taking no prisoners during his daybreak ambush of a Loyalist unit at Hanging Rock by arguing that the entire attack took place "under the eye of the whole British camp" so that "no prisoners could be safely taken." Abel Kolb, a member of the South Carolina Patriot legislature, was surprised in his home by Loyalist forces. He surrendered and was then murdered anyway. Constant invocation of Buford's Massacre encouraged Carolinians to adjust to these brutal realities of partisan warfare.[33]

Each side quickly found ways to justify executing the war prisoners they took, even after those men had surrendered and thought themselves safe. In some cases in the backcountry, quick courts-martial were conducted before the unlucky prisoners were hanged in the field. But Moses Hall, a young soldier, described an incident when some members of the Patriot militia suddenly went from milling around a group of Loyalist prisoners to attacking them after someone "cr[ied] out 'Remember Buford,' and the prisoners were immediately hewed to pieces with broadswords." Hall remembered the incident with "horror," yet he did nothing to stop it. He also gave no indication that anyone else in the camp lifted a finger to stop the murders. While it cannot be concluded that this sort of behavior was everyday practice in the militia war, it also should not be considered an isolated incident. The practice was widespread enough that a British officer complained that the Patriots used a "system of murdering every man (although unarmed) who is known to be a Loyalist." Such incidents served only to increase the anger of all people, especially those who suspected that their own relatives and loved ones had been murdered in just such a fashion.[34]

South Carolina's civil war encouraged inhumanity toward the enemy on and off the battlefield. Militia members tortured prisoners in order to gain information from them or just for the sheer pleasure of striking back at the enemy. In one example William Gipson, a Patriot militia soldier, testified decades later in his pension application that when his men caught two Loyalist militia members who they believed (with some justification) had been harassing Patriot civilians, they tortured them. First they dragged the two men fifteen miles to the Guilford Courthouse (later the scene of a pyrrhic victory for Cornwallis), where they convened an indecently hasty court-martial. While one Loyalist was immediately executed with a bullet, the other Loyalists was "sentenced" to a common backcountry torture practice—"spicketing." Gipson explained the torture device to the apparently fascinated person preparing his application: "that is, he was placed with one foot upon a sharp pin drove in a block, and was turned round by one Thomas Archer, to the best of his recollection, until the pin run through his foot."[35] Torture often served to harden both the soldiers who faced such treatment and the civilians who worried for them.

On the field of battle, men learned to treat the opposing side callously—even those they knew personally. While some of these stories are so colorful as to perhaps be apocryphal, the way Patriots and Loyalists repeated them with great energy suggests they spoke to a level of hatred required to conduct a civil war. The family legend about Patriot militia soldier Thomas Robertson from the beginning of this chapter illustrates how the very familiarity of the enemy could lead to danger. When that Loyalist neighbor used his own past relationship with Robertson in order to lure him to his death, he surely illustrated the worst instincts of a civil war. And Robertson clearly had all the same ways of suppressing any lingering positive feelings created over a shared lifetime when he shot the Loyalist and then refused to help him while he lay dying at his feet. Instead he told the dying man, "the devil help you." And Robertson was far from the only militia soldier in this civil war who felt nothing (or at least admitted no feeling) watching someone who had once been close to him die. Another wounded Loyalist begged his Patriot brother-in-law for help on the battlefield. The brother-in-law rudely told him to "look to your friends for help" and left him to die. Others still felt a prick of sympathy when faced with the human suffering of those on the other side but did nothing, since the cultural expectation during the war was to ignore or repudiate the suffering of those on the other side. Benjamin Sharp remembered passing the night after a battle "amid groans and lamentations," which nearby Patriots did nothing to assuage. One veteran remembered voices "begging piteously for a little water," but "these cries, when emanating from the Tories, were little heeded." Civilians and soldiers alike cultivated this numbness to the humanity of the other side—an enforced callousness.[36]

No one even accorded the dead much honor. In part practicality dictated that bodies were hastily stacked in careless piles and covered haphazardly in a way that did nothing to protect the corpses from the abuse of serving as food for animals. Survivors at Kings Mountain reported "all the hogs in the neighborhood gathered into the place to devour the flesh." But while practicality had something to do with it, so did hate. For days after the battle, Loyalist families picked through the pile of bodies, looking for their husbands and fathers. Neither Patriot forces nor local civilians made any attempt to bury the bodies of their fellow Americans properly or to help the distraught civilian relatives seeking only to provide a bit of honor to an inglorious death. Disrespect and weariness combined to create a complete lack of regard for human dignity in death. No wonder that persistent rumors held that some of the Patriot soldiers saluted the deceased Loyalist militia commander's body at Kings Mountain by stripping him naked and urinating on him. They probably did not bother, but they certainly all shared the same casual disregard for each other even as corpses.[37]

The desire for revenge and the very nature of militia warfare had pushed both Patriot and Loyalist South Carolinians into an unforgiving civil war in which they sunk ever lower in their efforts to win at any cost. They had trained their own soldiers and civilians to brutalize the enemy and ignore their humanity. The revolutionaries who had wanted to avoid paying higher taxes or to ensure home rule had ripped the top off of Pandora's box. No one knew if they could put it back on again.

✳ The Brutal Outcome of Civil War and the Redemption of Forgetting

Romantics love to dwell on the American Civil War as a war of brother against brother and consider that conflict to be the only civil war in American history. Yet the American Revolution itself was a brutal civil war in which both sides often chose abominable behavior. That bad behavior shaped the postwar period, complicating attempts at reconciliation and healing. The end of the war left shattered psyches, ruined physical structures, depleted fields, and battered social ties.

South Carolinians paid a horrifying price for this civil war. During military engagements in 1780 alone (during the thick of the guerrilla warfare), almost two-thirds of total American Patriot casualties fell on South Carolina soil. An astounding 90 percent of soldiers who were wounded but survived received those wounds in South Carolina engagements. These figures are for Patriot soldiers only. If the Loyalist casualties are added, the human toll obviously would be even larger. This is especially true because even the Patriot figures do not include the hundreds of minor skirmishes and confrontations of the guerrilla war in the South. Even when the entire eight-year war is taken into account, with almost five years of war bypassing South Carolina, we find that at least 18 percent of those who died in battle for the Patriot cause overall died on South Carolina's soil. This destruction of human life meant that few white families, rich or poor, were untouched by loss. If an immediate family member had not been killed, they knew a kinsman or neighbor who had. Henry Laurens bitterly reflected on his own greatest personal loss while contemplating the peace treaty he was shortly to negotiate and sign for all Americans. He eulogized his beloved fallen son, John, as "that good soldier and good Citizen, that dutiful Son and sincere friend" for whom he was "in deep mourning." He was far from the only bereaved father.[38]

Black families also knew deep and troubling losses arising from the Revolution. The human pluck and ingenuity that led 20 percent of enslaved South Carolinians to flee to British lines and make themselves free is rightly celebrated. For them the chaos of war offered the sweet taste of freedom. But it also left wives without husbands and children without parents. Slaves tried to preserve their families. Certainly many people had no intention of running toward freedom while leaving a spouse or child in bondage. But the grim reality of the physical exertions involved in the journey from plantation toil to a British warship in the harbor was such that not everyone could make it. Loved ones celebrated that their spouse, uncle, grandchild, or friend had found freedom while trying to squash the bittersweet realization that they would never see each other again. The psychic toll of loss for the survivors of the war affected black and white South Carolinians differently, yet it hit them both all the same.

In addition to the human toll, there was the crippling physical destruction of both the landscape and the infrastructure of the state. The total economic value of the destruction of property—in terms of the number and worth of crops and houses—is not known. Yet a sense of the devastation can be gained from the haunting reports of those who looked around postwar South Carolina and were moved to record with horror what they saw all around them. Joseph Kershaw complained that British troops had burned "the greatest Part of the best Houses" in Camden. In Georgetown observers noted that the British had burned down almost two hundred houses. William Drayton claimed he could follow the British path through the state by following the chimneys, which were the only things left standing after troops burned the houses.[39]

South Carolinians limped into the postwar state they had been so optimistic about creating in 1775. By 1782, when the legislature first met to consider what to do with the vanquished Loyalists, South Carolinians were concerned with not only the loss of human capital caused by wartime casualties but also the substantial economic losses in properties and crops destroyed and horses stolen. They were aware that their neighbors and friends were shell-shocked from the war. When Rev. Archibald Simpson worried that "all was desolation," he did not just mean the physical destruction he saw. He meant that the mood of the people was depressed. He recognized the signs of that moroseness in himself as well as in the people with whom he interacted. Capt. Francis Richardson spoke of the "general doom" in the population in the same breath he mentioned the widespread destruction he saw. When people looked around at the devastation on the landscape, their minds instantly turned to the emotional devastation of loss and uncertainty. These minds were scarred by the terror of the reality of unrelenting civil warfare.[40]

Victorious Patriots did not feel victorious. Instead they fed off each other's anguish. One Continental officer astutely noted this: "Wherever you turn the weeping widow and fatherless child pour out their melancholy tales to wound the feelings of humanity." Wherever South Carolinians turned, they saw destruction and depression to mirror the pain they themselves felt. Somehow from all this human pain, they had to find a way to release themselves from the emotional shackles of the past so that they could build a more prosperous and fulfilling future.[41]

It is no wonder, given this sad legacy of civil war, that South Carolinians wished to vent their rage by punishing Loyalists in their power. The amazing thing is that so little time would pass before they found it in themselves to be generous. And it makes it even more amazing that while South Carolinians could have rehearsed their wrongs incessantly to the next generation, guaranteeing these hatreds would live on from generation to generation, they did not choose to do so. Instead, they embraced the redemption of forgetting, and let the painful memories die with the Revolutionary generation.

TWO ✳ *1782*

The New State Government Confronts Its Loyalists

John Lewis Gervais, a member of the lowcountry elite, bitterly worried about his still-unknown losses from the war in the months before and after he joined other legislators to decide the question of Loyalist punishment. He was especially frustrated because British sequestration of estates during the war meant he had not laid eyes on his own property in years. Instead he relied on reports from friends as their wives and family members spread news (as well as rumors) about the state of such vital resources. He was worried that his entire estate had been singled out for destruction, because the Loyalists "have a great Spleen against me particularly": "Horses, Cattle & Stock of all Sorts they have either destroyed or carried off from the plantation, in a Word they have left me nothing but my Land, which thank God they could not carry away." Within the year his friends reported that he had nothing left but a single suit of clothes and a horse. That horse would have to carry him to Philadelphia in the fall of 1782 so that he could take his newly elected place in the Continental Congress.[1]

Yet when Gervais sat in judgment of South Carolina Loyalists in the early winter of 1782 as a member of the South Carolina legislature, he helped pass legislation that was actually quite generous to them. The Confiscation Act the General Assembly passed only proscribed 232 Loyalists, and a fourth of those were absentee landowners and British merchant houses. While he did help ensure that two men he blamed for destroying his own property ended up on the confiscation list, his personal revenge depended on the widespread agreement of many others in the legislature. Despite his own justifiable anger at his financial losses, he was able to exercise discernment as a legislator. He and others set aside their intense anger over their wartime anguish and losses and created a system of Loyalist punishment that was generous from the beginning and got steadily more generous over time.

Early American historians remember what U.S. history survey courses forget: that while the British surrender at Yorktown marked the conclusion of the last major British military offensive in their efforts to reclaim the American colonies, no one at the time was sure of that. Americans spent the next two years celebrating the likely prospect of independence while blanching at the fear that the British would send another army to reconquer them. Many Americans living in major cities had to deal with the anxieties and frustrations of occupation, wondering when, if ever, British soldiers would finally leave. It was in this context that several American states, including both Carolinas, Georgia, Virginia, New York, and Pennsylvania, decided to pass harsh legislation punishing and driving out Loyalists. A closer look reveals that while state legislators and governors wished for their constituents to see them dealing with the problem of Loyalists, the resulting solutions were not meant to be as harsh as they might sound on the surface. Instead Loyalist punishment was meant to draw wavering Loyalists back into the Patriot fold while their services were still useful to the cause. Only those Loyalists who remained with the British were singled out for official punishment. Of course, given the uncertainty of the times, many Loyalists chose to remain with the powerful British and only gradually gave in to the despairing realization that the British had chosen to abandon them and their efforts to subdue the thirteen mainland North American colonies.

For South Carolinians the problems were especially sharp. British forces still occupied their only city—the cultural, economic, and political locus of the state. Most wealthy South Carolinians owned property and had business affairs in Charleston even if they primarily lived on plantations elsewhere. This was increasingly true for the backcountry elite as well as the lowcountry denizens. The only functioning courts before the American Revolution were also solely in Charleston. Without the capital city, governmental life ground to a halt during the war. Even after the British surrendered their second large army at Yorktown, they still incontrovertibly controlled not only Charleston itself but much of the lowcountry. Guerrilla warfare continued to pick at British control but showed no signs of dislodging them from their secure berth—even after noted (if impetuous) hero John Laurens gave his life in a small skirmish designed to help force them out. Guerrilla warfare in the interior certainly disrupted British control, but it also disrupted everyday life. The war's dislocations had encouraged slaves to flee to freedom. From the perspective of white South Carolinians, their losses in slave property showed no signs of abating despite the surrender at Yorktown. All in all, as 1782 dawned and South Carolina Patriots faced the question of how to rebuild their society and deal with the Loyalists, there were many problems to work out.

✳ *The Emotional Logic of Loyalist Punishment*

When the legislature turned its attention to the question of what to do with the Loyalists—the likely losers—the war was not entirely over. South Carolinians had already lived through a bloody, violent civil war that ebbed and flowed throughout the entire eight-year period of the Revolution. Victorious Patriots faced the question of whether they should give into the very human desire for revenge—a desire that was widely shared. Many people suggested that inflicting painful punishments on the Loyalists was only fair, since Patriots had suffered themselves. Others tried to argue that pragmatism demanded Loyalist punishment, either because "the people" would demand it or because the Loyalists had proved themselves to be untrustworthy already and could not be depended upon to help build a strong new state and nation.

South Carolinians' desire for revenge was also enflamed due to the constant emotional whipsaw of often-changing alliances (brought on by often-changing governments). First the Patriots had controlled the state for almost five years and used the militia to control and even terrorize wavering Loyalists into submission. When the British gained the upper hand in 1780, Patriots discovered the pain of living under enemy occupation and experienced what it was like to have the militia and the government turned against them. So when they regained control in 1782, they were understandably interested in sharing the pain. Many Patriots also felt justified in doing so since the South Carolinians, like all Americans, were aware that the British had used the force of the state against those who dissented publicly, whether or not they took up arms against the state. In fact the remedy the Patriots settled on, confiscation and effective banishment, was already the one the British had used against them. Patriot leaders understood all too well the kind of pressure the sudden loss of home and income could wreak on a family. Henry Laurens complained about Patriot families' being "driven into the Woods reduc'd from affluence to the most extreme penury" after their estates were confiscated by the British. Gov. John Rutledge chimed in to remind Patriots that "many of our firmest Friends have been reduced, for their inflexible Attachment to the Cause of their Country, from Opulence to inconceivable Distress, and if the Enemy's Will and power had prevailed, would have been doomed to Indigence and Beggary."[2]

South Carolinians found themselves balancing conflicting, yet deep, emotional crosscurrents in shaping both official and personal responses to the Loyalists. At the same time as many people wanted revenge, citizens found it easier to condemn those whom they had never met and could therefore regard as merely a theoretical enemy. It would prove to be much harder to ignore the pleas and compensatory explanations and apologies of former friends and neighbors—people who had once shared the same emotional skin of close-knit communities. And claims for beneficence played into another overwhelming desire: the desire to create a more stable and prosperous society all whites could share in, one that would make the terrible memories of the uncertainties and tribulations of civil war recede into distant, hazy memory.

All South Carolinians—white and black, elite and ordinary, lowcountry and backcountry, Loyalist and Patriot—had suffered from the chaotic and harsh civil war. Prominent Patriots had ended up imprisoned in fetid British prisoner-of-war ships (as Lt. Gov. Christopher Gadsden was) or in the Tower of London (as was Henry Laurens). Others not only faced peril on the battlefield but also had their estates confiscated by the British, which meant their families were also thrown out of their homes and forced to rely on whatever other sources of income the family might have. Arthur Middleton, one of South Carolina's delegates to the Continental Congress, was warned that "it is said they also burnt your father's [house]" and possibly "carried off all his negroes" in the aftermath of a routine engagement after Yorktown. While some prominent Patriots could only imagine the devastation they would find, others were sure of the damages their property sustained from the war. Ralph Izard was furious that his house was in "a very ruinous condition," although his concerns for his "beautiful & elegant plaster" lares made him sound like an out-of-touch dandified aristocrat.[3]

South Carolinians would elect to treat the bulk of the Loyalist population generously from the beginning, but that was not for lack of rage. Aedanus Burke worried that "the inveterate hatred & spirit of Vengeance wch. they have excited in the breasts of our Citizens is such as you can form no idea of. The very females talk as familiarly of shedding blood & destroying the Tories as the men do." Burke was suggesting that the urge for revenge was out of control, and even though he was an advocate for leniency, he admitted that he too felt the "Love of Revenge natural to the mind of man," although he also felt the need to restrain that impulse. His admission of the naturalness of the desire for revenge opens up another possibility. While he condemned the loose talk of vengeance he claimed to hear in every parlor he visited, he seems to have misunderstood his fellow citizens. Up to a point, endlessly rehearsing vengeance served as an escapist fantasy that allowed South Carolina Patriots to release their anger rather than actually enact the vengeance they spoke of so frequently. Recent research in evolutionary psychology shows that our brains (at least the parts of the brain related to reward and pleasure) receive stimulation in the anticipation of watching someone receive punishment when the person watching believes it to be just. All that parlor talk was actually stimulating pleasure centers in the brain—a powerful incentive to continue talking about vengeance.[4]

Again and again Patriots let loose their rage against Loyalists in epistolary form. Laurens often expressed intense anger at the British and Loyalists for the immense destruction the war caused. From his vantage point as a prisoner in the Tower of London, he had no idea just how much physical destruction had been wrought on his own properties. He was well aware that other planters had experienced large losses of capital in slaves, as some 20 percent of the enslaved population freed themselves by seeking asylum with the British. So when a London merchant tried to collect a small debt from him, Laurens exploded with self-justifying rage. How dare this merchant ask about supplies and payments "now [that] the British forces have plunder'd him of all his property"? Matters did not improve much once he was able to assess his losses. In 1783 he railed at one of his occasional business partners that he was unable to make business decisions since he had "lost 30 or 40 thousand pounds sterling." This figure, derived from hazy accounts from his overseers, preyed on his mind right along with the painful loss of his son John, who died during a routine engagement in April 1782.[5]

While at first glance these constant invocations of righteous anger suggest the depth of Patriot rage and desire both to justify revenge and actually to end it, they can now be understood as coping mechanisms that activated powerful evolutionary pathways in the brain. Laurens put it frankly when he imagined a Loyalist trying to complain about being ill-used by South Carolinians who dared to levy harsh punishment. In his imagination all a Loyalist could muster in his own defense was "I am a Loyalist, I used my utmost endeavours to get you all hanged to confiscate your Estates & beggar Your Wives & children, pray make a provision for me or let me enjoy my Estate?" Yet tellingly, after the emotional release of imagining an unnamed Loyalist humbling himself with specious attempts at self-justification, Laurens was later able to consider "a few among the Loyalists whose Cases I shall truly commiserate, but the number is very small." His use of the word *commiserate* is telling as well, suggesting that when victorious Patriots were able to imagine themselves sharing the same emotional skin as the Loyalist they were judging, it became possible to share the ideas, thoughts, and emotions that Loyalists felt. Revenge talk could serve as a bridge to more positive feelings about Loyalists—feelings that ultimately enabled Patriots to empathize with and then reintegrate Loyalists.[6]

There are isolated examples of people moving from talk of revenge to actually taking revenge with their own hands, but these stories are few and far between. In the backcountry Patriots tried to round up and kill a roving band of Loyalist-identified men, but they were horse thieves first and Loyalist militiamen second by that time. In the years following legislative punishment, Charleston crowds occasionally acted against individual Loyalists. But even when those crowds turned to whipping individuals, the focus still remained on the traditional symbolic shame and humiliation that crowd actions were meant to signal.

Among the upper crust (who did not join the street crowds), personal revenge was symbolic. Christopher Gadsden, who had spent much of the last part of the war imprisoned by the British, encountered two Loyalist friends in a Patriot militia camp in December 1781, a month before the 1782 legislative session to consider Loyalist punishment began. As it turns out, Gadsden very much considered them to be former friends. Brothers Elias and Thomas Horry had just taken (late) advantage of the governor's proclamation of clemency for Loyalists who deserted the British and joined Patriot militias. Both Horrys had taken British protection only after the British conquered the state. Before then Gadsden and Thomas Horry had served together on the Committee of Correspondence. The Horrys evidently expected that they would be warmly greeted by their friend and fellow member of the lowcountry elite. They evinced no sign of hesitation as they approached Gadsden and expectantly reached out to shake hands. Yet they were in for a shock. Gadsden angrily spurned them and "told them he did not shake Hands wth. Rascals." When Elias Horry, in his surprise, pleaded that they had taken the clemency offer and come to give themselves up, Gadsden bitterly suggested that instead of getting pardon they should be "hang'd to be sure." Onlookers were amused to see the Horrys lose their nonchalant self-assurance as they "took fright, jumped upon their Horses, & dashed off." (They were then forcibly brought back to camp.) Even mild-mannered Patriots were extremely angry and willing to let that anger show. But like Gadsden many were more bluster than bite. Gadsden relieved his anger through such social opprobrium. The Horrys suffered a momentary fright as they realized the depth of their neighbors' anger. Yet others rode after them and returned them to camp—and therefore to legal clemency and reintegration. Even in moments of petty revenge, cooler heads prevailed. After all, compared to the vast losses Patriots and Loyalists suffered, a little personal humiliation over a handshake was merely the sting of an insect bite. [7]

While anticipating the chance to see someone be punished stimulates the pleasure centers in the brain (at least in studies of contemporary American undergraduates), actually punishing them is not nearly as pleasurable as people anticipate it to be. In fact enacting revenge or seeing it enacted can lead people to dwell on their wounds. That constant rumination actually makes people less happy. Instead people feel better when they stop dwelling on their injuries and move forward with their lives. Or at least this is what recent research in psychology suggests. In fact this makes intuitive sense and is what South Carolinians were actually doing as the Revolutionary War wound down. They felt better by working out their anger in lots of rabid talk about vengeance, but in practice they would start to move away from constant dwelling on their losses and thereby ensure that they would feel better about themselves, their lives, and the solidity and direction of their society. Their angry words and strictly symbolic personal revenges started to yield to an increasing empathy with

Loyalists and a willingness to cut the vast majority of them some slack for their wartime actions.[8]

The understandable desire for payback was tempered by the empathetic understanding that many Loyalists had simply been faced with nothing but bad choices and had made the one that seemed most likely to protect them at the time. As Burke, the leading voice advocating for Loyalist clemency, later pointed out, people only owed allegiance to a government that could protect them. At some point during the eight-year war, everyone had experienced the realization that their preferred government could no longer protect them. Should the legislature punish everyone who simply took protection? Edward Rutledge, the author of the eventual punishment legislation, derisively called these Loyalists the "protection Gentry" and resented their audacity in continuing to conduct themselves publicly as if nothing had happened. Many especially resented them for taking the easy path, describing them as "trimming" like a sailboat avoiding the winds. Yet the beginnings of empathy were important. Political science literature on contemporary conflicts suggests this recognition of the humanity of the other is essential to crafting a lasting reconciliation. Laurens charitably described his Loyalist neighbors as those once "called a good sort of, or, good Men" who had beaten the drums for the Patriot cause when it seemed safe but "shrunk from all principles . . . [and] chose the strongest party" when danger arrived. Yet many of these men were lifelong South Carolinians with deep roots in the community and a long history of conducting themselves as upright neighbors, giving credit, aid, charitable contributions, and personal favors. Which spoke more deeply: their wartime actions or their lifelong commitments to social networks as trustworthy community members? As South Carolina's legislature met to consider how to punish Loyalists, this growing empathy and implicit realization that constant rumination would prolong people's emotional recovery swayed the legislature to be merciful.[9]

❋ Behind the Legislative Curtain: The Realities of Designing Loyalist Punishment

Wags say that one should never watch sausage or legislation being made. On the face of it, the 1782 Confiscation Act was harsh, putting a definitive end to the "Loyalist question." Retrospectively, though, it is clear that it was part of a longer-term effort to bring Loyalists back into the fold. Even at the time of its passage, elite South Carolinians in and out of the legislature opined that the legislation would soon be undone—at least in piecemeal fashion. Shortly after the passage of the Confiscation Act, Christopher Gadsden, who was in the legislature and opposed passage, wrote to Gen. Francis Marion (who also was a proponent of leniency to Loyalists) and argued that "we must patiently wait till the next Assembly to endeavor to have its severities at least mitigated where there is room." He was indeed right—by early 1784 a new legislature junked most of the Confiscation Act.[10]

Aedanus Burke was even more realistic, as well as caustic, when the same year he told Arthur Middleton (a signer of the Declaration of Independence and a perpetual South Carolina delegate to the Continental Congress) that the Confiscation Act was passed "to satisfy publick justice, and as you would throw a Tub to a whale to satisfy the vengeance of those who have suffered."[11] He believed that some wavering legislators were pushed into such harsh legislation by the public demand that someone pay for all the loss around them. In other words the human desire for vengeance meant that there should be many sacrificial lambs. But other legislators defended the Confiscation Act as a just law that actually already exempted many from its punishment. These legislators also supported the idea of retributive justice and saw nothing wrong with the Confiscation Act. Despite their support there is a clue here in these epistolary discussions between elite South Carolinians concerned with the potential long-term effects of an act they had helped create. From the beginning the act was both a carrot and stick designed as much to pull wavering Loyalists back into the Patriot fold as to punish those recalcitrant holdouts.

Tellingly, even before calling together the 1782 Jacksonborough Assembly, Gov. John Rutledge offered two separate public proclamations trying to persuade wavering Loyalists to return. Despite his noted hostility to the Loyalists, Rutledge issued a proclamation on September 27, 1781, offering many Loyalists the chance to return to the Patriot side with full forgiveness (and no confiscation) if they were willing to serve in the Patriot militia for six months. Male Loyalists who chose to take this offer were further assured that their wives and children could immediately resume living on the family estate, which everyone recognized was an ideal strategy for securing full, lasting control. In an effort to make sure wavering Loyalists were aware of the offer, the government had them printed on handbills and distributed by the army as widely as possible. Notice of the proclamation certainly made the Charleston Loyalist newspaper, although the publisher wisely avoided reprinting the most moving part—where Rutledge correctly predicted the sad fate that awaited many Loyalists who did not take the offer. He brought pressure to bear on wavering Loyalists by frightening them with the coming need to move to "some strange and distant land" where they would suffer "all the miseries and horrors of beggary, sickness and despair." This indeed was the experience of many ordinary people who ended up in Nova Scotia.[12]

South Carolina politicians pursued reconciliation with Loyalists for cold-hearted, practical reasons. As much as they might have liked simply to punish as many of them as possible, the circumstances they confronted mandated a more lenient policy. After the British surrender at Yorktown, Loyalists could see that the tide had turned and the British position in America was weak at best. Yet it was not at all clear to either side that the war was truly over. In 1782 there was no peace treaty, the armies were still in camp and, in the Carolinas, still skirmishing. Military and civilian strategists believed Britain might send a third major force to reconquer the colonies. Rutledge argued to the legislature that it was "probable [Britain] will not only endeavor to keep possession of our Capital but make another attempt to subjugate the Country." South Carolinians still did not control their largest city and state capital, Charleston, which was firmly in British hands. The 1782 legislature was a true wartime assembly, requiring protection by Patriot troops during its term. In fact its meeting place in Jacksonborough was chosen because Marion (who also voted in the assembly) and Gen. Nathanael Greene (commander of the southern Continental Army forces) felt they could protect it. Since many, including Greene, believed that the best-case scenario for a peace treaty would recognize the current military lines of control as the final territorial concession, South Carolinians were very motivated to continue to try to gain back control of the lowcountry and even Charleston—although getting control of Charleston was a long shot. Col. John Laurens, son of Henry Laurens and leader of a crucial Patriot spy ring, was killed in routine skirmishing in August 1782 while trying to gain the advantage in the lowcountry. Despite the pain and sacrifices of the eight-year war, it was almost unthinkable to the victors that the British army and navy, the mightiest in the world, would give up their own colonies.[13]

Further, across America in garrison towns such as Charleston and New York, where Loyalists and Patriots had been uneasily mixing for years, authorities who thought the war was finally coming to an end took the opportunity to solidify their control by pushing out the families of people on the opposing side. One Patriot wrote the South Carolina Continental Congress representative that the Wilmington, North Carolina, authorities "sent out the wives and families of those who had not joined them." South Carolinians were therefore justified, he suggested, in "collecting the wives & families of the Tories to send in return, &c. &c." Military officials on both sides were trying to secure the towns against the transmission of evidence and goods that porous borders allowed. Such forced evictions also deliberately increased the pressure on the opposing side by sending waves of panicked displaced persons into the opposing camps, where the other side had to care for them out of often-scarce supplies. As an effort to secure garrison towns from the transmission of information and goods, it failed miserably. Burke laughed at how the commandant at Charleston "winks at a little traffick carried on by our people." But it certainly increased pressure on the Loyalists and made it a good time to try

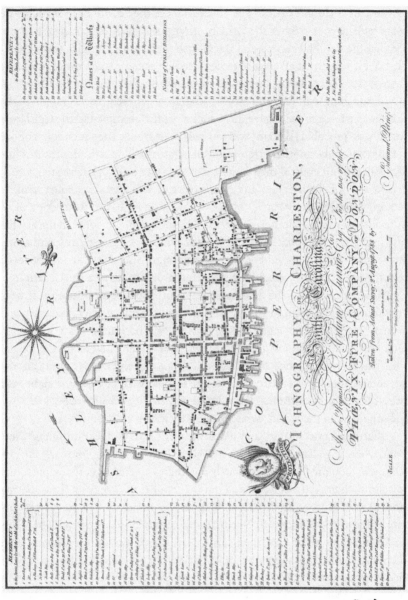

Ichnography of Charleston, 1788. Courtesy of the South Caroliniana Library, University of South Carolina, Columbia.

to woo them back to the Patriot side at a time when their military aid could change the situation on the ground.[14]

Rutledge's strategy worked well. Burke confidently told a friend that "above one hundred of their adherents (the inhab^ts. Of Chas. Town & the Country) have deserted over to us, and more are daily coming over their Lines." While there was officially a thirty-day deadline, in fact refugees trick-led into American outposts up to and during the Jacksonborough Assembly. In the two months before the legislature met in 1782, Loyalists felt intense pressure to take the proclamation before it was too late. When the legislature came to draw up legislation punishing Loyalists, the governor was able to report that more than a hundred male Loyalists had returned to the Patriot cause and taken up arms in the Patriot militia.[15]

The legislature rewarded those Loyalists who responded to Rutledge's proclamations (as well as other backdoor offers of lenient treatment) with an official legislative pardon act in the 1782 session. The Pardon Act helped the legislature consolidate control by insisting that South Carolina's government had the right to determine whether individuals were entitled to citizenship. It protected the rights of former Loyalists, but it also required them to serve nine months of active duty in the Patriot militia in order to secure the full protection of the act. The earlier proclamations had only required six months. The act also did not bother to list individuals by name but rather incorporated any Loyalist who was certified by the Patriot military command. This increased the pressure on Loyalists to come forward and was a de facto extension of the deadline for return. Overall South Carolina guaranteed protection and citizenship only for former Loyalists who were willing to make personal sacrifices on behalf of the independence of South Carolina at a time when they would still have to take a risk in coming over the Patriot side. Loyalists protected under the Pardon Act also were expected to pay a one-time amercement (tax penalty) of 10 percent of the total value of their estate.[16]

Rutledge had offered the Loyalists a carrot; now it was time for the stick. That stick—Loyalist punishment—also gave the fragile new state government and its central authority, the elected legislature, a chance to assert its own primacy. Rutledge had been functioning as the entire civil government of South Carolina for several years, including years in exile. As much as he enjoyed wielding power (and he had been strongly disciplined earlier for his autocratic tendencies), he understood that legislative power was the key to legitimacy in the post-Revolutionary world. Having fought a war for direct representational government, Americans needed to see their government in action. Jealous leaders were far more likely to support legislative decisions that they had a part in creating, and voters had been conditioned to expect real representation on concrete local interests. As historian Robert Weir has noted, one reason the

General Assembly passed punitive anti-Loyalist legislation in 1782 was to assert legislative power.[17]

Actually holding elections, however, presented problems. Several prominent South Carolina Patriots were still imprisoned by the British, and Rutledge wanted them to be able to serve in the new legislature in order to give it legitimacy. An even more ticklish issue was ensuring the safety of elections and the ability of all South Carolina citizens to cast their votes. Since the British still held about a third of the state, many citizens could not vote, and British troops and Loyalist raiding parties could make the election unsafe if they wanted to. In response to this problem (which could hardly have a perfect solution), the governor called for elections only after generals Greene and Marion were able to gain reliable control of more of the state. Still there were very few lowcountry voters who voted in the 1781 elections that put into place the 1782 Jacksonborough Assembly, which meant that the backcountry was more influential in this election than in any before. And yet most of the proscribed Loyalists were from the lowcountry.

How much influence did the backcountry representatives have in the Jacksonborough Assembly? To put it in perspective, before the war backcountry leaders complained loudly, often, and justifiably that they had little representation in the legislature relative to their population. But given how important backcountry people (and their terrain and leaders) had been in the war, it was clear that the lowcountry would have to yield a fair share of political power to the backcountry. And since most of the lowcountry was, for all electoral purposes, under occupation, backcountry representatives were important in the resulting 1782 assembly—much more important than they had ever been before, and in many ways more important than they would be in later years. For example in the 1782 senate only seven of the nineteen senators represented Charleston District, and those seven could not claim a mandate. Embarrassingly St. Andrew's Parish in the lowcountry sent six representatives and one senator, elected by a grand total of four voters—fewer voters than elected officials.[18]

Why does it matter that the legislature that would actually enact Loyalist punishment had more backcountry power than any assembly before or after it? Everyone in South Carolina suffered from the war, but backcountry residents had suffered more. Male backcountry residents were also more likely actually to have fought in a militia in either side and therefore to have experienced the war up close. The Patriot militia leaders who backcountry voters chose as representatives were less likely to sympathize with Loyalists, especially the elite lowcountry Loyalists whose main argument in their favor was that they had just signed congratulatory addresses, taken offices, and then done nothing while in those offices. And while all South Carolinians experienced the pain of brother against brother and cousin against cousin in the war, the tendency of backcountry men to choose the same side as the most prominent men in the district meant that often (although not always) backcountry legislators were less likely to be linked by marriage to a family with Loyalists. Some historians have overemphasized this situation and concluded that later reconciliation was merely because self-interested lowcountry elites offered clemency to their extended family members. While it is unlikely that this is the primary reason for reconciliation or even a factor in it, it did apparently color the way legislators in 1782 saw each other's motivations. Lowcountry legislators who privately favored generous policies toward at least some Loyalists—their friends, neighbors, and relatives—found it easy to paint the newly dominant backcountry politicians as backwoods rubes who sought vengeance above all else. They were aware that under these electoral conditions, they lacked the moral suasion to protect their friends from the justice they were prepared to mete out to others. Given this pressure, it is especially impressive that in the end, out of thousands of white male Loyalists, only about 220 men found themselves the subject of confiscation and banishment.[19]

The 1782 legislature was composed of men who had suffered greatly for the war. They had suffered financially and made great personal sacrifices. Benjamin Kilgore (from the backcountry Little River District) and Christopher Gadsden were British prisoners of war for quite some time, and other legislators had also found themselves imprisoned. Prisoners of war in the South found themselves held in dirty, disease-ridden ships or in faraway military outposts such as Saint Augustine, Florida. Burke, who opposed confiscation, uncharitably suggested that many of his fellow legislators were so battle-hardened, and even coarse, that they could not possibly find it in themselves to offer empathy to the plight of the Loyalists. "One of our Members of this present Assembly kept a tally of the number of men he has killed on the barrel of his pistol, and the notches amount to twenty-five. I know another who has killed his fourteen, &c. &c." While it was not guaranteed that men who bragged of their double-digit wartime kills would take every opportunity for revenge on the enemy, it was certainly a crowd that would be skeptical of Loyalist claims for clemency. All of them had made sacrifices for the Patriot cause, and they were sitting in judgment of men who had not made those sacrifices—men who had "trimmed," meaning they had taken the safe course. Of course it was tempting to force them to feel what it meant to lose everything. This intense anger at their own losses also makes the insistence on financial penalties for Loyalists more understandable.[20]

Despite Burke's fear that his fellow legislators (especially from the backcountry) were coarse soldiers, most South Carolinians elected these men because they considered them both distinguished war leaders and fine men in peacetime. Edward Rutledge described his fellow assembly members as "the Flower of the Country" and was pleased with the "Competent Appearance of the House." Even Burke, when not angry about confiscation, admitted that the legislature was "composed of very respectable good men." South Carolinians had broadened who could serve in the legislature, but the traditional rules of status and deference ensured that the leading men of each region took up the task of considering how to punish Loyalists and who specifically should bear that punishment. While they had every reason to be bitter about what they had lost in wartime, they had not lost more than many of the people they represented. This wartime legislature was well-suited to represent the desires of a war-weary populace.[21]

Despite having the best of intentions, the legislators did not agree on who was culpable enough to face confiscation. While few legislators spoke out against the theory of Loyalist punishment, when it got to the specifics of exactly who would suffer these punishments, the legislative debate got much rockier. In the House full floor debate began with a list of more than 700 names, and members on the floor quickly added another 240. Burke, a member of the House, bitterly complained that the list kept growing because "every one gives in a List of his own and the State's Enemies."[22] There may be something to his uncharitable suspicions, but it is also possible that individual legislators found it easier to empathize with and therefore protect those Loyalists who they knew more intimately (from the same community). Revenge was certainly not the sole consideration in generating the list of Loyalist names, even if it may have explained the fate of a few.

That same empathy helped to explain why a few men managed to dodge confiscation even though legislators added their names back to the draft confiscation list time and time again. At the end of the initial week of debate, the House had managed to whittle their list down to a mere 118 names, but the Senate rapidly added back almost 300 more. Edward Rutledge, Speaker of the House and the chief architect of the act, was insulted by the Senate's demand to expand the list. In his mind the Senate had "increased the List to such an amazing Length & have added so many insignificant Characters that it must undergo very great alteration." His characterization of many of those names as "insignificant Characters" suggests that the House had already agreed to a concise list of names chosen as much-needed sacrificial lambs. In practice Rutledge must have been frustrated that the Senate threatened to undo the delicate compromises his House had already made. In addition some of those names were men he personally empathized with and was trying to protect from the confiscation he advocated. For instance both John Wragg (Christopher Gadsden's brother-in-law) and William Blake were the subject of hard-fought battles. In the end both were saved from confiscation due to their friends, although both paid an amercement. Rutledge, the author of confiscation, fought to protect Blake and later told a mutual friend that "your old Friend, Billy Blake, has had a very narrow escape indeed."[23]

South Carolina badly needed quick and easy sources of money, as the state was flat broke. Wealthy Loyalists made a tempting target, since their properties could be auctioned off and used to fund the state's pressing bills. In fact those funds could also be used to fund all manner of pet projects of legislators, from new schools to fine mahogany chairs. Burke claimed that discussions of which Loyalists to punish revolved not around "what he has done, as what Estate he has." Other legislators confirmed that the discussion often involved the net worth of individual Loyalists. Alexander Garden later told the perhaps apocryphal tale that when confiscation was discussed, members of the legislature would listen for certain names, calling out "a fat sheep—prick it! Prick it!" when the names of especially wealthy men were called.[24]

Wealthy and well-situated Loyalists were attractive targets of confiscation for another reason. While their estates could certainly help pad the depleted finances of the state, the sales of their property, including prime male field hands and well-tended and well-situated lowcountry estates, could also benefit individuals trying to make up for the wealth they had lost during the war. Edward Rutledge personally profited by buying scores of confiscated properties on easy credit terms.

Loyalists did not take lying down the effort to confiscate their estates and drive them out. Instead several rallied to try to save their estates from confiscation while the legislature was still debating the final terms. Rutledge noted with a certain wry amusement that "since the Confiscation List has made its way into Town" (during the session), there had been "several broad Hints from our quondam Enemies wishing that we wd. permit they would return to their *Countrymen*." People circulated drafts of the confiscation lists, or at least heated rumors about what names were on it. Some legislators wrote their friends and warned them that they were in danger of facing confiscation. Rutledge himself tried to save well-connected Charles Drayton from confiscation as a courtesy to his brother-in-law. He tried to get Drayton to come over to the Patriot militia camps as a show of good faith so that Rutledge would have political cover in removing him from the confiscation list. To his disgust Drayton was "as inactive as ever, for which he has been placed on the Sequestration List. He has been written to repeatedly about the Matter, but all to no purpose—He stays at Home, & returns no answer." Despite Drayton's fear or obstinacy, Rutledge and his allies managed to save him from confiscation by moving him to the amercement list—but it was touch and go for a while. Sarah Steward also was "informed" that her husband's name was on the draft Confiscation Act, and she responded by petitioning for clemency while the legislature was still in session. She argued that her husband had "always been a friend to the American cause," that he had "befriended many American prisoners," and that if he was "restored to his Country," he would be appropriately grateful. All of this was despite the fact that she had to admit that her husband was in England at the time of the appeal. In an effort to bolster her case, she also pleaded her own distress and poverty if the family was stripped of their land. Given that her husband's name was the subject of considerable back-and-forth negotiation between the House and Senate, it is likely that a Steward ally contacted her and coached her on how to approach the legislature. And just like in Drayton's case, this seemingly flimsy approach gave Seward's allies enough cover to move him from the confiscation list to the amercement list.[25]

A handful of Patriot relatives of Loyalists used this opportunity to try to take their relatives' property through the official auspices of the legislature. Alexander Garden Jr., the son of a Loyalist, apparently spent the entire month and a half of the assembly buttonholing acquaintances into protecting his interests. He annoyed Rutledge, who described him as "full of Trouble . . . lest we should touch *his* Plantation at Goosecreek." In addition to protecting his own property against any misidentification, he also petitioned to be granted his father's estate in the light of his own "invariable attachment" to America. William Henry Harvey tried to claim his brother's property. Both Garden and Harvey were more concerned with the potential for personal profit than for their relatives' interests or the interests of the state in raising money through the sale of confiscated estates. The General Assembly did waver in the face of these efforts, briefly considering an amendment to the law that would allow Patriot male family members to assume their Loyalist relative's property. However greater reflection stopped them. Most of the lowcountry Loyalists named on the confiscation list had Patriot relatives. The state desperately needed to raise money from the confiscated estates. Even if relatives did not quickly claim all the confiscated estates, the possibility that relatives would later emerge to take those estates would make potential purchasers leery of making such an investment. Instead the legislature stuck to making unseemly backroom deals. In one they even admitted in writing that their decision "militates against the whole Tenor of the Bill now under consideration."[26]

In the end Henry Laurens would conclude that after a "moment for Reflexion" the legislature had confiscated property with "necessary & magnanimous reservation," forbearing from committing injustices.[27] Loyalists who faced confiscation, and even amercement, would vigorously rebut this presumption in the coming years. It was certainly financially advantageous for these Loyalists to do everything they could to preserve the full value of their often considerable estates. Yet Laurens had a point. While on the surface confiscation, amercement, and the use of the court system in future years seems like a comprehensive and harsh system of punishment for Loyalists, in the end the numbers make it clear that the vast majority of Loyalists dodged a bullet. Those who escaped official legislative notice still had one important barrier to overcome—the acceptance of their communities. But for the majority who managed to effect personal reintegration, the legislature had just opened the door to their full thriving.

✳ Anti-Loyalist Legislation: Retributive Justice and Reparations

South Carolinians chose to join all other Americans in adopting severe legislative penalties for Loyalists between 1777 and 1782. Every single state chose to confiscate all of the property of some Loyalists and banish those people from the new United States. This move for retributive justice was popular across the board. Most states also created or acknowledged some system by which a few Loyalists might pay reparations in order to absolve themselves of harsher punishment. Those payments might be to individuals (as in Virginia) or to the state (as in South Carolina), but in both kinds of reparations the pain inflicted on Loyalist families by substantial transfers of wealth helped reassure other Americans that they had paid for their poor choice of loyalties. Yet it becomes clear that South Carolinians, like other Americans, actually chose to only punish a handful of Loyalists and ignore the rest. On the surface anti-Loyalist legislation was very harsh, but in practice only a small number of people actually found themselves scrutinized and banished or forced to pay reparations. Most American Loyalists actually found themselves working out their own reintegration through personal negotiations.

When South Carolina joined other American states in enacting Loyalist punishment in 1782, they were firmly in the mainstream of American thinking about the position of Loyalists in the postwar nation—at least on the surface. What is distinctive, however, is the extent to which even confiscation was far less harsh than it could have been. Just because every American state ultimately confiscated estates and pushed out Loyalists does not mean they all did it to an equal share of their population or even of their Loyalist population. What actually stands out about South Carolina's efforts to craft a legislative solution is twofold: first in the end confiscation covered fewer than three hundred families, and that number includes British families who owned land in the state but did not live there at the time of the Revolution. The legislature considered more than twice as many names as were ultimately subject to confiscation. Legislative confiscation turned out to be quite mild, given the ferocity of the civil war in South Carolina. Second the legislature actually decided that confiscation alone was too blunt an instrument to deal adequately with both the desire for Loyalist punishment and the reality that *Loyalist* was a label that covered a wide variety of wartime actions from simply accepting British protection to leading a Loyalist militia. While some in the legislature were blindly bent on retribution, others from the beginning sought to temper the necessity of punishing some with the desire to use mercy as a method to create a freer, more stable, and more inclusive state and nation.

As the 1782 legislature began, it looked as if the Loyalists would find no mercy. Gov. John Rutledge warned the legislature at the opening session that "Justice and Policy forbid their free readmission to the rights and Privileges of citizenship." By judging their conduct "reprehensible," Rutledge argued for retribution over empathy or moderation. Of course he was a vocal advocate for Loyalist punishment, along with his brother, the Speaker of the House, and used his bully pulpit to advance the cause of harsh retribution against Loyalists. For the Rutledges and many others, the security of South Carolina's hard-won independence required that the state expel many former Loyalists as unreliable and unredeemable citizens—a fifth column waiting for a chance to destroy the security of the Republic. They could not be citizens of the independent state precisely because they had already sold out the interests of South Carolina once.[28]

But how to craft Loyalist punishment that balanced this very human desire for retribution (however justified) and the competing desires to forgive at least some Loyalists? That was the task of the 1782 General Assembly, and it was one they largely stumbled through without a clear vision of the outcome. But what they created at the end was theoretically a sophisticated and interlocking system of punishment and redemption that would punish both backcountry and lowcountry, elite and ordinary Loyalists. But whether they knew it or not, what they in fact designed was a system that largely ignored ordinary Loyalists and many backcountry Loyalists. Or at least that is the way it worked out.

What did this legislation look like, and what did it actually do? In the end the General Assembly passed four separate acts—the Confiscation Act, the Amercement Act, an act for using state courts to prosecute wartime actions, and an act confiscating the lands of those who left the state even when their names were not on the official Confiscation Act. In sum these acts were meant to punish a wide variety of Loyalists whether or not they were prominent enough to come to the attention of the legislators. Yet in practice most of these acts quickly became dead letters, and very few Loyalists ever faced official sanction from the legislature.

The Confiscation Act, which dominated legislative discussion for the entire month-plus session, named some 230 male Loyalists and confiscated all of their South Carolina property including personal items, real estate, and property in slaves. That property in slaves was very valuable but hard for either fleeing Loyalists or the state to capitalize since these human beings used the chaos of the war to claim their own freedom through arriving in British camps. The Confiscation Act followed Governor Rutledge's prior categorization in dividing these approximately 300 people into six categories of ever-increasing culpability for wartime actions. These categories tried to take what could seem random (why might one man find himself punished while another one seemingly got off scot-free) and overlay a sense of order and rationalism to it. In practice some men would have qualified under multiple lists, and some men who avoided confiscation had in fact committed one or more of the specific acts in the list.[29]

Among resident South Carolinians who demonstrably had Loyalist connections, the Confiscation Act mostly singled out elite men who had taken officer-level positions in either the civilian British occupational government or the Loyalist militias or had otherwise publicly supported the British cause by signing congratulatory addresses welcoming the British to Charleston and complimenting them on conquering the state. Therefore the majority of men on the eventual confiscation list had supported the British in public ways, not to mention ways that could not be easily disavowed later. Thousands of men took allegiance oaths and protection from the British once they controlled the state. But a much smaller number, often concentrated in Charleston proper, signed the official welcoming addresses. It is for this reason that historian Robert Lambert called the signers "marked men."[30] At a time when South Carolina's Patriot fortunes were at their lowest ebb, these men had used their public personas to support the Loyalist cause.

Public appearance and character were important to eighteenth-century Americans, with a sense of palpable urgency hard to recapture now. From a contemporary perspective, it is difficult to understand why more than 20 percent of the proscribed Loyalists were singled out for signing a public address and punished just as severely as those who commanded Loyalist militias. Yet from the perspective of the eighteenth-century concern for public reputation as a vital part of the demonstrated self-mastery required of dependable neighbors and citizens, it makes more sense. Further this insistence on the importance of personal reputation in oath-taking and signing addresses speaks to the eighteenth-century American insistence on a politics of personal, face-to-face relations. In a world where voting was by public voice affirmation at local gathering places, public political reputation was paramount. A "blot" on a man's character reduced him from equality with other men, undermining these Loyalists' claims to honor and citizenship. Self-sacrifice was part of the code of honorable citizenship. Well-off and professional men who should have understood the necessity of resisting personal self-interest in their public roles as citizens had instead massively failed—lending their names to the destruction of their own government on behalf of their own self-interest.[31]

Yet even in this moment when the General Assembly crafted harsh anti-Loyalist legislation, they opened an escape hatch from the consequences of the act for at least some savvy Loyalists. Technically all proscribed Loyalists had been deemed traitors by legislation from 1777 on, yet the Confiscation Act of 1782 explicitly stated that despite this designation, in the interests of "extend[ing] to those persons as much mercy as may be consistent with justice to the public," the legislature would waive the penalty of execution from the vast number of Loyalists subject to confiscation—even if they stayed in the state for some time after the passage of the act. The act itself gave them forty-five days to stay before facing forced transportation out of state, but this provided an opening many of these proscribed Loyalists would take and use to petition and even pester later legislatures until the 1784 legislature ultimately restored most of them to full citizenship. In practice the state never enforced the rule to leave and never forcibly deported individual Loyalists. The only thing that could dissuade these Loyalists from ignoring the legislative order to leave was the concerted hostility of the Patriot neighbors. And as will be seen later, only a handful of Loyalists found their neighbors implacably opposed to working out some sort of accommodation.

The legislature also used the opportunity to confiscate the valuable properties of nonresident landowners and British merchant houses. A quarter of the total confiscation list comprised these people, accounting almost certainly for more than half of the total value of the confiscated property. This total is even larger when one considers that at least thirty other individuals named on the other lists were merchants, albeit often of longer South Carolina residency. The Confiscation Act justified this seizure of nonresident property by describing the nonresidents as not necessarily culpable but of dubious loyalty. Charles Cotesworth Pinckney, a supporter of confiscation and Jacksonborough Assembly member, later argued sheepishly that these estates had been included because "it was not known who were the Heirs or Devisees," and it was easier to restore property later than to allow "our Enemies" to get their hands on it. Of course at the time Pinckney was arguing as the paid attorney of an absentee owner who was trying to reclaim this confiscated property, so his halfhearted explanation seems dubious. It seems more likely that these estates were confiscated because they made a compelling target. These absentee owners and merchant firms possessed economically valuable property and were in no position to defend it during the legislative session of 1782. It would be more difficult for them to litigate or otherwise make a case for redress later, given such a great distance and lack of local ties—although in the end some of these "foreign" owners did pursue such redress and with the aid of prominent local Patriots such as Henry Laurens. Perhaps a legislator had his eye on choice Charleston property when the legislation even threw in the "Owners of a Lot in Gadsden's Alley" (a valuable tract of land right by the water). This long list of absentee owners also made it easier to disguise the most tempting targets of all: the British merchant houses. Many South Carolinians owed sizable debts to these merchants, which they sometimes found difficult to repay. Confiscation effectively erased these debts.[32]

The confiscation list also singled out a few notorious Loyalist militia leaders for their longtime military leadership in the Loyalist cause, dubbing them proven "inveterate enemies of this State." These eleven individuals (or a mere 5 percent of the total number) were singled out for the harshest terms. In addition to the complete confiscation and banishment that all the other targets of the Confiscation Act faced, these men faced a much stronger legislative order to leave the state. While all proscribed Loyalists were told to leave the state, only these eleven were pointedly excluded from measures that changed loyalism from a capital crime to a banishable offense. The Confiscation Act made them still subject to the death penalty for treason. And yet even these men turned out to have the possibility of reintegration. Half of them were able to achieve clemency in 1784 along with scores of other less-hated Loyalists.

The legislators were also careful to define the fate of the wives and children of proscribed Loyalists. Legislators responded to their felt obligations as merciful patriarchs concerned with the fate of women and children they considered without independent political affiliation or even independence of action. As practical taxpayers they also realized that if they did not make some sort of financial provision for these Loyalist families, they would make individual South Carolinians bound to pay to support these families. Burke, a foe of confiscation generally, worried that if women were cut off from support from their family estates, it would "bring so many families & their children to beggary & ruin, that I most devoutly detest it." And the legislators, as wealthy leaders, would find themselves dunned personally by desperate women arriving on their doorstep. Further savvy Loyalist families often stationed women and minor children on the property even if the father took refuge in occupied Charleston. Few buyers would agree to purchase confiscated estates if the family was still living there. The state would need to dispossess them of the property, and to do so in practice the state needed to provide a minimum income guarantee. The Confiscation Act did this by promising to "make such provision for the temporary support of such of the families . . . as shall appear to the said commissioners, or a majority of them, necessary." The legislature further promised to consider later a final settlement to support Loyalist dependents. The legislation carefully offered a minimal level of support to Loyalist dependents while keeping it vague enough and economically insufficient enough that those wives and children would find it advantageous to give up their American claims and leave the state along with the rest of the family.[33]

These restrictions and punishments focused on the wives and minor children of the male Loyalist were in fact harsher than those of most other states, including other southern states such as Virginia and North Carolina. For instance Virginia at least protected women's traditional dower right in the estate, whereas South Carolina swept it away under the Confiscation Act. Why might South Carolina take a harsher stance? The answer lies in the obvious loophole they would create by recognizing women's rights to family estates. It would be easy for a woman to protect lands for the benefit of the entire family, including her Loyalist husband, if the General Assembly did not close off that avenue. In fact when the assembly offered many families clemency in 1784, they did respond to many female claimants who made a complicated mélange of protests based on their own financial needs, their own political commitments, and their traditional dower rights.[34]

The Confiscation Act also sought to spread economic opportunity to Patriots in South Carolina through a careful disposition of the confiscated estates. Five commissioners were charged with a quick and orderly disposition of all confiscated property including land, slaves, personal property, and goods seized from merchants in Charleston. In order to attract a wide variety of purchasers and to offer this unusual buying opportunity to a wide cross-section of the white population, the legislature arranged attractive five-year financing. Only a small percentage of the total payment price had to be paid up front. While this meant the state was slow to get much-needed financing from the confiscated estates, these terms protected both middling sorts and cash-strapped elites. Land was to be divided into parcels of between two hundred and five hundred acres each, so that ordinary South Carolinians had a chance to participate in auctions of confiscated estates. South Carolinians also hoped to use democratized land auctions as a way to "increase as much as may be the number of white inhabitants": maintaining the tiny majority of whites in the state depended on increasing the number of smaller landowners, especially outside the lowcountry. While South Carolina was a place rarely concerned with the democratization of anything, in this effort to use confiscated land sales to democratize landholding, they were in line with the confiscation practices of other American states. Unfortunately the best evidence is that none of these efforts democratized landholding at all—in South Carolina or anywhere else. The same people who already owned land bought more land, roughly in proportion to the amount they already owned. In South Carolina this pattern holds true for the disposition of all confiscated property, including slaves.[35]

But confiscation alone was not enough to create an equitable and effective system of Loyalist punishment, at least if the end goal was indeed to punish Loyalists. After all only approximately 230 Loyalists (almost all male, with a handful of female absentee owners and British merchant houses) were subject to the 1782 Confiscation Act, and only 30 more were legally banished before 1782. Thousands of South Carolinian males had served in the Loyalist militias or otherwise made common cause with the Loyalists when the British were in power. More than three times as many names were considered for the confiscation lists than were ultimately included. And legislators were aware that the Confiscation Act overwhelmingly singled out lowcountry Loyalists, with the exception of a handful of backcountry Loyalists who were prominent high-ranking militia leaders such as Moses Kirkland and Patrick Cunningham. In some cases the backcountry Loyalists named in the Confiscation Act were infamous across the Carolinas for their wartime conduct, such as William "Bloody Bill" Cunningham, who was accused of several atrocities against Patriots. (His atrocities may well have been exaggerated, but that does not change the reality that his widespread reputation as a native South Carolinian willing to commit atrocities against his neighbors made him an irresistible target for harsh legislative punishment.) An equitable and comprehensive system of Loyalist punishment would require a system that also punished the scores of backcountry Loyalists who were militia leaders. For that matter the legislature also needed a system that could bring to justice Loyalists from outside the elite—men who had not ranked high enough to serve as officers but whose own wartime conduct was sufficiently cruel that their former communities would no longer accept them.[36]

At its heart the 1780s General Assembly originally intended to create a two-tier system of justice—a legislative system aimed at the elites, which was created as the confiscation and amercement acts, and a system aimed at more ordinary people that depended on both local persuasion and the justice system. The legislators assumed that many other ordinary Loyalists would flee with the British at the end of the war, in large part because they attempted a dance of negotiation and reconciliation with their local Patriots, and only some Loyalists would find reintegration a possibility. Hundreds of Loyalists, many enlisted men and noncommissioned officers who did not meet the elite requirements of the Confiscation Act, did "withdraw themselves" as anticipated by the state in 1782. The act called for surveyors to fan out across every district in 1783 and prepare a return of all abandoned estates. These were then sold as confiscated estates in the same manner as those mentioned specifically in the 1782 act. This system worked to bring ordinary people under the umbrella of confiscation and increase further the state's profits from the sale of confiscated property.[37]

The second part of democratizing Loyalist punishment went even further. South Carolina authorities might have chosen to model their policies on those of other states such as Virginia. Through the Pardon Act, the South Carolina legislature intended to use both the civil and criminal courts as a vehicle for local people to pursue actions against Loyalists for financial damages and wartime atrocities. While South Carolina never ultimately used the court system to prosecute Loyalists, Patriots on Virginia's eastern shore utilized the civil court system as a system of reparations, forcing Loyalists to face their accusers in court and at least partially reimburse them for their losses. Tellingly this remained a local process in the places that did use court systems; as in the Virginia example, eastern shore residents would testify in local suits but refused to testify when those cases were filed in the state capital of Richmond. Civil suits functioned as a form of ameliorative justice that allowed local Patriots to reintegrate many Loyalists they believed would make good community members in the future, based on their previous actions before the war. Patriots used the civil courts to even the score economically and provide themselves with an emotional release that allowed them to move forward with what historian Adele Hast has termed "some degree of reconciliation." Other states used the criminal courts to prosecute war crimes: by singling out a few Loyalists and punishing them for wartime cruelty, Patriots were able to reintegrate a far greater number of Loyalists who had simply obeyed military orders. In North Carolina, Margaret Balfour testified in a 1783 criminal case against a member of Col. David Fanning's Loyalist militia who she believed was involved in her brother's murder. She recalled with evident pleasure that "my story was so affecting that the court was willing to give me every satisfaction in their power; and in order to do this they broke a little through the usual course, for they had the villain tried, condemned, and hung, all in the space of the court." Of course the fate of this North Carolina Loyalist, who was convicted and summarily executed by an angry crowd willing to take matters into their own hands, makes it clear why using the court system was a poor solution to the problem of Loyalist punishment and eventual reintegration.[38]

Despite imagining the court system as an additional resource on pursuing Loyalist punishment, South Carolina ultimately never used this method. As cooler heads prevailed in 1783, South Carolinians became convinced that court trials would only stir up and further stimulate bad feelings at a time many were putting those wartime emotions behind them. Judge Aedanus Burke, a member of the 1782 legislature, had been opposed to using the court system from the beginning and used his pen to crusade against it in private letters in 1782 and in grand jury addresses as the courts finally reopened in 1783. From the beginning he was afraid that such courts would be merely kangaroo courts "to gratify the fierce revenge of the people; For you cd. not enter a Company that some do not talk of hanging many hundreds." When Gov. John Mathews pressed Burke to open special court sessions to follow the law and prosecute "about a hundred Scoffs wch. is the term we have for a Tory," Burke resisted. He was later proved correct when he oversaw a 1783 court term in which an angry crowd hanged Matthew Love for murdering wounded Patriots on the battlefield.[39]

Love had fought in "Bloody Bill" Cunningham's Loyalist militia, which gained a reputation for indiscriminate slaughter of Patriots even after they tried to surrender. Testimony established that after an engagement near Edgefield, "Love traversed the ground, where lay the dead and dying, his former neighbors and acquaintances, and as he saw signs of life in any of them, he ran his sword through and dispatched them. Those already dead, he stabbed again. And where others seemingly without life, and who were pierced with his sword, gave involuntary convulsions from the pain, to these he gave new wounds."[40]

On the basis of this testimony, his former community wanted to execute him. Burke refused and tried to convince the gathered crowd that the Treaty of Paris of 1783 forbade such criminal prosecutions for wartime conduct. And as a matter of fact, a strict reading of the treaty would support that conclusion, although it is also the case that much of the treaty was written so that it could be cheerfully ignored by both sides. In any case the crowd waited until Burke left the courtroom and then dragged Love out of sight of the courthouse, where they proceeded to hang him. Burke used this isolated incident as a way to persuade other members of the elite that the court system was an inappropriate way to deal with the situation of Loyalists. Despite the original intentions of the 1782 legislature, this avenue for ordinary people to seek the punishment of ordinary Loyalists was quickly closed in 1783 and never tried again.

Originally the legislature only intended to confiscate and banish a few select Loyalists. Otherwise local justice, either from the official court system or from unofficial pressure and threats, would separate the few Loyalists who could not be redeemed from the many who would be reintegrated. Yet very quickly both the practical problems of agreeing on an official confiscation list and the theoretical problems of defining what kind of behavior really merited full confiscation and banishment led the General Assembly to pursue a secondary, lesser form of official legislative sanction for some prominent, largely lowcountry Loyalists. As the eventual Amercement Act declared, a "due discrimination should be made" between committed Loyalists and those who merely chose to take the coward's path by taking British protection. Unfortunately there was little difference between the actions of many who ended up subject to confiscation, amercement, or no penalty at all. In practice the Amercement Act allowed the General Assembly a way out of their most intractable debates over whether specific individuals could be moved from the confiscation list to the amercement list without generating as much opposition as simply removing all penalties. It also meant they embraced the use of reparations, paid to the state, as a strategy for Loyalist reintegration.[41]

The Amercement Act levied a one-time tax of the entire value of all the Loyalist's property (land, slaves, and personal property) to be paid to the state within a year. For forty-seven men named in the act, the legislature settled on a 12 percent tax after debating figures between 5 and 20 percent. A later legislative committee, when faced with blacksmith James Duncan's appeal of his penalty, justified the tax because we "think as he must have made large Profits by his Occupation during the British residence here, that he ought to pay Twelve per Cent." Edward Rutledge justified amercement as merely a small recompense for the costs Patriots had borne during the war in paying and equipping soldiers. Rutledge argued that he did "not know one [Patriot] who would not be very glad to have lost no more than 25 per Cent^m." A small additional number of amerced men had to pay a 30 percent amercement. Rutledge bitterly suggested of one Loyalist on the amercement list that "he will be amerced 30 per Cent, & justly too." As a matter of equity, the legislature decided also to levy an amercement on Loyalists pardoned by the Pardon Act, who had come back over to the Patriot side late in the war.[42]

Reparations went hand in hand with expulsion from the voting pool and therefore from government power. This aspect of the Amercement Act continued the governor's policies for the late 1781 election that had ensconced an all-Patriot legislature. On the face of it, this would be uncontroversial—traitors against the state would hardly be appropriate voters in the new government. Yet to see it that way was to buy the arguments of the Patriot elite who had defined loyalism as an incontrovertible vote against the American cause. Most Loyalists saw their individual actions as part of a continuum of choices that were all bad. Months after the election, one legislator remembered that "the numbers thus excluded were considerable in some parishes, and they murmured exceedingly for a few days." Since in many cases entire communities had elected to follow their most prominent male citizens into a Loyalist militia, an exclusion of all Loyalists would deprive entire districts of representation in the new legislature. Some South Carolinians resisted this as an undemocratic power grab. In the months and years to come, South Carolina Loyalists would continue to protest vigorously any suggestion that they were anything but full-fledged citizens.[43]

Even outspoken foe of confiscation Burke approved the result of this denial of Loyalists' full citizenship. He told a friend that the "Tory dead weight" had been removed thanks to Governor Rutledge's "good policy in excluding [the Loyalists] from voting." While at other times he resisted any imposition on the full citizenship of Loyalists, in the practical matter of the makeup of the voting pool, he concluded it was "madness to allow men to influence our Elections who had borne arms against us without giving some Test of their attachm^t. to us." The 1782 act addressed this concern by requiring oaths for returning members and future oaths from Loyalists seeking to vote or serve in the assembly. In 1783 the General Assembly made this restriction of Loyalist voting lasting and explicit. Legislators argued that it was "repugnant to, the spirit, intent, and meaning of the constitution" that Loyalist men who had once "acknowledged themselves subjects of the king of Great Britain" should get the franchise in a state organized on republican principles. This went against the general trend in Revolutionary America to expand voting rights. While other states were making cautious experiments with female suffrage and the rights of free black men as voters, South Carolina was busy limiting the rights of elite voters—based on their Loyalist past. Generally South Carolinians fell into line with other states in the choice to create a second-class citizenship for former Loyalists in which those Loyalists could maintain their possession of land but lost the vote—an essential component of republican citizenship.[44]

In the end despite the ad hoc nature of the attempt to come up with defensible confiscation lists, the 1782 legislature achieved its aims. From the beginning what could have been an unlimited attempt at harsh punishment for Loyalists, born out of the intense anger South Carolinians felt at how much they had suffered from the war, turned into a carefully limited and even merciful legislative response to the problem of what to do with the Loyalists. The final legislation officially pardoned many more individuals than faced official confiscation and banishment. While the tenor of other parts of the legislation, such as the call for prosecution in the courts and the confiscation of abandoned estates, could potentially have levied harsh punishments on many more people, in the end these acts never punished more people than faced the anger of their Patriot neighbors in 1782. That year was the high point for revenge-oriented rage in South Carolina. The war's devastation was both fresh and ongoing, and all South Carolinians—white and black, Patriot and Loyalist—were unsure of how the war would finally end. Given that the legislators and the numerous South Carolinians who elected them spared most Loyalists at this most vulnerable moment, it must be concluded that a generous reintegration and reconciliation was in the cards from the beginning.

THREE ✳ *Hope for Reconciliation*

How Loyalists Built Their Case for Reintegration

The vast majority of white Loyalists dodged a bullet in 1782. Despite the intense anger of those who had suffered for the Revolutionary cause, the legislators had found it within themselves to be merciful and generous in crafting Loyalist punishment. While the total package of laws had the potential to punish thousands, in fact fewer than three hundred people found themselves subject to official legal notice. Any Loyalist not named in the confiscation or amercement acts would be subject only to the loss of their property and citizenship if the people in their own local community were unwilling to forgive the past and allow them to return to a peaceful life together. From the moment the ink began drying on the official announcements of the Confiscation Act in Charleston's Loyalist press, Loyalists began planning how to effect their own reintegration. Aedanus Burke noticed two months after the passage of anti-Loyalist legislation that the "Confiscation Act began to work on them [the Loyalists] some time since, and still continues to sweat them considerably." Well aware of their vulnerable position, the Loyalists would "give the world now for an opportunity, even to cringe, like Spaniels" in the hopes of securing a place in postwar South Carolina. Edward Rutledge believed that by late spring the "Tories in general seem heartily tired of their situation" and were seeking a more palatable option.[1]

Loyalists following the Charleston press found nothing but terribly depressing news. In July 1782 the newspapers reported that the Patriot government had already begun selling confiscated property. As the stifling summer humidity of the lowcountry gave way to the beautiful balmy days of fall, the paper began to fill with official notices to sign up for a spot on the British-provided convoys to take Loyalists away from their homes to Saint Augustine and a diaspora around the British Empire. The end was coming, and Loyalists knew it. As fall gave way to winter, William Carson and others desperately advertised the need to sell "ALL . . . HOUSEHOLD GOODS and FURNITURE" for "cash only." Everyone was trying to sell, but there were few people to buy, and those who would buy would only take Loyalist goods at a deep discount to the real value. No one would touch the real estate of most Loyalists, since the Confiscation Act made it worthless. One Patriot spy reported to Gen.

Francis Marion that in the last weeks before the British evacuation, "the lamentations of the Poor Going Away almost destitute of every Comfort of Life" filled the air as soldiers prepared the city for departure. Even the spy, in a brief moment of sympathy, concluded the whole place was a "most Melancholy Scene."[2]

White Loyalists, even the minority facing official proscription, were casting around for a better option than joining the Loyalist diaspora abroad. They quickly realized that it was worth making every effort to secure a prosperous future in their home—the state of South Carolina. Black Loyalists did not have a choice. Death or enslavement were the only choices facing them if they stayed in South Carolina, and so unsurprisingly they chose to hope that the British would offer them dignity and economic self-sufficiency wherever they were transported. But white Loyalists did feel as if they could change the legislature's decree—and in the majority of cases, they were right. They began to lay the groundwork for a return by apologizing and making sure their neighbors were willing to let them live together without violence. From that start Loyalists worked to knit their communities back together and in so doing made themselves an integral part of the American understanding of citizenship in the new Republic. In the end the vast majority of white Loyalists were able to reintegrate successfully into their prewar communities and move on with their lives.

✳ *Why the Petition Was the Best Form for Loyalists to Make Their Case*

Psychological research (introduced in the previous chapter) suggests that humans enjoy the anticipation of watching the infliction of just punishment more than they actually enjoy watching the punishment itself. Legislators had salivated over their chance finally to inflict the pain of punishment on a small subset of Loyalists and in the end were moved to exempt the vast majority of white Loyalists from official punishment. Yet they had not found it as satisfying as they had expected. Instead they found themselves receptive to carefully worded petitions from Loyalists they had punished. And while they wanted to see some demonstration of those Loyalists' pain, they were also looking for evidence of their shared humanity. Petitions were a form of polite abasement on the part of Loyalists that granted legislators license to take pleasure in their suffering. These petitions also allowed Loyalists to demonstrate their own humanitarianism in the face of the trials of civil war. Empathy depended on mutual recognition of shared humanity.

Petitions were also the right form for beginning the process of official governmental postwar reconciliation because the understood norms of petitioning guaranteed Loyalists that the General Assembly would read the petition aloud and consider it seriously. Petitions were not just a request but commanded the duty of formal legislative consideration, including a reading on the floor of the legislature and committee action. Petitioning was so embedded in early American political life that the right to petition was enshrined in the First Amendment to the Constitution, although the institution of the gag rule in the antebellum Congress has made this a dead right today. (The fact that Americans no longer actually have the right to petition may help to explain why very few Americans even know that it is part of the much-vaunted First Amendment.) In colonial assemblies petitions were the primary way that bills originated. In the American colonies, the use of petitions was rooted in the link between individual petitioners and their local legislators, who were presumed to have local familiarity with the issues raised by petitions. Certainly the South Carolina General Assembly assumed the importance of using legislators with personal knowledge of local issues in that they always referred Loyalist petitions to a subcommittee with at least one legislator from the same district as the petitioner. Some Loyalists were reassured by that local knowledge, while others rightly worried that it might sink their efforts at clemency.[3]

Petitioners also knew that the eighteenth-century right to have petitions read aloud and debated carried with it the expectation of a hearing in which evidence could be presented on both sides. Petitioners expected their grievances to be subject to countertestimony. Historian Raymond C. Bailey has termed these exchanges of evidence-laden petitions a "polling device" and has found that counterpetitions badly hurt the chance of success. This suggests that the united support of the local community was important to legislators and was required for them to approve a petition. As will be seen later in this chapter and in the next, substantial local support was also vital for Loyalist petitioners, and without it they could not gain clemency. Loyalists made it clear in their petitions that they expected that a hearing in which they could offer exculpatory evidence would clear any tarnish from their name. Maurice Simmons was just one of the many Loyalists who argued that "if he were allowed a hearing he will be able to Explain his Conduct and Situation (Supported by good Evidences) to the Satisfaction of his Countrymen."[4]

Petitioning was also a rare form of public political action that was available to people who had no other official voice. Americans who could not vote could petition their local legislature (at least as long as they could write or find someone who would write on their behalf). Colonial assemblies considered petitions from slaves, women, Native Americans, and convicted felons. Especially in the case of women and poor men, "the right to petition vested these groups with a minimum form of citizenship" and offered a route to political power for those denied the franchise.[5] In the hands of male Loyalists, petitions made an assertion of citizenship. For female Loyalists petitions provided an acceptable method of seizing the chance to represent themselves and their families in the vital question of securing their futures. Black Loyalists still found themselves shut out of even this most basic mechanism of redress.

Petitioners followed widely understood conventions that required language that was at least outwardly polite. Pre-Revolutionary petitions were inherently written in the voice of dependence, but during the Revolution petitioners, especially white men with some property, "became less obsequious" in their language and demands.[6] White male Loyalists followed other Revolutionary-era men in choosing forthright language. In fact these petitioning Loyalists come across as a self-assured bunch. They reacted with the expectations of people used to the rule of law—and full social inclusion. They believed in their equality of citizenship, and it showed in the language of their petitions. And while the legislature could have simply chosen to ignore their complaints, the strong conventions of the form of petitions and the growing desire to reintegrate Loyalists led the General Assembly to receive these petitions and take them seriously.

Patriots assumed that the petition process was the correct form for Loyalists to use in seeking legislative clemency and even counseled their friends to pursue legislative reintegration via a carefully worded petition. Henry Laurens counseled one friend to "send a proper message to the House," since with "all Parliamentary probability" it would be accepted.[7] For Laurens the accepted legitimacy of petitioning guaranteed an orderly process for considering Loyalist appeals. And with the waning anger he and others felt by late 1782, he was ready to counsel friends as to how best to approach efforts to regain their property and citizenship.

Loyalists also quickly figured out that the petition offered a reliable yet flexible format for pursuing clemency. The vast majority of those named in the official confiscation and amercement acts submitted petitions to the 1783 legislature. Some of them seem to have started writing their petitions, or hiring a lawyer to write them for them, as the ink was drying on the Confiscation Act. One hundred and thirty-eight Loyalists submitted petitions that are still extant out of just over two hundred resident men named on the Confiscation Act. That is, some 70 percent of these Loyalists targeted for punishment petitioned quickly for clemency. The pace picked up steadily when the British abandoned Charleston in December 1782. Edward Rutledge had noted in August 1782 that many merchants had already submitted petitions. By the opening of the 1783 legislative session, Loyalists and their supporters had already filed 104 petitions. Loyalists went through the effort of writing and submitting petitions because they felt the expenditure of energy had a reasonable chance of success. They went to even more effort to apologize to friends and neighbors and then convince those community members to submit supporting petitions. Loyalists were convinced that the moment was auspicious for their reintegration and that petitions offered a reasonable format for persuading the legislature to consider again the "Loyalist problem." They would turn out to be right.[8]

✳ *The Position of Female Loyalists: In the End Not a Special Case*

Margaret Colleton, a British absentee landowner whose family descended from one of the original eight Lords Proprietors, was the only woman named in the 1782 Confiscation Act. As an absentee owner, she was a convenient target for a legislature with an eye for easy profit. Further the Colleton name had symbolic value. The fact that only one woman was named on the act punishing Loyalists makes it seem as if the legislature saw women as an invisible entity, unworthy of official notice from the governing authorities. Yet at least fifty women pursued the return of family property in the 1780s through a wide variety of avenues such as occasional court cases, epistolary campaigns, and petition campaigns. These women worked to make reconciliation possible for themselves and their families.

The Revolution did not automatically change everything about the political or social position of women in America. Recent research in the cultural history of the Anglo-American eighteenth century certainly suggests that the long shadow of the Enlightenment was causing men and women to value women's independence more highly and that this played out in even the most private decisions, such as how many children to have. American women began to limit their fertility deliberately. Other women pursued increasingly public political roles, given the wide range of political venues outside of official legislative debate. Women's forthright petitioning might seem to be part of this increasing emphasis on their autonomous personhood and political participation. Yet women continued to be denied the perquisites of full citizenship. The very language women (and their lawyers) used in crafting petitions presupposed them as humble supplicants before the august power of the male legislature. Women came before the legislature careful to maintain the illusion that they were duly humble people begging rather than expecting a hearing. In fact men were noticeably not humbled in their petitions, whereas women understood the need to be circumspect in the language with which they chose to make their best appeal. Women in more privileged positions may well have felt that Revolutionary ideals freed them to pursue a greater say in American life, but Loyalist women were aware of the need for great caution, as well as great savvy, as they attacked the problem of how best to position themselves to save their family estates.[9]

South Carolina's legislators made it perfectly clear in the way they punished Loyalists that loyalism, as a particular kind of political decision and political orientation, was presumed to be a male domain. The entire logic of the enterprise assumed that those subject to the Confiscation Act had the economic and social independence required to have chosen a political affiliation and had pursued that choice in military and government service for the British. That is why they limited the confiscation list to white male citizens of independent economic means who had signed official welcoming addresses, taken officer positions in the Loyalist militia, or been officials in the occupation government. In short they imagined someone who could achieve full independent citizenship, and they understood that to be an exclusively male prerogative. Obviously this book argues that many men did not have an ability to choose their political affiliation and that the legislature often recognized this fact. Nonetheless this was the operating political theory behind legislative anti-Loyalist actions. This theory presupposed women could not have independent political affiliations, since they were not expected to serve either side militarily or by holding office. The legislature made this assumption explicit by confiscating all family property claims, including extinguishing any claims on the historic dower right to one third of the estate. In the 1782 legislation, the General Assembly elected to make sure Loyalist families could not protect their wealth by using women as foils in order to maintain residence or ownership. It was one of the harshest confiscation acts in the nation in the way it treated women and dependent children. In no way did the legislature consider women as independent political actors.[10]

Loyalist families worked together to use women's traditional protections as vulnerable people, and the assumption that women themselves did not have political affiliations, in deliberate strategies aimed at protecting the position of the entire family. From that perspective the legislature was actually astute in choosing to deny the dower right in law. Female Loyalists remained on family properties as long as possible in an effort to maintain their claim. Their continued presence on family estates both gave families continued support and made it functionally difficult to sell those properties at confiscated estates auctions in 1783 and 1784. Astute, or wary, investors were leery of purchasing what they saw as encumbered properties. If they paid full price for those estates, and women were later able to reinstate the traditional protections of the dower right, those investors would instantly be out of at least one third of their investment. Further no one wanted to be the person who had to evict piteously weeping Loyalist women and children from their homes. So the strategy worked very well. For example the Cunningham name had become infamous by the end of the war as the surname of a committed Loyalist family. The male

Cunningham brothers and cousins (with the exception of John Cunningham) left the state in 1782, although some were later able to return. Despite their shaky case, the family left Margaret Cunningham behind to assert a lasting claim on "the Tract of Land on Rayburnes Creek Containing Two Hundred Acres, whereon she formerly lived." While the commissioners of forfeited estates sold some other Cunningham parcels, they and the legislature turned a blind eye for three years to this situation. In the end it paid off, as Cunningham's effort to assert "squatter's rights" led to the official grant of the property to her by legislative action in 1785.[11]

On the surface the Confiscation Act was very harsh toward Loyalist dependents, including women. Yet the reality is that the legislature backed down pretty quickly and that elite South Carolinians expected them to do so, even though they understood that conveying property to women ultimately benefited their Loyalist husbands as well. In 1782 Henry Laurens warned his friend Richard Champion to be cautious in purchasing confiscated estates when he immigrated to America. He cautioned Champion that those estates might come with many legal obligations that were not immediately apparent. He may indeed have had in mind women's dower rights when he made that caution, although he was not that explicit when he warned Champion that the seemingly below-market costs for confiscated estates might harbor all kinds of expensive traps for the unwary. He certainly was correct in worrying that confiscated estates would be encumbered for years with dower rights claims by women, and in fact some women launched a series of expensive lawsuits in later years (when other avenues of clemency and redress failed) that tied up estates for years and therefore depressed the value and utility of those lands. Laurens even encouraged Anne Burns to pursue a claim to her husband's estate despite its official confiscation. He reasoned that "in honor to my Country I cannot believe that the property of the innocent Widow & Children" would permanently be seized by the state. He suggested to another woman that after the "Pell Mell" had subsided, some "proper Reservation in favor of his family" would be made. His land investment advice to Champion certainly makes even more sense in the light of his support for individual Loyalist wives in their efforts to regain at least their one-third share of the family estate.[12]

Male and female Loyalists worked hard at achieving face-to-face reintegration and reconciliation within their community networks. They were able to capitalize on this in 1783, when the General Assembly moved to codify more generous legal arrangements for Loyalist dependents. They were allowed to draw monies to maintain their households, including the trappings of elite life such as carriages, horses, and household slaves to wait on these white Loyalist women. The bill also allowed women their "plate." Since household plates, linens, and clothing were traditionally women's property in early America, this could pass as clarification rather than a genuine amelioration. On the other hand, since these were valuable goods, and in families outside of the elite, they could be worth as much as the family lands, this was a real move toward reintegration of former Loyalists. In 1783 Loyalist men subject to confiscation did not receive clemency, but their wives already found a distinct loosening of anti-Loyalist resolve. From the perspective of the family unit, this was progress on the path to the ultimate aim of reconciliation.[13]

South Carolinians offered clemency to women first because it was easier to imagine them as lacking the political will to have stood against American independence. Laurens had been correct in his reading of the intentions of the legislature when he advised Anne Burns (and Elizabeth Stead Izard) to pursue her property claims after people had several months to cool down. Other South Carolinians also shrank from the idea of "reducing a whole family for the Sin of one." Arthur Middleton, South Carolina's representative to the U.S. Congress, mourned the "inhuman Sentence of visiting the Sins of the Fathers upon the guiltless women, [and] Children."[14] While this was generous and served the desires and needs of these Loyalist families, it relied on an understanding that women were simply victims of their husbands' political allegiances without any of their own. Women might be punished as the wives of Loyalist men, but their own political feelings were beside the point. The Confiscation Act had placed a high bar on what kinds of Loyalist activities justified total confiscation. Women did not fit that definition, and it was therefore easier to refuse to acknowledge any indications that these women had exercised their own desires when their husbands opposed American independence.

Women's petitions show that they (and sometimes their lawyers) understood that as women, they were not judged to be independent political actors. In the first wave of petitions in 1782 and the first part of 1783, women did not make dower rights claims. They focused on supporting their families' claims by submitting supporting petitions or petitions on behalf of their husbands (or sometimes fathers). They wrapped themselves in the rhetoric of female submission and helplessness. While they certainly experienced the war through gendered experiences, they found no benefit for themselves in making claims that advanced women's rights. Instead they chose collusion as a family, which meant making any claim that seemed likely to win legislative favor. Women did not begin to make representations on behalf of themselves as political individuals or to assert the dower right until after the 1783 legislative session ended. They only made claims of their own beliefs and their historic dower right when they believed that their united family approach to full clemency for their husbands was going to be rejected.

Women's petitions used submissive and self-effacing language and emphasized the helplessness of Loyalist dependents. Mary Cape positioned herself as a desperate but loving mother whose "Innocent Children" had not themselves taken part in the war. Ann Legge reminded the legislature that she was "left with three helpless Children ... That if wholly deprived of her property, which the Act directs, She and her family must be reduced to a situation truly distressing." These women did not miss the opportunity to remind legislators subtly that if women and children could not draw financial support from their families' resources, then they would turn to Patriot relatives and neighbors for charity. Sarah Scott used this strategy when she worried about her children turning into an "incumbrance" to the community. Ann McGillivray made this equation of public support in lieu of use of the family property explicit. "If the Laws should take the Estate, she must be reduced to the necessity of Soliciting the Bounty of her friends or the Officers of the Parish, for the support of herself and her Children." Even McGillivray's bold threat to the legislature to stay in South Carolina and force the local taxpayers to support her was couched in the theatrics of female submission and helplessness.[15]

Occasionally female petitioners tried to have it all—a woman's right to support for themselves and their children and family appeals on behalf of husbands in the joint effort to reunite the family with full possession of all property. And these women only had the two or three handwritten pages of these appeals in which to do so. Ann Legge offered a very legalistic petition (almost certainly drafted by an attorney) with two claims. If the legislature "dictat[ed] a refusal" to her claims on her husband's behalf for his claims to clemency, then she wished the legislature to consider her secondary request for support on her own behalf so her "poor inscent children" would not be left penniless. As a practical woman, she pushed the General Assembly to "vest" property in her own name. In fact she may have pursued this line of argument because she anticipated that her husband's case would find favor in the legislature. She was right in that calculation, and her own separate claims for maintenance disappeared when her husband, Edward, was relieved of confiscation and instead amerced.[16]

Women only turned away from submissive appeals intended to reunite the entire family with their property when they believed there was no more chance that their husbands would prevail in their efforts to achieve clemency and reintegration. In other words when women made independent claims, it was part of a family strategy in which men had already tried to petition and were not successful. Women then moved in to try to claim part of the property in order to salvage as much as possible. The only women who made these claims were married to men with unusually weak cases for clemency. James

Mackey petitioned the legislature for clemency, but pointed questioning at his 1783 hearing (scheduled in response to his petition) revealed that he was widely suspected of deliberately sabotaging American Patriot efforts to hold Charleston in 1780. As a cooper he had been tasked with making the barrels to hold preserved meats for the defending garrison. The meat spoiled, and Mackey was accused of not only having deliberately destroyed the meat but also bragging about it later when the British controlled the city. Therefore when his wife, Eleanor, appealed to the tender hearts of legislators in 1784, she did so in the knowledge that her husband's case was falling on deaf ears. In that light she worried that she would "be completely wretched & deplorable cast forlorn on the wide World, friendless & hopeless destitute of all resource & Subsistence with a mind preyed upon by Sorrow and a Body weaken'd by care and the approaches of age." She asked for financial support from her husband's estate.[17]

Women made explicit claims to their historic dower right to at least one-third of the property only when they, like Mackey, believed their husband had little chance of official clemency. In 1783 Florence Cook argued that the legislature had "deprived [her] of her right of dower." She went on to position herself as the ideal Republican mother (in historian Linda K. Kerber's formulation) who had "always endeavord to inculcate . . . the love of Liberty of this her Native Country" in her own daughter. Republican motherhood promised that women would serve a vital role in the new nation by inculcating virtue in their children, especially their sons, and training them as useful, self-denying citizens. In this respect she exemplified the ideal qualities of a female citizen of the new Republic. Unfortunately for her, she was the mother of only a daughter, but her petition shows she understood the equation of republican motherhood. "If providence had blessed her with a number of Sons," she would have worked to "render them fit for the defence and Support of their Country." Even with her daughter, her Patriot political allegiance led her to give her child "a Confirmed aversion to our enemies." Cook made a case for herself as the right kind of woman for the new republican South Carolina and therefore as someone who should be welcome in the new order. Kerber uses her petition as an example of women's self-confident voices in claiming patriotism and her confident assertion of her dower rights to her belief in equal protection under the law as part and parcel of the Revolution. Kerber was also struck by how she explained away her husband's conduct as the weak thinking of a man in "a Mechanic employment." Yet this petition may not reveal anything about women's independent political status. The Cook family was running out of options when Cook submitted this petition for the January 1783 legislative session. Her husband, a Charleston carpenter, was believed to have been the main author of the decision to shut out all neutral and Patriot artisans from the ability to practice their trades in British-occupied Charleston. The artisan community was united in their strident opposition to readmitting James Cook. Florence Cook only petitioned for her own dower right to their property when his multiple petitions had fallen on deaf ears. Her efforts to denigrate her husband's class status also speak to a desire to stimulate the worst snobberies of the legislature in an effort to get them to sympathize with her. In fact, as will be seen in the next chapter, James Cook was so hated that his effigy became the target of a mob action, and he indeed never achieved legislative clemency and died abroad.[18]

The only other woman to claim openly that her political beliefs were the opposite of her husband's was also married to a man who, despite several rounds of attempts at legislative clemency, never could convince South Carolinians to readmit him. Margaret Brisbane took pains to reassure the legislature that "her Sentiments with respect to the present Contest, ha[ve] always differed from her husbands." Yet Brisbane certainly did not let her appeal hang only on her own political beliefs. She also reminded the General Assembly that the political opinions of women did not matter. "From their Sphere in Life," they could not be considered "promoters of the War" or "disadvantageous to the Contest." She used the expectation of women's political passivity against the legislature. If women could not be presumed to have political wills, how could they be punished for that lack of will? In later years (and in the midst of litigation), Attorney General Alexander Moultrie tried to claim that the legislature had ended women's dower right for Loyalist wives "upon the idea, that husbands are oftentimes influenced and governed by the sentiment and conduct of their wives." Both Cook and Brisbane would disagree with this sentiment, but in very different ways. Yet what lay at the bottom of each woman's strategy was the reality that the only claim left to their families was a dower right claim divorced from their husband's claims to the properties. And in both cases the husbands failed ever to win any clemency from the banishment and confiscation of their properties.[19]

Women submitted several petitions to the General Assembly, but in the end women petitioners were not a special case. Loyalist women, in the eyes of the legislature, were women who were married to, or the unmarried daughters of, Loyalist men. The legislature did not accord them political agency. In the end women went along with this conclusion because it suited their purposes to do so. While most of them relied on the assumption that women were helpless dependents who needed support, even the two women who went out of their way to claim their own political commitments to the Patriot cause did so because they saw it as a last-ditch effort to regain a fraction of the total family estate. What ultimately made these families truly loyal was their loyalty to each other.

❋ *The Importance of a Sincere and Penitent Apology*

The most difficult part of the process Loyalists had to pursue to achieve reconciliation was the one that slips out of the historical record—the difficulties in proffering personal apologies to a wide number of former friends and neighbors. Loyalists mostly apologized personally. The sensitive work of personal reconciliation required the daily face-to-face social interactions that relaid the trusting relationships each side had experienced before the war. However, because of this most of the direct evidence of the work Loyalists did in apologizing has disappeared from the historical record. For that matter even when Loyalists did resort to writing letters trying to heal their friendships (a necessary first step to physical return for many), they were understandably circumspect in putting anything in writing that might later be used against them. Yet their friends and neighbors demanded that apologies radiate sincerity. In order to do that, Loyalists had to apologize directly and have difficult conversations about their wartime behavior on and off the battlefield. Letters were important but could never do the work alone. The hard work of apologizing with enough humbleness and sincerity could only be accomplished face-to-face and therefore only enters the historical record through the end result—hundreds of Patriot South Carolinians who were willing to sign statements to the legislature endorsing the return of property and citizenship to those Loyalists who had come through this humbling process successfully. Still there are suggestive moments where supporters made it clear that their postwar embrace of a former Loyalist depended on their efforts at apologizing and working to be good community members again.

Loyalists sometimes felt it was important to reach out for forgiveness before physically returning home in order to lay the groundwork for their smooth return. In some cases they wished to ensure that their neighbors would not use this opportunity to take revenge on them—up to and including killing them. John Wigfall was living in British-occupied Charleston when he reached out through a series of personal letters to his oldest friends from home. He attempted to apologize and seek a rapprochement that would at least allow him to return home safely and be able further to heal the wounds of war and reinvigorate his community relationships through the intimate conversations and rounds of personal favors only possible through proximity. While Wigfall ultimately succeeded, at the time several community members rejected his efforts to return. In fact at least one person returned his attempt at apologizing with a written threat to "take his Life" if he dared show his face in the community again. One of the more gracious recipients of these written apologies later testified to a legislative subcommittee that Wigfall had then written him to say he would gladly come back and start the process of face-to-face reconciliation and even serve in the Patriot militia (as ordered by the pardon offer made by the governor in 1781), if he "could have the least assurance that his Life would not be taken." In the end supporters such as Benjamin Quark accepted Wigfall's apologies, welcomed him home, and then testified on his behalf before legislative hearings. So even with a rough start, many Loyalists could persevere and find a way to apologize and continue to pursue a harmonious and mutual reconciliation.[20]

Apologizing certainly worked out well for Richard Wayne. What he said to his former neighbors is unknown, but he was able to apologize in a way that allowed his local community to embrace him. They turned out in force to support him in his efforts to achieve legislative clemency. Their supporting petition emphasized that he "express[ed] a Sincere penitence for the part he acted in behalf of the British." It was his willingness to apologize properly, and in so doing embody the sincerity of penance that victorious Patriots demanded, that gained him widespread support. And his ability to live up to the expectations of continued neighborly involvement meant that his neighbors were willing to support him with the legislature. This community support was crucial in the legislature's 1784 decision to lift the decree of confiscation and banishment.[21]

Both sides found apologies difficult to give and difficult to receive. Yet apologizing turns out to have been a crucial—and inescapable—part of renewing the ties of friendship and community that people continually identified as the very heart of citizenship and belonging. John Joachim Zubly, a Loyalist and a Calvinist minister, should have found apologizing easy since his religious convictions supported humble contrition. Yet even this devout and well-intentioned man found it almost impossible to abase himself in apology when it was called for and when it could have gone far to mitigate the personal damages he would suffer as a Loyalist. Zubly had been born and educated abroad (like many ministers), yet he had spent most of his adult life leading a well-established church in Savannah, Georgia. In the years before fighting broke out, he had actually been a leading southern voice against British policies in America. Yet when he was unable to support a final break with Britain, he found himself suffering the harsh consequences—driven from his church and his home and forced to move around the South, landing in British-occupied Charleston. Zubly got the chance many Loyalists did not have—to apologize face-to-face to a former Patriot friend. Benjamin Andrew visited him while he lived in Charleston, and Zubly felt that he offered forgiveness, which Andrew should receive with a mutual apology and then reciprocal forgiveness. To his amazement, despite Zubly's willingness to offer contrite Christian forgiveness, his visitor "does not seem to feel that he ever did me any wrong."[22] Zubly was frustrated that his supreme emotional struggle to practice Christian forgiveness was brushed over and ignored. But of course he went about it the wrong way. He still attempted to hold the high ground and expected the other party to offer mutual apologies—and that was simply not going to happen.

Patriots expected contrition from those Loyalists who sought their personal understanding and forgiveness and their further willingness to extend the courtesies of neighborliness to them. Henry Laurens reflected in advising one woman how best to approach efforts to achieve clemency that she must "remember that the Minds of the People are sore & many of their Bodies too from Oppression and Grievances. Give them a decent Time for recovery and deliberation." Loyalists whose own minds and bodies were sore from the emotional and physical devastations of war would have to put aside their own anger and craft personal apologies to Patriots that allowed them the grounds for emotional healing. However much both sides might need that healing, only Patriots were in a position to demand it. Those Patriots expected the apologies to be frank and comprehensive, and most important, they expected them to reek of contrition. Loyalists found these standards difficult to meet. When Laurens received an apology from his wife's nephew, Elias Ball of Comingtee, he held it to these intense standards. It took Ball at least two attempts at apologizing by letter before Laurens finally deemed him sufficiently contrite.[23]

Ball became a Loyalist out of no particular conviction. He was of the many Loyalists who switched sides once the British were in possession of the state and therefore made loyalism the more lucrative option. Like many lukewarm Loyalists, he took an officer's commission in the Loyalist militia, yet he made sure he and his men actually did very little. His unit saw few battles and avoided serving as the enforcement arm of British occupation despite the pressures on the militia to do so. After the war Ball repeatedly wrote his uncle trying to apologize and gain his prominent kinsman's aid in effecting his removal from the Confiscation Act of 1782. When he finally constructed a letter that assuaged Laurens's anger and was taken as a sincere and penitent apology, he was rewarded with both personal reconciliation and practical aid. Laurens was pleased to note that Ball had finally "discuss[ed] the matter of [his] political conduct & the part [he] took in the late cruel and unjust persecution of your Country" with "reflection." Ball had explicitly apologized for his political decisions and the effects his alliance with the British had on his family, his friends, and his state. Laurens was especially pleased with this "reflection," which might better be understood as the emotional tenor of his apology. The Laurens/Ball correspondence also makes it clear how important uncomfortable conversations could be in convincing Patriots to accept former Loyalists. Laurens was finally moved by Ball's confessional apology, but he could not resist his chance to admonish his nephew for his lack of principles.

He railed that Ball had lacked the "resolution to persevere in a cause which you had engaged in & knew to be righteous." Laurens not only needed to hear a full, frank, and contrite apology, but he also needed to achieve the emotional release he found through uncontested verbal recrimination. Only after he got to have the last angry word was he willing to extend the olive branch to Ball.[24]

Yet once Laurens accepted an apology, he went to work on Ball's behalf. He offered his nephew a position as his plantation overseer on his Georgia lands while Ball pursued legislative clemency from South Carolina, which gave him a secure berth nearby while he continued to build his case for a successful reconciliation. This was a generous offer, but one that also benefitted Laurens's own bottom line. Ball had saved considerable property in slaves both from wartime disruptions (including the mass migration of slaves to British lines to secure their own freedom) and from confiscation. Laurens expected him to set those slaves to work on the Laurens plantation, where their labor would benefit him much more than Ball. With a kinsman who owed him as his overseer, and that kinsman's slaves adding to his own productive capacity, he could expect a temporary windfall in return for his willingness to get over his anger at his wife's nephew. In a sense he exacted a price for his willingness to support Ball in his efforts to gain prominent Patriot supporters who might convince the South Carolina legislature to return his property. Laurens was undoubtedly being honest about his own emotions when he hoped that "the time is coming when I shall take [Ball] again into my arms as a friend." But he demanded much from a former Loyalist before he was willing to consider that possibility.[25]

In the end Ball's repeated efforts to apologize in a way that actually moved his uncle to consider his plea worked. Undoubtedly he, like others, reached out to other family and friends just as he did to Laurens, even if those letters are no longer part of the historical record. He obtained legislative clemency in 1784 and got back his estate and citizenship. No doubt Laurens's support helped. A little abasement, while temporarily disconcerting, allowed him a lifetime of comfort.

✳ Excuses, Excuses: Practical Explanations for Loyalist Affiliation

Loyalists had already done the hard work of making personal apologies—even abasing themselves in epistolary and face-to-face conversations with former friends and neighbors. The vast majority of Loyalists had laid this groundwork before ever formally petitioning the General Assembly—and as will be seen later in this chapter, it was that painstaking work of personal apologies and reconnecting frayed social networks that ultimately led to clemency and then reintegration for the majority of white Loyalists.

When it came time to craft and submit petitions seeking legislative clemency, Loyalists were more circumspect. Few of them actually apologized in their petitions, although when they did it must have seemed a refreshing change from the evasions and excuses that all the petitions shared. John Wagner hoped "he may be pardoned the Errors he has Committed," although he pointedly did not get any more specific about what kind of errors the legislature may have thought him guilty of. William Rees apologized for his embrace of loyalism, stating that with the benefit of time he "is truly sensible of the Errors he has been guilty of." While these Loyalists apologized, they stayed clear of any specific instances of their political or wartime behavior—the

Petition of William Rees, 1783. Courtesy of the South Carolina Department of Archives and History, Columbia.

things that led to them facing confiscation. Heated stories of wartime atrocities, and the routine use of civil and military offices to harass Patriot-identified civilians, had enflamed many against the Loyalists. Yet Loyalists (even those who ought to have apologized for some specific acts) were wary of hurting their case further with frankness about the realities of civil and military service in a civil war. The closest any Loyalist petitioner came to admitting even the appearance of questionable and violent acts against others was Charleston merchant William Glen. Glen argued "that altho' he might have been Guilty of some Improprieties [he] hopes it does not amount to Criminalities." These Loyalists gambled that a show of remorse would put their listeners in the proper frame of mind to offer them clemency, without reminding their listeners of any behavior that might preclude their clemency case from proceeding. Honesty was not necessarily the order of the day—but apologizing helped so long as the person apologizing had a relatively clean record (meaning no active harassment of many individuals).[26]

Even fewer Loyalists admitted a real political preference. Edward Fenwick was unusually honest when he admitted that "during the late contest between these United States and Great Britain your Petitioner unhappily engaged in the service of the latter; in consequence of which he acknowledges that the Resentment of his Countrymen hath been justly shewn against him."[27] In many ways this is indicative of just how nonideological adherence to loyalism really was in South Carolina during the Revolution. There was no point in apologizing for something that could only antagonize those listening to one's case. It was not worth it. In fact most Loyalists were motivated by a brutal calculus of self-preservation, not by political philosophy. Petitioners steered clear of discussing political sentiments and instead focused on offering more practical excuses for their wartime adherence to the Loyalist side.

Loyalists used their petitions to offer exculpatory evidence in order to minimize their public Loyalist actions during the war. In so doing they walked a delicate line between presenting themselves as upright, honorable men worthy of citizenship in the new Republic and abasing themselves just enough to convince both the locals who read and signed their supporting petitions and the members of the General Assembly who then received and read those petitions that they had truly repented of their loyalism and been humbled by the dislocations of civil war. While it might seem as if Loyalists would have been better served to present themselves carefully as lacking in flaws that might make them seem like poor candidates for the rigors of republican citizenship, in fact some humiliation in their self-presentations was actually an important strategy in putting their best foot forward with those who considered these petitions. Justice demanded that Loyalists abase themselves—at least in rhetoric. They did not need to apologize outright, and few actually did. But they did need to reassure their listeners that they too had suffered the privations and dislocations of the war and yet that they recognized that their listeners had every reason to resent them.

Loyalists rushed to offer convincing evidence that they had no realistic choice except to join the British after Charleston and the rest of the state fell into British hands. This exculpatory evidence took many forms, including accusations of fraudulent behavior by others, admissions of poor health, and concerns about financial strains on dependents. In all cases Loyalists sought to offer plausible explanations for their wartime adherence to loyalism, and they clearly decided that practical explanations would be far more persuasive than any attempt to debate ideology. Certainly it would not have behooved them to cling to Loyalist ideas at a time they were seeking legal citizenship in the Republic, but it also speaks to the ways in which these Loyalists by and large were not and never had been primarily swayed by ideological concerns in the war.

A handful of male Loyalists tried to excuse their loyalism by arguing that they had signed congratulatory addresses due to the fraudulent actions of others. In other words someone else made them do it. No one tried this route to evade punishment for serving as an officer in the Loyalist militia or the civilian occupational administration. Presumably it was easier to deny culpability for a signature than for the ongoing public commitment of public service. In one especially cheeky suggestion, Aaron Loocock tried to convince the legislature that "some person inserted his name in an Address to Sir Henry Clinton, he believes contrary to his Knowledge or Consent." Loocock tried to support this rather flimsy excuse by saying he had not even been in Charleston at the time the address was circulated for signatures. Yet he could not bring himself to make such an audacious assertion without hedging. Should any future witness in the legislature or in a later public hearing contradict his assertion, he had left himself an out. Thomas Buckle went even further and tried to exculpate himself by claiming it was all a case of mistaken identity. "His nephew Thomas Buckle Junior did Sign his name to an Address to Sir Henry Clinton and Arbuthnot, Contrary to his Knowledge." These excuses seemed jarring to Patriot South Carolinians even at the time—which is one reason that only a handful of men resorted to such naked efforts at evading responsibility for their actions. These attempts to deny responsibility undercut men's attempts to show themselves as trustworthy neighbors and therefore honorable citizens. Most important for Loyalists, these claims did not work.[28]

Other Loyalists tried to evade responsibility for their actions by suggesting that they were simply the unfortunate victims of character assassinations by personal enemies. They either denied the actions entirely or suggested that the true level of their assistance to the British had been drastically misrepresented. William Burt tried to dismiss peremptorily what he felt to be unfounded accusations that he had sought to curry favor with the conquering British by delivering intelligence (through protected government books) to the British Navy. He characterized these suggestions as "owing to erroneous opinions formed from reports of his being an Enemy to America which are destitute of foundation." Evidently this attempt to blame his inclusion on the confiscation lists on false information fell on deaf ears, as he never returned to South Carolina. (His family did ultimately reclaim a part of his total estate, however.) Planter Andrew Hibben was more successful when he argued that his inclusion in the confiscation list was "owing to the misrepresentation of Some unkind person, that he is not conscious of any Crime to deserve such punishment."[29]

Loyalists of the middling sort, especially artisans, sometimes claimed that their limited educations and lack of experience in the elite-dominated political culture meant that they did not have the ability to discern the real consequences of their actions on the war effort and therefore should not be punished as if they had the independence of thought and action that the 1782 legislature had presumed when they fashioned the Confiscation Act. Charleston cooper William Cameron used this excuse successfully when he argued that "his signing the address, was occasioned by the example of Men, he thought more Capable of judging in political affairs than One of his narrow understanding." James Mackey tried the same type of argument (unsuccessfully) when he claimed he had not known what he was signing since "the address was fabricated by artfull & designing men. . . . Many persons were invited and persuaded to sign the same who were totally ignorant of the Nature or contents thereof." Cameron and Mackey certainly tried to play to the worst pretensions of the elite political class (who dominated the legislature) in suggesting that artisans, who had spent the pre-Revolutionary period asserting their own importance in the body politic, should now be excused from the consequences of their actions. These excuses relied on widely shared eighteenth-century understandings of political causation, which historians from Richard Hofstadter to Gordon Wood have called the "paranoid style." This belief that conspiracies lie behind political action might have worked with the legislature, as they shared these basic assumptions about how politics worked. However, this was a dangerous strategy. These Loyalists were arguing for their return to republican citizenship, and that citizenship imagined men were capable of independent discernment. This strategy relied on rejecting the norm of independent discernment while simultaneously arguing that men who had lacked independent action during the war would somehow be ideal exemplars of such independence after the war. This contradiction meant that only a tiny handful of Loyalists actually relied on this strategy.[30]

When Loyalists were not denying culpability altogether, they offered practical explanations to rationalize their wartime behavior. Of course they wanted to put the best face possible on their wartime conduct. They stayed away from ideological explanations and instead reinforced the widely understood practical peril many South Carolinians had found themselves in when the British occupied the state in 1780. Loyalists had to balance exculpating themselves with not sounding like men easily bent by the troubles of the world. Some petitioners used their own ill health, including physical debility, as a practical and sympathetic excuse. Thomas Eustace tried to convince the legislature that he had taken British protection because "being advanced in life, and infirm for many Years," he was unable to undertake the physical strains of fleeing Charleston indefinitely. John Walters Gibbs argued that he had been forced to sign not one but both public welcoming addresses to the conquering British commanders due to his "bad State of health." He went on to argue that his health continued to decline during the occupation, rendering him unable to act on Gov. John Rutledge's repeated offers of clemency in return for military service in the Patriot militia after Yorktown. Since "he had lost the use of his limbs by the Gout and Rheumatism," he could not be expected to ride out of the city. In citing their age and infirmities, these men argued that they did not possess the necessary freedom of action to make the choices that a republic demanded of its citizens. They essentially argued for diminished capacity and accepted appearing pathetic as the price necessary to win back their property.[31]

Many Loyalists admitted that they had been swayed by economic incentives when they took British protection and then kept it by signing welcome addresses and taking positions in the Loyalist militia. Loyalists who chose this strategy assumed that Patriots would understand the delicate reckoning involved in keeping a family and business afloat—even when Patriots had themselves suffered financial reversals due to their own wartime adherence to the cause. Alexander Rose tried this strategy but struck a sour note when he admitted that he made common cause with the Loyalists in order "to save a large Quantity of Indico" during the fall of Charleston. Complaints solely about financial losses were destined to fall on deaf ears as Patriots continued to ruminate over their own painful economic losses. Instead financial calculations needed to be tied to more sympathetic concerns about the welfare of others. Loyalists were far more likely to seek clemency by arguing that they allied with the British in order to protect their property and income and thereby support dependent wives and children. Both Jacob Deveaux and James Brisbane claimed that they took civil commissions under the British occupying administration because they needed a steady source of income to support their families. Brisbane put it most eloquently when he suggested that "he was obliged to apply to the British for Some place by which he might be enabled to Support a Numerous family." Brisbane's pleas did not actually convince the legislature, since in his position as sheriff of Charleston for the British occupiers, he routinely harassed Patriots. In the end the legislature emphatically rejected his application, saying that "he had taken the most early opportunity to evince his attachment to the British cause, that he had been rewarded for it by being appointed to a lucrative office under the police established in Charles Town, that he acted so as to obtain the thanks of that truly honourable Board, and therefore they recommend him to remain where he is and enjoy the favours of his beloved masters." On the other hand, Deveaux did convince the legislature to grant him clemency. Loyalists could be successful in arguing that the pressing realities of financial hardship forced their need to take British protection so long as they made their fear about financial hardship a concern about the plight of their vulnerable dependents. This strategy also only worked as exculpatory evidence when combined with evidence of strong support from members of the local community. These excuses, mired in the practical details of ordinary life, privileged the real constraints of interpersonal relationships that made up the network of dependency obligations that governed the lives of seemingly independent men of honor.[32]

✳ Proving Oneself a Good Citizen: Volitional Citizenship and the Ideal of Neighborly Good Character

South Carolina needed good citizens for its experiment in republican government. Loyalists strove to show fellow residents and legislators through their petitioning that they could be those good citizens. Certainly they offered practical excuses for their wartime behavior, but they understood that was not enough. Instead they needed to muster convincing evidence that they were honorable men who always engaged in upright conduct. One way that they could display their command of these traits was to show that they were linked to local networks that could vouch for them. Through the long-term maintenance of those networks, they could demonstrate a history of honorable service. They could also demonstrate the lived reciprocal obligations of neighborhood and community, such as lending money and offering emotional and physical support to friends and community members. Loyalists were aware that all Americans had come to understand neighborliness as a primary determinant of citizenship for eighteenth-century Americans, no matter what the law said about oaths of allegiance or birth obligations. Citizenship was an active entity, dependent on the norms of a face-to-face society. Loyalists used their petitions as a chance to offer evidence that they personified the ideal manly citizen.

A few Loyalists took the risk of combating the legislature's assumption that signing an address or taking an officer's commission should be considered punishable behavior. Under the circumstances these men were polite, but nonetheless firm, in rebutting that assumption. These men moved beyond offering evidence to exculpate themselves to cataloging their own bitter lack of choices in the context of the state's inability to protect its own citizens. John Wigfall pointedly reminded legislators that he "did accept of a Commission under the British, at a time when he thought no effectual opposition could be made in defence of the State, and that he never expected to be Called upon to Act against his Fellow Citizens." In so doing he reminded the legislature that legally he had done nothing but taken British protection when there was no other protection to be had. As will be seen in greater detail in the next chapter, this was an accepted legal principle and one Aedanus Burke used at length when he argued for Loyalist clemency. Since the vast majority of South Carolina "Loyalists" were in fact people who only took open Loyalist affiliations after the state was in British hands, this was a category that encompassed most of the petitioning Loyalists in 1783 and 1784. As a committee of legislators uneasily pointed out in recommending clemency for John Deas, confiscation and banishment were "too large an Imposition for doing no more than what the Bulk of the Citizens had done before him." Very few Loyalists chose to point this out so explicitly, however, since the strategy was not without risk. If it worked as planned, it openly questioned the motives and ultimately honor of the legislators themselves. If legislators missed the point, on the other hand, they might simply conclude that these petitioners were weak-willed and therefore made poor citizens. This may explain why few Loyalists openly pushed back against the assumptions of the legislature about what kind of behavior was culpable. Instead the vast majority of Loyalists worked to shape the reality of their wartime actions into a form they thought the legislature would find acceptable.[33]

Loyalists further sought to burnish their claims to good character, and therefore to honorable citizenship, by demonstrating that even under the tribulations and constraints of a brutal civil war, they always conducted themselves honorably. They then positioned both their wartime (despite their loyalism) and postwar actions in securing and enhancing their community networks as a natural outgrowth of their own fine character. Honor was the fundamental qualification of citizenship for free men of the Republic. America was to be a republic of virtue, where democracy depended on the willingness and capability of all men to behave continually in an upright fashion. Historian Joanne Freeman has shown that honor "was integral to the 18th century mindset— part of a larger body of pervasive cultural assumptions."[34] A man's character and reputation established him in the hierarchy of meaning that determined how others should treat him, and it was also a crucial part of men's self-conception. Character was not only one's personality but also one's moral standing in the public eye. Men had to manage honor, making sure that they convinced themselves and others of their possession of this important quality. Most of the Loyalist petitioners were men who had once been of clear character and reputation. By choosing the losing side, they had shaken any assumption of honorableness. In order to reassure Patriots, they would have to agree to face scrutiny to reestablish their honorable character, allowing their neighbors and legislators to sit in judgment of them. In return they expected to be able to reestablish the assumption of good character and through that unquestioned access to citizenship.

Petitioning Loyalists showed themselves to be men of charity as part of their process of claiming honorable character. Many petitioners cited their service to American prisoners in their attempt to portray themselves as vital supports to stressed wartime communities. Charles Johnston simply asserted that he had "endeavored to alleviate the distresses of many," but he also submitted a petition from Benjamin Villeponteaux, a prominent Charleston merchant, testifying that "Mr. Johnston has rendered him great Services while a prisoner." John Hartz's supporters were careful to testify that he spent substantial sums of money "reliev[ing] the distresses of the American prisoners, on Board the prison Ships and Hospitals in this Town by supplying them with Money and Necessarys." The legislators who heard these petitions knew without being reminded that these charitable visits exposed the visitors to rampant infectious disease. Loyalists were especially keen to show that their charity included not only those they knew personally, such as neighbors and friends, but also those from a much wider circle. The best charity, therefore, was not reliant on personal connections but on an empathy that led men of sensibility to care for those who could not demand it—or, more cynically, later return the favor. In this vein several Loyalists were quick to point out that they were now caring for orphaned children of Patriot soldiers. Three women who petitioned in support of Hartz applauded him for keeping "an Orphan child of a deceased American soldier, which he has and does now treat as his Own." In the absence of orphanages, individuals stepped forward to care for and protect vulnerable children. Taking on the paternal role for other men was a sign of neighborly investment and charity without expectation of recompense.[35]

Other Loyalists showcased their proper command of sensibility, and their willingness to stick out their necks against British interests during the war, by involving themselves in efforts to persuade British authorities not to execute Col. Isaac Hayne. John Scott reassured legislators that "he was particularly Active in promoting a petition in favour of Colonel Hayne." The British executed Hayne as a warning to all Carolinians who had taken oaths of allegiance to the Crown in 1780 and then joined the Patriot military efforts. For southern Patriots the colonel's execution became a cause célèbre, since Hayne and his supporters always maintained he was a man of honor who had been released from his oath of allegiance to the British and was therefore perfectly free to resume his actions on behalf of the Americans. Hayne's execution stirred people on both sides to protest and therefore was an effective way to showcase Loyalists' willingness to finesse the difficulties of resisting unsavory (and unpopular) British antihumanitarian efforts despite living under British protection.[36]

Some Loyalists sought to demonstrate their humanity by their own recognition of the terrors of civil war. Edward Fenwick made the connection between wartime conduct and honor most explicit when he argued that he used his position in the British service to "lessen the horrors of war by every office of Humanity and attention towards the Persons and property of those who fell within his Power."[37] His "humanity" in the face of the tribulations each side faced during the war was meant to show his ability to behave as a man of discernment and a good neighbor. By empathizing with the other side, they displayed the character traits of a respectable republican citizen.

Loyalists made it clear that wartime political affiliations were themselves the product of community-wide strategies aimed at protecting people and their property throughout the war. For every committed Loyalist who sought fame and glory through an officer's commission in the Loyalist militia, there were many more Loyalists who took those commissions out of a sense of duty to protect their neighbors. In one example John Adamson "accepted of it [the commission] at the Earnest request of his Neighbours (now Subjects of this State) to prevent its falling into the hands of a person whose intentions was well known to oppress them." And while contemporary audiences may imagine that the claims that men took commissions only with the agreement of Patriot-identified community members were met with incredulity, in fact so many Loyalists offered this testimony, and were able to find willing Patriot supporters to affirm it, that the General Assembly must have found it persuasive. Adamson's twenty-three Camden supporters chimed in to inform the legislature that he had "used all the Influence he had with the British in favour of Such persons as avowed their attachment to the American cause."[38] The only way legislators could have found these claims persuasive is if they had personally experienced such community collusion to stymie British efforts to use the militia as a tool of political enforcement.

Other Loyalists used the same strategy in painting their appointment to the Loyalist militia as part of a community collusion against the effective use of the militia. In so doing Loyalists burnished their bona fides as good community members with strong, trusting ties before, during, and after the war. Joseph Seabrook emphasized that he had been "prevailed upon by his neighbors to take a Militia Command under the British Government in order to prevent plundering." Since plundering was a major concern of both sides during the war, it stands to reason that communities would seek to arrange anything that would lessen the chances that serious militia incursions would lead to both plunder and heavy demands on foodstuffs. Lowcountry planter James Casells tried the same tack in explaining that he protected "the persons and properties of his neighbors from violence and plunder" while serving as the Loyalist militia captain for his area. Yet unlike others who tried this strategy, Cassells was not able to translate these claims into legislative clemency in 1784. He probably failed because despite his apparent reluctance to plunder, he was an unusually devoted Loyalist military leader in other ways. British lieutenant-colonel Nisbet Balfour dubbed Cassells more "manly, & worthy of credit" than any other Loyalist militia leader in the Carolinas. Still the fact that even unlikely applicants tried to use their wartime actions as evidence of neighborly honor and investment in local communities suggests that was widely understood to be an essential part of establishing a man as a good citizen.[39]

Military service had long been considered a vital part of manly citizenship. Adult able-bodied men were required to serve in the militia until they were in late middle age. Militia service, while often avoided, was crucial in cementing individual citizens' standing as free men. Militia service was legally required, but it was expected as well as a part of one's community contribution. Men who did not face up to their military duties chose to shirk their vital duties of community defense, and the community could rightly choose to doubt their commitment. Such men were not good community members and not good citizens. For Loyalists after the war, this was a difficult problem, since they had avoided service in the Patriot militia, unlike the legislators who sat in judgment of them. If they had served in the Loyalist militia, they had to present their service as compatible with notions of honorable manly conduct during war, which usually assumed active heroism in battle. Yet the kind of claims that would bring renown to the winning side after the war would only bring Loyalists disapprobation at best and continued confiscation and banishment in the worst case. Loyalists used their petitions to argue that they had served with honor while avoiding the battlefield entirely—and their supporters were willing to back these claims. In one telling example, backcountry Loyalist Patrick Muckle Murray testified that he had "ever had the goodwill of his neighbours in particular, and others in general" during his sixteen years as a South Carolina settler. When they chose him to serve as an officer in the Loyalist militia, in order to save his neighbors from the "oppressive and violent measures were Carrying on in other districts by the British owing to men being put into Commission not known to the Inhabitants," he served faithfully to protect his community from the harshness of the civil war. Yet

Murray also took pains to assure the legislature that "he never fired a Gun against his Countrymen." Normally military men would be embarrassed to admit that they avoided battle. Yet in this context, Murray saw it as an important part of his claim of honorable conduct during a fraught moment in a civil war. And forty neighbors from the proud Scots-Irish settlement of Crackers Neck signed on to support his contention that his honorable wartime service included avoiding military service entirely.[40]

Petitioning Loyalists sought to build on their efforts by reassuring both their neighbors (who became their supporters) and legislators that they could be dependable citizens going forward in the postwar world. This meant that not only did they have to demonstrate their dedication to the ideals of the Republic, but also they needed to demonstrate within themselves the willingness to let bygones be bygones in the spirit of healing the wounds of war. Christopher Williman claimed he had always been "warmly attached to this Country," while John Harth, who was subject to confiscation for signing a welcoming address to Sir Henry Clinton, claimed that when he did it "he had no design of Injuring the American cause, for which he has the highest Veneration." Neighborhood supporters were willing to echo these claims as well. Dr. James Lynah's supporters were clear that they "look on him as a Steady Friend to America" despite the fact that he took British protection. Loyalty to America was important for potential citizens of the new nation. South Carolinians were looking for both new citizens and reintegrated former Loyalists to show their dependability as citizens.[41]

Implicit in the American understanding of citizenship was that it was the product of voluntary choice, not unwavering birth allegiance. Historian James Kettner showed how Americans went from a traditional early modern British legal and popular understanding of subjecthood that held that political belonging was immutable and owed to the king by virtue of birth to a notion that citizenship was changeable. England did allow noncitizens to gain subjecthood through naturalization, but the practice was very unusual. To become naturalized, men had to be made subjects by a special act of the Parliament, so in practice only a few wealthy and determined men became naturalized. In the American colonies, naturalization became easily obtainable, since all of the colonies sought to attract willing white migrants. A 1740 act of Parliament specifically authorized American colonies to create British subjects through their own naturalization procedures. American naturalizations (unlike those in Britain) allowed all rights of citizenship, including the right to hold public office, ensuring that naturalized citizens in America truly enjoyed all the privileges of British subjecthood despite their birth. Citizenship to a state and a nation required the American Revolution, and even with the Revolution, it took years to progress from a bumpy sense of citizenship as allegiance to a state to a truly national conception of citizenship. After the Revolution South Carolinians continued to make it easy to become a naturalized citizen. In fact a perusal of the 1780s naturalization applications in the legislative records shows that many defecting British soldiers were warmly welcomed as new South Carolina citizens with all the rights of native-born Americans. In fact they faced a much easier path than proscribed Loyalists.[42]

Over time, with the rise of easy naturalization and the logic of an immigrant-friendly society, Americans had come to understand citizenship as based on the volitional actions and attitudes of individuals rather than the lifelong duties of subjecthood. This privileged the importance of showing the lived reality of citizenship through local affections and ties as a way of demonstrating the daily choices on which volitional citizenship rested. After the Revolution Loyalists proved they embraced the American understanding of citizenship with the same fervency as those Patriot legislators who were sitting in judgment of them. Loyalists understood that their society rested on a folk understanding (supported by some law) that citizenship was an active obligation for men that rested on the continuing choice to be a citizen. In so doing Loyalists helped to establish the lived norms of citizenship for all Americans. All South Carolinians shared their understanding of volitional citizenship based on a demonstration of public character, as evidenced by the fact that this was the argument that persuaded the General Assembly to pass an omnibus clemency act for Loyalists in 1784—less than two short years after they had passed confiscation originally.

A handful of Loyalists made the connection between honorable character and citizenship explicit. Philip Porcher's lowcountry supporters made this connection when they argued "in private life he is an honest Man and in public character, a friend to his Country." Character was the very basis of volitional citizenship in the American imagination. Isaac Delyon made the connection between public character and the lived obligations of citizenship his main argument for his readmission. In his defense he reminded the legislature that he had "always maintained the Character of a good Citizen." And the legislature concurred with this definition of citizenship as the product of the many everyday life choices that were summed in the public character of a man.[43]

Throughout the early national period, Americans continued to understand citizenship as local and character-based, just as they continued to identify with their state over the nation. The grand claims of American universal democratic citizenship, despite James Madison's theories, were in practice based on the comforts possible in a face-to-face society. The rise of universal male voting and the fraught abolitionist politics of the antebellum period redefined citizenship again, but Americans made it through the crucial early

To the Honorable *John Lloyd* Esquire President
and the rest of the Members of the Honorable the Senate

The Petition of Philip Porcher of the Parish of
St Stephen's in the State of South Carolina.

Most humbly sheweth

That your Petitioner is under the deepest sorrow and distress on account of a Law passed by the last
General Assembly whereby his Estate is Confiscated
and himself Banished, and of consequence his unhappy
wife and numerous Offspring will be reduced to misery
and want.

Your Petitioner therefore begs leave to throw himself
at the feet of your Honors, humbly imploring the favor of this
Honorable House to indulge him with their attention while
he lays before them a faithful and just recital of his Conduct from the commencement of this unhappy war to the
present time with the principles on which he acted and
the necessity he was under in so doing, and hopes from a
view of the whole That you will in your goodness and clemency find him an Object not altogether unworthy your
Protection and regard, and that you will be pleased to
relieve him from his distress.

Your Petitioner on the first commencement of this
unhappy war, was called upon by his Parish to represent
them, not only in the General Committee but also in the
Provincial Congress and Assembly where he continued a
Member until the surrender of Charles town, during which
period he served his Country faithfully and to the utmost
of his ability. that so far were his intentions ever to surrender himself as long as he could possibly avoid it, did
during the Siege of Charles town send on the North side
of Santee a considerable quantity of Rice for his Family's use, and built a couple of log Houses there, for their
reception in case it should be found practicable

5 —

Petition of Philip Porcher, 1783. Courtesy of the South Carolina
Department of Archives and History, Columbia.

years of this nation with a notion of citizenship based on the local and the character-driven. Volitional citizenship may have been new, but like much of the grand Enlightenment ideals of the eighteenth century, it rested on far older norms of a face-to-face society with a dense web of obligations.

Just as historian John Murrin has argued that the early Republic had a "roof without walls," meaning that our Founding Fathers erected the roof, a Constitution, with no national identity (the walls) to support it, here is a case where the implicit notion of citizenship resting on much older ideas of what made a good community endured well into the early nineteenth century, waiting for the reality of everyday understanding to catch up to the grand words of the founders.[44] These older ideas bridged the crucial gap that existed because there was no genuine, strong sense of national identity to make an American citizenship based on documents and ideology at all coherent. Loyalists used this folk understanding to write themselves into American citizenship. In so doing they helped construct a vision of citizenship based on demonstrated continued involvement over time in all the mundane details that made a community work. And in so doing they provided Americans with a conception of citizenship that has proven to be elastic, accepting people of different ideologies, religions, cultural preferences, and skin colors—so long as they all can be relied on to pitch in with the routine niceties that neighborliness demanded then and now.

✳ Why Demonstrating Local Support Was the Only Strategy That Actually Worked

In the end Loyalists had to demonstrate local authentic support in the petitions to the General Assembly to be offered legislative clemency. Loyalists were interested in what was efficacious, and showcasing vibrant neighborhood and community ties was what actually convinced the legislature to offer a mass clemency in 1784 that returned property and full citizenship to the majority of Loyalist petitioners. Everything else in the petitions—the rare apologies, the exculpatory evidence of practical obstacles to supporting the Patriot cause, the evidence of honorable conduct both before and during the war—was necessary to position these men as worthy of clemency. But what sealed the deal was convincing evidence that local community members accepted them. The legislature was unwilling to buy these seemingly facile claims from the Loyalists themselves unless others in a position to know were willing to vouch for them. Loyalists bet that if they showed substantial and resilient local neighborhood and community ties by doing the hard work of convincing neighbors to forgive them and vouch for them before the legislature, then the legislature would regard them as dependable citizens and community members—the kind of people who any thriving society would want to keep around. And that bet paid off. Loyalists were savvy interpreters of the social and cultural expectations of their world—at least after the war. They had to be.

Members of the General Assembly were looking to make sure that Loyalists had already achieved the social reconciliation necessary to settle quietly into the normal routines of life. Legislators were afraid of anything that might roil the waters of social stability after such a calamitous civil war. Their greatest collective nightmare was that their postwar efforts at stabilization and growth for the entire society would be submerged under a wave of mob violence and vigilantism such as that which had terrorized the Carolinas and Georgia during the war. Only former Loyalists who clearly were not going to be the target of the mob could even be considered for readmission. When petitioners demonstrated their social capital, they also made a convincing case that they ultimately chose people over ideas and could therefore be expected to do so again in the future. This is why Loyalists were so quick to assure both the legislature and their neighbors that they had "always been a friend to the United States" or "always appeared to be a friend to his Country."[45] Instead of the dreaded fifth column, Loyalists would be dependable citizens (at least in the future) precisely because they valued their inclusion in and service to local communities more highly than more theoretical concerns. The supposedly ideological Revolution on behalf of human liberty and a government resting its authority on the consent of the governed seems to have been a lot more concerned with lasting issues of harmony in culture and functional government—at least when viewed by the questions the new state legislature ultimately used to evaluate chastened Loyalists for clemency and reintegration after the war.

South Carolinians had long imagined citizenship to hinge on local community ties and had recognized that when they crafted the original Confiscation Act. As seen in the previous chapter, friends and neighbors organized epistolary campaigns to warn their Loyalist compatriots that they were facing the danger of confiscation and to offer practical suggestions and then aid in their efforts to evade confiscation and banishment. While Charles Drayton may have failed to take adequate action, multiple members of his social network went out of their way to offer him the evidence of local support that would have convinced the legislature to protect him from punishment. The legislators who enacted the legislation were aware that the fate of Loyalists, both those already punished and those not named in any official act, would depend on their reception by their own communities. Edward Rutledge, the chief architect of the Confiscation Act, expected the Loyalists returning to their communities in 1782 to be allowed to live without molestation if they were judged to be "peaceably inclined." He foresaw the importance of local support in differentiating between Loyalists who would reintegrate and those few who would not be able to persuade their neighbors. For them the outlook was ominous. The legislature would not need to step in because "the People in that part of the State will soon make their Situation very uncomfortable."[46]

Loyalists consistently offered to demonstrate their high level of local support. When they petitioned individually, they sought to assure the legislature that if they were granted a hearing, they could prove that they did have substantial support. James Gordon told legislators that he "appeals to his Neighbors, to prove the Services he has rendered many of them." Maurice Simmons bluntly offered "if he were allowed a hearing he will be able to Explain his Conduct and Situation (Supported by good Evidences) to the Satisfaction of his Countrymen." These Loyalists recognized that they needed to showcase their successful efforts to rebuild their social capital.

Merely asserting that their community supported them was not enough—they would have to show it. Loyalists also realized that they needed to show widespread support. As Henry Laurens had sardonically noted, "Every man has his friends & none of those, whose Estates have been justly forfeited, but may find a friend to pen a letter in his favor." Loyalists realized that it would be easy to reject the recommendation of only one supporter, and therefore they responded by cultivating widespread community support and then demonstrating it to the legislature.[47]

Loyalist petitioners realized that they needed to demonstrate tangible evidence that they possessed vibrant community networks that were accepting of them after the war. While it could help to produce evidence at later trials, it would be more effective to demonstrate that social capital at the time of petitioning. So they made great efforts to produce supporting petitions from their local communities. These petitions were almost certainly drafted by the same person who wrote the Loyalists' own individual petition, whether it was a paid attorney (in some cases) or the petitioner. For the most part, the claims in both petitions are identical. Sometimes the nuances of the phrasing changed, but much of the time the two petitions said exactly the same thing in exactly the same way. This excessive similarity makes it clear that the real point of the supporting petitions was not in the language of the claims but in the fact that they carried the weight of local community support. Community supporters indicated their support by signing their names. Up to a point, the more local community members who were willing to sign a supporting petition, the more the legislature was convinced that this Loyalist should receive legislative clemency.

A significant minority of Loyalists submitted these supporting petitions (along with their own individual petition), with anywhere from 13 signatures to a high of 114. In these primarily agricultural communities, individual houses

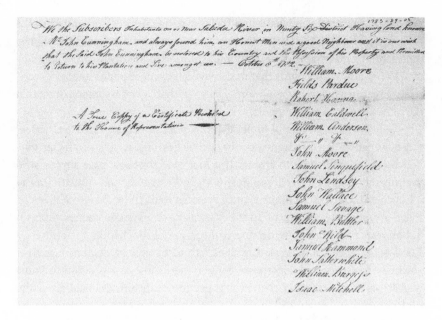

Petition by inhabitants of Ninety Six on behalf of John Cunningham, 1783.
Courtesy of the South Carolina Department of Archives and History, Columbia.

were spread far apart from each other on the landscape. While most communities had de facto gathering places, South Carolina's backcountry communities lacked the courthouses that served as a site for the collection of petition support in more established places such as tidewater Virginia. People literally had to go out of their way to sign a supporting petition. In that light these high numbers of signatures seem very impressive—and it impressed the legislators, who understood well how difficult it was to collect them and therefore how convincing this was as a sign of true support. Loyalists who produced these petitions were almost always offered clemency from confiscation when the General Assembly passed a mass clemency act in 1784.

The legislature continued to value evidence of local support when they began actually to consider these petitions. Each petition was referred to a legislative subcommittee comprising at least two legislators from the same area as the applicant so that people from the district could evaluate these claims of good service to the neighbors and high community social approval. In addition these local legislators were in a position to evaluate not only the number but also the quality of the signatories. Local legislators were aware of community ties and personal relationships that are hard for contemporary historians to reconstruct. In short they were in a much better position to analyze the names on each petition than are contemporary scholars. Unfortunately the hearing records do not preserve debate, and the committee records are limited to the final report. But these committees must have considered whether the signers represented a reasonable cross-section of the landed members of the community. What also stands out is that in the end it was more important to demonstrate a reasonable level of community support than it was to demonstrate that the local leaders were in support.

Legislators were careful to publish the dates of hearings in the Charleston newspapers far in advance of the actual hearings to give character witnesses every opportunity to attend. This long lead time also gave anyone who passionately desired to testify against the good character and admissibility of a Loyalist the chance to prepare and appear as well. These should perhaps be called anticharacter witnesses. In the rare cases where anticharacter witnesses did appear, such testimony destroyed those Loyalists' chances for clemency. Local support cut both ways. Loyalists had to be able to demonstrate convincingly that they had widespread support, and those in a position to know (legislators from the same area) would get the chance to evaluate all of the evidence.

By handing what had been statewide judgments off to a system of local decision making on an individual basis, the legislature bowed to the greater knowledge of the localities while preserving their own ultimate prerogative of control. In making these decisions based on local opinion, they guaranteed that pardoned Loyalists had shown that their communities welcomed them. These were people with enduring ties who would indeed make good citizens. And in the end the General Assembly would be able to put their own imprimatur on local decision making, which could only aid their own efforts to establish firmly the supremacy of the state legislature as the foremost governmental authority in the newly republican state. Historian Robert Weir has argued that the South Carolina General Assembly used the lengthy individual and "piecemeal" consideration of Loyalist cases in order to "legitimate the authority of the Revolutionary legislature."[48] Yet in fact reconciliation was bottom-up rather than top-down. What made reintegration work was the actions and words of people willing to support individual Loyalists all across the state. Rather than the leaders leading, the leaders followed.

In the end Loyalists had to do the hard work of apologizing to their neighbors. Their social networks, which were vital to economic, political, and social success in the eighteenth century, required extended efforts at revitalization. Once Loyalists had undergone these efforts and had success, they were ready to demonstrate this cohesive network to the state legislature. Petitioners represented themselves as loyal Americans who routinely undertook honorable service to community and state. The way to predict confidently that a white man would rise to the demands of volitional citizenship in a republic that demanded much higher standards of reasoned participation was to study his public honorable character. These assertions of honorable character were essential in proving themselves fit citizens of the new Republic, but honorable character was not enough by itself. The legislature needed proof of the reality of that character. This is why the only Loyalist strategy that really mattered in the end was securing substantive local support and then offering the legislature convincing evidence of that support. The General Assembly eventually endorsed this notion of citizenship when it offered these Loyalists clemency in 1784.

Loyalists who failed at these tasks suffered the consequences even if their neighbors and the legislature had been willing to let them try to make their best case for clemency. When William Drayton made a leisurely tour of the backcountry in April and May 1784, he was no stranger to the extremes of violence people in the backcountry had experienced during the civil war in the Revolution. Yet what Drayton encountered on his spring 1784 journey was the saga of a former Loyalist whose neighbors had permitted him to live peacefully among them for more than two years after his armed wartime actions (and infractions). Drayton was spending the night in Thomas Box's public house when he noticed how uncomfortable the entire accommodations were. Drayton, ever the aggrieved consumer, complained to his "sour looking" host about the state of the place. To Drayton's dismay Box tartly replied he would be moving away and therefore saw no reason to maintain his property. This Loyalist taverner boasted to Drayton that during the war he had killed two men from his own community. Drayton was shocked that Box spoke of these murders "coolly . . . as if they had been Bucks or Wolves." He planned to leave the area, if not the state, one step ahead of his likely executioners, calmly telling Drayton that "his neighbors already talk'd of hauling him over the coals for having killed only two of them." Drayton was understandably shaken by his encounter with a disagreeable and unrepentant Loyalist who still relished his wartime stories counting up his battlefield exploits and mourning his missed shots.[49]

Drayton and Box's neighbors all agreed that Loyalist reintegration was a worthy pursuit. Box's community members had clearly been open to healing those former social bonds, since if they had not been open to reconciliation they would have used violence to "convince" him to leave long before the spring of 1784. Box was about to be run out of town well after most white Loyalists had been successfully reintegrated into their communities, had demonstrated evidence of that successful community building to the legislature, and had been granted clemency because of that. Yet Box did not do any of the things other white Loyalists did to further their own acceptance in the community. As a common man who only owned four hundred acres in the backcountry, he had never risen high enough in the Loyalist militia to serve as an officer and therefore end up subject to confiscation. Yet despite this luck he would not do what it took to build on his Patriot neighbors' willingness to give him time to apologize and be an unusually thoughtful neighbor. The tenor of his conversation with Drayton certainly paints a picture of a man who routinely missed social cues and probably did not care about those cues anyway. A man who could live among the families of the men he killed on the battlefield and still publicly obsess over the shots he missed lacked both the desire to pay attention to other people's emotions and the social finesse to use any understanding of them he might have had. He probably never apologized for his wartime behavior, and if he did he almost certainly did it in an offensive way. His boorish behavior must have been well known to his neighbors before the war, so it is a marker of their strong appetite for reconciliation that they tolerated him for over two years before finally giving him the boot.

Drayton's later reflection on his meeting with a churlish Loyalist reveals the extent to which all South Carolinians relied on an understanding of volitional citizenship reliant on the honorable character of male citizens that could be convincingly demonstrated by neighborly service. A stunned Drayton was moved to record in his journal that one "unhappy consequence of the late war" was the destruction of the ties that bound South Carolinians together. For Drayton the civil war had "dissolv'd not only the Ties of Friendship & Neighborhood, but even of Humanity."[50] Drayton's understanding of South Carolina citizenship rested on those ties, precisely the ones that Loyalists worked so hard to cultivate after the Revolution and that the General Assembly consistently considered in deciding how to deal with individual Loyalists. If an educated member of the elite considered the ties of belonging that held society together to rest at the heart of "Friendship & Neighborhood," how much more so must ordinary people have relied on their gut instinct that neighborliness denoted honorable character and that men's honorable public character was the best guarantee of fitness in citizenship. Loyalists had seized on the shared folk understanding of citizenship shared by all South Carolinians (or at least all white South Carolinians) and bent that into a tool to regain unquestioned access to citizenship in the new Republic.

FOUR ✳ *Uneasy Neighbors to Trusted Friends*

How Loyalists and Their Allies Built Reconciliation

In the summer of 1783, Stephen Mazyck wrote to his anxious young nephew Peter Porcher, who was studying in England at the time. Porcher was understandably concerned because his father, like so many other South Carolinians, had elected to embrace publicly the Loyalist cause after the British invaded in order to preserve his property and had been branded a traitor and stripped of that property by the 1782 Confiscation Act. Porcher was no doubt worried about both his father and his own chances without the inheritance he was undoubtedly counting on, and his anxiety was palpable. But his uncle was able to reassure him that the situation was really much better than it seemed on the surface. He bluntly told young Porcher that his father "was fully determined to stay in this Country not withstanding his Estate was confiscated." Philip Porcher understood well that despite the harsh tone of the Confiscation Act, he and other elite men who had changed sides during the war but not committed violent acts were likely to find increasing sympathy as time wore on. Gambling on his understanding of the situation, Porcher "stayed at Santee" on his family's property throughout 1782 and 1783, going up to Charleston for the meeting of the General Assembly and clemency hearings. Mazyck was optimistic about Porcher's chances and soothed his nephew that "your Father amongst others having a great many Powerful Friends" and being known for his "Universal good character" would gain legislative favor.[1]

In fact Mazyck's letter to his nephew was prescient. Rather than offering empty reassurances, he had a good understanding of the real situation for Loyalists by 1783. The legislative committee on Loyalist petitions did recommend exempting Porcher from the Confiscation Act, and in 1784 he was given his property and his citizenship back, although he was still temporarily subject to amercement.

In many ways Porcher is representative of the experiences of Loyalists during and after the war. He had been a Patriot early in the war, even serving two terms in the provincial congress of South Carolina. When the British occupied Charleston in 1780, he made the decision to accept protection and took a British commission. In his own defense, he told the General Assembly in his 1783 petition that he first laid "whole nights in Santee River Swamp" hiding from the British, giving up in fear after a few very uncomfortable weeks. In addition he made his decision to take a commission as a lieutenant in the militia after hearing persistent rumors that every member of the legislature would be apprehended and imprisoned on an island outside Charleston. Given the smallpox outbreak, Porcher pleaded that imprisonment seemed to promise "certain Death." Forty-some members of his parish filed a supporting petition on his behalf. For them his character was "that of a man attentive to the Duties of his Station," and he was "beloved and respected." He explained that he took the commission hoping that he would only have to run slave patrols, not participate in the war. When he realized that combat training was required, he resigned the commission, and his neighbors seconded his account. He was the perfect picture of many Loyalists: a supporter of American independence who made the best accommodation he could with the British after they took Charleston. He tried to protect his family and his property without actually harming the American cause. Maintaining good relationships throughout the war with neighbors and kin, he had warm ties to augment his own direct appeal to the General Assembly. And for the assembly, those ties were solid proof of his honor and fitness for the responsibilities of citizenship.[2]

As the war wound down, Porcher, like so many other Loyalists, strategized to reconcile with his community and present the best possible case to the legislature for official clemency in order to maintain his comfortably enjoyable life in South Carolina as well as his family's economic prospects (those prospects his son was so anxious to see preserved.) He secured help from war hero Gen. Francis Marion to gain official permission to live on his own plantation. He must have spent many months reaching out to his neighbors—his community—in order to heal lingering resentments. While those conversations are lost to the historical record, the end result is not. He savvily marshaled additional testimonials from those Patriots he had reconciled with as evidence to persuade the legislature as they moved toward ending confiscation for many Loyalists by 1784. His reconciled supporters argued that any "inconsistency of Conduct into which he may have been betrayed" came from his efforts to protect his family and his community. And in the end his hard work paid off, and the legislature lifted his confiscation and banishment in 1784 (along with many others). Even the rudimentary restrictions they levied on him to suggest some punishment (a 12 percent amercement and a seven-year restriction on voting and office holding) were gradually eliminated in the intervening years. Porcher died on his own plantation in 1800, fully restored as a citizen.[3]

His anxious son Peter finished his schooling in England and returned to South Carolina, where he eventually received the inheritance he was so anxious to secure. Peter served eight terms in the General Assembly. His political ambitions were aided by his father's recovered wealth and unharmed by his father's loyalism. Today Philip Porcher's home in Charleston is a pricy bed and breakfast in the heart of the historic district. Advertising materials and guidebooks make no mention of his Loyalist status. By convenient silence he has become just another Revolutionary Patriot.[4]

Philip and Peter Porcher turn out to be representative of the experiences of the majority of South Carolina Loyalists and their children. Despite the seeming harshness of confiscation, comparatively few Loyalists were ever even subject to it or to amercement. While the legislature may have originally proposed a concurrent system of criminal justice through the courts, it never actually came to fruition. Of the minority of South Carolina Loyalists who did find themselves singled out and publicly punished in 1782, a majority of them were forgiven and offered full governmental clemency in 1784—a short two years later. South Carolinians came to empathize with defeated Loyalists, eventually recognizing that harsh punishments were "too large an Imposition for doing no more than what the Bulk of the Citizens had done."[5] Loyalists rapidly slipped back into the same social and economic positions they had held before the war, and their children went on to suffer no limitations because of their father's history of loyalism. All in all South Carolinians offered their former Loyalist neighbors and friends a generous reconciliation—one that those very Loyalists had worked hard to bring about. South Carolina's prompt and widespread governmental clemency and societal reconciliation looks extraordinarily generous in comparison with other American states. So why did South Carolinians choose to work so hard to reintegrate the losers? Loyalists such as Porcher clearly represented themselves in ways that so resonated with Patriot South Carolinians that they joined in a shared project to heal their society and reintegrate the Loyalists completely.[6]

✳ *The Effort to Build a Public Culture of Reconciliation*

South Carolinians, elite and ordinary, sought to shape a public culture that favored reintegration of the Loyalists and reconciliation with them. Despite the occasional bubbles of frustrated backlash, usually against a few individuals, by 1783 white South Carolinians were increasingly receptive to arguments in favor of Loyalist reintegration. The hard work the Loyalists themselves were doing in socializing with their neighbors and rebuilding their war-torn communities soothed angry Patriot hearts. Public culture became a font of the effort to create unity in which former Loyalists were actively embraced back into the community. Public intellectuals, drawn from the elite, joined in the effort to define a viable reconciliation for Loyalists and for a society still suffering the scars of civil war.

The American Revolution was itself a testament to the persuasiveness of a generation of public intellectuals to shape public culture profoundly—especially when they were pushing with the desires of middling sorts instead of against them. While scholars such as Woody Holton have vividly shown that ordinary colonial Americans, including Native Americans and enslaved African Americans, helped fuel the Revolution, nobody disputes that men such as Thomas Paine and Thomas Jefferson helped create and shape the Revolution with their skillful evocations of natural law and intrinsic political rights. While South Carolina's public intellectuals never rose to the heights of those from Virginia, they were locally influential. These writings were widely distributed, in South Carolina benefiting from the Charleston-centric nature of information (and social) distribution. In other words most elite South Carolinians, who still had significant roles as opinion makers for the wider society, visited and lived in Charleston part of the year and knew each other personally. Most important, public intellectuals were influential in early national debates because public writing still captured the imagination. Newspapers were still one of the primary means of conducting something approaching a society-wide discussion of how to handle the "Loyalist problem" (as it was sometimes known.) The middling sort yeoman farmer who South Carolina relied on, especially in the backcountry, to solidify public support for the inclusion of Loyalists was interested in joining the best of the elite culture.[7]

Three South Carolinians joined a small but outspoken chorus of American leaders (including Alexander Hamilton) who used public persuasion to try to ameliorate the position of Loyalists after the war. Judge Aedanus Burke, Judge John F. Grimké, and Christopher Gadsden all opposed confiscation for legal, moral, political, and economic reasons. Gadsden and Burke ventured into public advocacy for Loyalist reintegration and official clemency, although they never tried to create an alliance among public supporters of the Loyalists or even tried to coordinate their efforts. Crucially these outspoken Patriot defenders of the Loyalists had impeccable Patriot wartime credentials themselves and therefore were immune to potential aspersions on their own wartime character. In speaking out they provided cover for other, more moderate leaders to lift confiscation for many Loyalists. Their public pronouncements helped create a public culture oriented toward a generous, if not universal, reconciliation.

Christopher Gadsden (the wartime lieutenant governor) and Francis Marion opposed the Confiscation Act from the beginning, but neither was willing

Aedanus Burke. Emmet Collection, Miriam and Ira D. Wallach Division of Art, Prints and Photographs, New York Public Library, Lenox and Tilden Foundations.

Christopher Gadsden. Courtesy of the South Caroliniana Library, University of South Carolina, Columbia.

to risk all their political capital to oppose it vigorously. This was despite the fact that both had enormous political capital to burn. Marion was a beloved war hero, and Gadsden had been a leading light in Charleston radical revolutionary circles. After Charleston's surrender the British made an example of Gadsden; he suffered in prison in Saint Augustine for eleven months, complaining often that he was deprived of even the sight of the sun. But both men relied on their sizable political skills and chose to try to exempt as many Loyalists from punishment as possible while avoiding a frontal attack on anti-Loyalist legislation. Marion was generous in granting military passes to Loyalists to return to their own estates in 1782, which enabled men such as Porcher to assert their claim to their property aggressively. Gadsden opposed the Confiscation Act of 1782 while he was a member of the legislature, although he worked harder behind the scenes to protect as many individuals as possible from ending up on the eventual list. Even his delicate and mild public opposition to the act attracted hostile notice. He told his ally Marion that he had "met with continual rebukes from my friends, and not a few gross affronts" for his efforts to "restrain and to mitigate their rage and impetuosity." He did vote against the act, but later he suggested he had been more outspoken than he really had been, grandiloquently recounting that he threatened to cut off both his hands before he would vote for it. Gadsden and Marion waited for the healing effects of time to soften ardent opposition to Loyalist reintegration and forgiveness before pressing their case. They correctly anticipated that South Carolinians would be willing to reconsider. Gadsden suggested to Marion that in the wake of their legislative defeat, "we must patiently wait till the next Assembly to endeavor to have its severities at least mitigated where there is room."[8]

Burke, a recent immigrant and trained British lawyer who had become a Patriot during the war, was one of the only members of the legislature to oppose the Confiscation Act when it was first proposed in 1782. Yet despite his early public opposition, he also believed the Confiscation Act could serve a valuable temporary purpose in slaking the strong public desire for revenge—a desire shared with the elected legislators. He suggested that a confiscation act or similar piece of legislation would be required and that any Loyalist relief would have to have "some exceptions to satisfy publick justice, and as you would throw a Tub to a whale to satisfy the vengeance of those who have suffered."[9] In other words a few notorious and highly noticed (and perhaps very wealthy) Loyalists would need to be singled out for public punishment in order to preserve leniency for everyone else. A limited confiscation act was the cost of doing business in 1782.

So even the most public opponents of confiscation in 1782 had acceded to the reality of public condemnation and punishment of the Loyalists and planned from the beginning to allow time to pass before stepping up their public efforts to end Loyalist punishment. The next year Burke and Gadsden began to mount a more public and more confrontational advocacy campaign for Loyalist clemency, although the two men often disagreed with each other about strategy and tone.

Marion chose to limit his opposition to Loyalist punishments to his private correspondence, serving as a cheerleader for Gadsden as he pushed forward in arguing for greater clemency for former Loyalists. In contrast Burke felt alone (and reveled in the challenge) in his quest to persuade his fellow South Carolinians to accept Loyalist clemency. Both men sometimes chose to publish their newspaper writings under a pseudonym, although in neither case did this truly protect their anonymity. But only Burke was willing consistently to use his own public reputation to promote Loyalist clemency and reintegration into South Carolina society, and only he was willing to carry that message beyond the safety of the printed page and into direct conversation with those who disagreed. The only other figure who was willing to argue directly for Loyalist clemency outside of newspapers and the elite was a fellow jurist, John Faucheraud Grimké, and he only interceded publicly once. Why did Burke stand alone, the only elite voice in favor of Loyalist reintegration to step outside of his own comfort area to travel into the backcountry and try to persuade skeptical middling sorts of the value of Loyalist reintegration, and do so repeatedly? In part the answer is that he was the kind of man who reveled in being crude, hotheaded, and argumentative. He delighted in creating controversy and often went out of his way to court it. While his forceful intellect helped him rise in South Carolina society, many members of the elite could not stand him. His propensity for riling people up and his recent entry into society also gave him an outsider's perspective that allowed him to enunciate forcefully a convincing defense of Loyalist reintegration that did not depend solely on local ties and therefore could rise above accusations of favoritism and backscratching among the elite. To be fair the white South Carolina elite often did deserve charges of backscratching and favoritism, which is why Burke's contribution was so important.

Burke utilized multiple methods of public persuasion, calling upon his position as a circuit judge. He also used his superior education and entrée to elite social networks to make sure his writings were published in several local newspapers, albeit often anonymously. In 1783 he used the occasion of an address to the grand jury in a backcountry South Carolina town (in a region split between Loyalists and Patriots) as a forum for kick-starting the public conversation he wanted to have about repealing the confiscation and amercement acts. In so doing he personally made the argument for Loyalist reintegration in a region that badly needed reconciliation. He knew in his bones it took some courage, and he discovered anew a year later how angry some former Patriots were with at least a few notorious Loyalists when an angry crowd, frustrated that he had ruled that a former Loyalist could not be prosecuted for murder when he had killed people after a battle, seized the prisoner and hanged him from a tree just out of sight of the courthouse. (The crowd hanged the man out of sight in deference to Judge Burke.)

All three men, Gadsden, Burke, and Grimké, made both legalistic and psychological arguments for Loyalist clemency and reconciliation, just as Hamilton and his allies did in New York. In particular both Gadsden and Burke argued that the confiscation and amercement acts were ex post facto laws that created a dangerous precedent for the security of citizenship in a free democratic state. Yet ultimately all three men emphasized practical arguments based in psychological arguments about human nature. In the end South Carolinians were more convinced by arguments that spoke to the realities of how to craft a stable and thriving society after unleashing the dogs of war. Loyalists made their own arguments on the basis of how they could contribute to a stable, attractive white society, and their outspoken defenders took up the public argument on the same terms. While these public intellectuals would be more eloquent, at bottom they had the same concerns. If South Carolinians gave in to revenge and hatred, they would ultimately drive out good members of society and make their own society less attractive and robust. On the other hand, if they rose to the occasion and offered Loyalists reconciliation, they could build the foundations of a generous democratic state attractive to all. Ironically this robustly inclusive democracy required that black people be excised from social belonging so that white people could learn to be tolerant of each other's missteps and failings.

Burke's legal arguments were the most sophisticated of the three men, befitting his legal training at the Inns of Court. When he argued that Loyalist punishments made citizenship more capricious and insecure than a democratic state should countenance, he went for the legal and political jugular, predicting that such ex post facto laws would come back to haunt South Carolinians: "If so obscure a man as *Paddy Hinds*, or so obnoxious a one as *Bob Williams*, can be banished, amerced, or put to death without trial, hearing, or examination; whence comes security to you, or even to J_ R_ himself." Here Burke carefully moves the question from whether former Loyalists deserved their punishment to the question of how to construct a secure future for all South Carolinians. He also takes a swipe at former governor John Rutledge ("J_R_ himself"), whose family was personally profiting from confiscated properties. Burke was convinced that Rutledge and his supporters were deliberately stirring up hatred toward former Loyalists as a cover for their systematic attempts to disenfranchise voters in order to maintain their own shaky grasp on power.[10]

Burke further pointed out that now-proscribed Loyalists had every legal and moral right to choose to take British protection at a time when the Patriot government had ceased to be able to protect its citizens. Loyalist confiscation hinged on legally designating the Loyalists as traitors, but under English law a government must exist in order to bind the affections of its members. As Burke argued, "the obligation of subjects to the State is understood to last so long, and no longer than the power lasts by which it is able to protect them." When many men protected themselves by signing congratulatory addresses and taking positions in the British-organized militia and local governance structures, proscribed Loyalists had simply made accommodation with the victorious party. Burke pointed out that while such public pronouncements of loyalism "did not show much political wisdom," they were not "crimes against the laws or government, for neither law nor government existed." In the end he concluded that confiscation and amercement risked creating "disabilities [that] degraded them below the rank of freemen."[11] South Carolinians risked creating a two-tier system of white male citizenship that ultimately undermined white racial solidarity and the robust protections of Anglo-American citizenship that Americans had fought the Revolutionary War in order to preserve.

So what made total amnesty for Loyalists the best choice, given the realities of human nature? Burke's legal arguments came together with his concerns that South Carolina's political leaders risked a secure future on a misreading of human nature. His conclusion that legal restrictions created a second-class citizenship was the key to his arguments that punishments would only embitter former Loyalists and lead to long-lasting resentments instead of healing. Tellingly he turned to history to show that punishing the losers in a civil war was a poor choice and that in the past offering generous amnesties created more prosperous, secure, and stable societies. In his reading Charles II of Great Britain had promoted a program of amnesties out of strength instead of weakness, deliberately choosing to secure the affections of those on the other side of civil war. In Burke's hands Niccolò Machiavelli also preached amnesty as the best solution to civil war.[12]

Burke and Gadsden independently came together to press an argument for complete Loyalist clemency as the wisest decision. They were not friends, and they did not consult each other throughout their writing binges in 1783 and 1784, but they independently came to argue for what Burke termed "moderation, and reconciling principles" and Gadsden explained as forgiving in the service of the future. In this they joined Judge Grimké in arguing that forgiveness was in fact the best way to secure peace, prosperity, and the promise of democracy. Burke convincingly argued that punishing former Loyalists would only lead them to agonize over their sense of being treating unjustly. They would seethe. Since South Carolina had de facto allowed many former Loyalists to stay in the state and deluge the legislature with petitions for clemency, they had already cast the die for former Loyalists to live among them. In that case the worst possible solution was the Amercement Act, which served only to "irritate one half of the people against the other, and disgrace both. It will also serve to keep alive the memory of the troubles of the present day, which should be buried in oblivion." Burke's understanding of human psychology highlighted the risks South Carolinians were already taking in dithering—admitting many Loyalists while officially punishing them. Former Loyalists were already mounting successful personal campaigns convincing their neighbors that they were reliable citizens worthy of inclusion. If they achieved social reintegration but not legal clemency, they potentially would become the festering, traitorous fifth column that Loyalist expulsion was originally designed to avoid.[13]

In the end both Burke and Gadsden worked to convince other South Carolinians that reconciliation was a matter of self-interest, the best way to guarantee the kind of government and society they wanted. If punishing the Loyalists risked creating permanent animosities, than offering them generous pardons and full social, political, economic, and legal reintegration into society would produce a grateful set of citizens. Their insight into human nature showed them that while those who felt wronged might stew over perceived injustices, those who felt that had been showed mercy, especially unwarranted mercy, would redouble their loyalty and affection for the society that offered them that mercy. As Burke put it (in two different pieces), if South Carolinians would only bury "in oblivion past injuries, and past errors, [so that] a disposition of benevolence may go out through the land," then they would "make them our Friends by Pardoning." Generosity and empathy would ultimately build stronger social ties than continually drawing distinctions, at least between whites. All in all Burke was picking up on and using his voice to amplify the kind of argument former Loyalists had been making over and over again in their personal relationships and in their official legislative petitions—that Loyalists were "friends," meaning people deeply invested in the warp and weft of society and deeply trustworthy. And in advocating that South Carolinians bury their memories of wartime division, including personal losses, Burke anticipated an approach to the careful management of historical memory that South Carolinians eventually adopted.[14]

Both public advocates of Loyalist clemency ultimately argued that it was the wise duty of triumphant Patriot South Carolinians to set aside their personal anger in order to embrace full Loyalist reintegration. Burke argued that if South Carolinians embraced the "reconciling principles" he urged, they could then "connect our citizens in ties of harmony and common brotherhood."

Gadsden put it more eloquently when he counseled his fellow South Carolinians that "he that forgets and forgives most, such times as these, in my opinion, is the best citizen." Loyalists had persuaded many people to forgive them with their own personal, face-to-face conversations and apologies. Now it was incumbent upon all to build on those instances of personal forgiveness to participate in deliberate reconciliation. That deliberate reconciliation was the marker of the "best citizen."[15]

How could the elites who shaped public opinion move beyond intellectual, often legalistic, arguments on the printed page to forge a vibrant culture of openness to former Loyalists? Successful long-term reconciliation depended on it. As it happens, like other places in the Atlantic world, newspapers and print culture more generally provided a widespread, nonviolent, and often unattributed forum in which the issue of Loyalist reintegration could be probed.

South Carolina's newspaper culture was important to allowing the public a sense of full discussion of the problem of what to do with the Loyalists after the war. Even a cursory examination of Charleston's newspapers from 1783 and 1784 shows avid discussion of Loyalists in South Carolina, other states, and British dominions. Public discussions allowed everyone to feel that their opinions had been aired, even if they did not get everything they wanted in the end. South Carolinians opposed to Loyalist reintegration, or even just the reintegration of a few specific people, were able to slake their rage through rhetorical violence in their reading, rather than actual violence in the Charleston streets. Newspapers offered a way to communicate across class boundaries, as white Charlestonians had almost universal literacy and 80 percent of rural white South Carolinians could read. Presumably, with such a high degree of literacy, many people were exposed to the debates carried out in Charleston newspapers, and they worked to diminish their desire to seek revenge. In the end, while South Carolinians read about violence toward former Loyalists across the United States, there were only a few isolated instances of even the threat of violence against the former Loyalists by 1783. Those isolated instances certainly stirred up brief chaos and local color (for instance one mob brawl in Charleston's streets that year turned into two weeks of breathless coverage in the local paper), but in the end what is actually remarkable is not that a few individual Loyalists were threatened by crowds and encouraged to leave or face real personal violence, but that so little violence actually greeted the increasing reintegration of the Loyalists. By late 1783 and 1784, while the legislature would entertain the petitions of hundreds of former Loyalists seeking reintegration, readers of Charleston newspapers began to consume a steady diet of stories of successful Loyalist reintegration and forgiveness in other American states— leavened with occasional revenge humor, which was a definite step up from actual violence.[16]

Certainly in the month before the final Treaty of Paris resolved the war, American anxiety grew, and that anxiety was reflected in public discussions of what the treaty should and should not include. Americans who were open to reintegrating men who had lived their entire adult life in America quailed at the prospect of opening the United States to a new wave of British merchants with no ties to the community. Americans also were largely resistant to British insistence that they pay back all prewar debts in full. Both issues were vital to British interests in the peace treaty, yet neither really had anything to do with the question of clemency and reconciliation with American former Loyalists. But in the public anxiety surrounding the treaty, the issues were conflated. In South Carolina (much like in New York), British occupation encouraged a new generation of British merchants to establish themselves. As the war ended, those merchants petitioned to be able to stay. Instead they were given a twelve-month reprieve in order to collect debts and put their affairs in order. Given the way Loyalists had seized on those kind of merciful arrangements to craft a strategy for long-term reconciliation, and given British pressure to protect British merchants as the price for continuing trade with the British Empire, South Carolinians were right to be concerned that these merchants would become permanent denizens of Charleston, like it or not. Even forthright defenders of Loyalist reintegration such as Gadsden fought against the new British merchants. Gadsden spoke for many in the artisan class when he suggested the real elite plot against everyone else was to protect these merchants. He had in mind the way in which Governor Rutledge had protected the merchants when the British withdrew from the city in order to negotiate the return of many valuable slaves. And when crowd violence finally broke out in Charleston near Independence Day, 1783 (one of only two incidents in the period between the end of the war and legislative Loyalist clemency in 1784), the precipitating incident did not even involve a Loyalist but an especially cocky and self-assured British merchant who had only recently moved to South Carolina when he decided to publicly pick a fight with a French citizen. Like this incident, much of what seemed like anti-Loyalist propaganda was actually antimerchant (or anti-paying-justly-contracted-bills). Real anger dissipated quickly after 1782, concentrating on pockets of anti-British feeling rather than hostility to those Loyalists who were working hard to convince their communities of their trustworthiness.[17]

What did South Carolinians read in the newspapers by the middle of 1783 in addition to the carefully penned arguments of elite public intellectuals such as Gadsden and Burke? For one thing they read about Loyalist amnesties in other states. For instance the South Carolina press approvingly reported Connecticut's, North Carolina's, and Georgia's debates over legislative clemency acts. South Carolinians could read that Connecticut had agreed that

Americans who offered Loyalists clemency would create a nation "distinguished for justice and magnanimity." All of this evidence helped convince the literate middling sort that reintegration was a worthy project that deserved their buy-in.[18]

Hamilton's outspoken defense of Loyalists and the wisdom of Loyalist reintegration in New York even made it into the South Carolina press when the *South Carolina Gazette* published one of his pseudonymous circulars. Hamilton's postwar law practice specialized in defending Loyalists and British subjects in their efforts to regain control of their property in the United States. In the same year he won the case of *Rutgers v. Waddington* (1784) protecting the property rights of former Loyalists, he vigorously defended Loyalist rights in the press through a series of circulars published under the pseudonym Phocion. Phocion was an Athenian military commander who advocated reconciliation with former enemies as the key to preserving a peaceful postwar society. Hamilton took on his persona to amplify his current arguments for Loyalist reintegration with the historical gravitas of the classics. South Carolinians could read Hamilton's arguments for the "generous" spirit of Revolutionary ideals. He admitted that it was "common ... for a free people, in times of heat and violence, to gratify momentary passions" by seeking revenge, but that wise societies turned away from revenge and strove to reintegrate former enemies and move on.[19]

Of course South Carolinians also continued to slake their anger at Loyalists in the popular press—often as a way of relieving it that allowed them to then reintegrate most individual Loyalists. South Carolinians, like other Americans, enjoyed a moment of schadenfreude when they read the satirical poem "The Tory's Soliloquy" in the pages of the local newspaper. Echoing Hamlet's "To be or not to be" speech, the poem asked whether Loyalists should "go, or not to go" to Nova Scotia or try to stay in the United States. The poem predicted that Loyalists would not inspire welcoming feelings among victorious Patriots but rather, "by our stay, rouse up their keenest rage." While the poet advocated that Patriots respond by "crush[ing] [the Loyalists] for the countless wrongs" they had committed, it certainly seems that in practice many South Carolinians read this as escapist literature. Based on what South Carolinians did rather than what they read, they ultimately, despite reading competing claims for reconciliation and punishment, chose reconciliation.[20]

In the end South Carolina's press reflected the average South Carolinians' focus by late 1783—moving ahead rather than dwelling on the pains of the past. Both elite and ordinary South Carolinians had suffered to bring independence to the nation. But most people were practical even as they grieved their economic, personal, and psychological losses. While Henry Laurens may have brooded about the pain of "beginning the World anew" in the face of his

"Oh fly," cries *Peace, the Soul of Social Life,*
Far from this Fiend of dire destructive Strife:
Ingenuous Youth, these Scenes attend no more,
But turn to Britain's once maternal Shore:
From Her fair Liberty's celestial Flame,
Religion, Language, Arts, & Commerce came."

Thomas Stothard, "O Fly, Cries Peace." Prints & Photographs Division, Library of Congress, LC-USZ62-45560.

considerable losses during the war, by 1783 most South Carolinians were working to put themselves and their society on a successful peacetime footing. Rice
crops that were abandoned in 1781 were replanted by 1783. South Carolinians
(and not just in the lowcountry) rapidly began importing new slaves to service
an expanding agricultural economy. Optimistic plans for postwar betterment
filled men's minds and hearts. In just one example, the General Assembly
turned considerable attention to plans to build a substantial waterway network

into the interior for the purpose of expanding commerce. In the postwar rush for personal and societal wealth building, South Carolinians correctly divined that a society in which men were focused on getting rich was a society with better things to do than rehearse old wrongs.[21]

While they worked to rebuild personal, business, and state finances, they also tried to put their society on a more solid footing through targeted philanthropy. While Thomas Jefferson's Elementary Education Act for Virginia called for the creation of a system of universal education "to avail the commonwealth of those talents and virtues which nature has sown as liberally among the poor as rich, and which are lost to their country by the want of means for their cultivation," South Carolinians in both the lowcountry and the backcountry worked to spread educational opportunities to the poor and orphaned. South Carolinians were in step with the rest of the country. For instance backcountry and lowcountry residents joined together in creating the Camden Orphan Society on Independence Day in 1786 as a more organized way to provide support and education for war orphans as well as children orphaned in the normal, if tragic, run of late eighteenth-century life. Camden, near present-day Columbia, had been struck hard by the civil war of the Revolution, and that damage lingered after the war. A visitor to the town in 1784 remarked that the war damage was so extensive that it offered "evident Proofs of . . . wanton Barbarity & Desolation" because British and Loyalist troops had "burnt the Court House, Gaol, & the greatest Part of the best Houses. They cut down all the Fruit Trees; & destroyed all the Furniture, which they could not carry away." And yet in joining other Americans in a vigorous pursuit of philanthropy in the years after the war, they healed their own infrastructure, land, society, and people—all by working to build a more prosperous nation. South Carolinians were in step with the rest of the country even as they were more generous toward former Loyalists.[22]

✳ Loyalists Helped Build Their Own Relief

Philip Porcher's experience related at the beginning of the chapter was representative of the real-life experiences of South Carolina Loyalists in shaping their own reintegration and reconciliation. At the same time the victorious Patriots shaped policy with both carrots (to bring Loyalists back into the fold) and sticks (to punish visibly at least some "recalcitrant" Loyalists), the Loyalists responded in kind. They wailed to themselves about how viciously fate was treating them while they looked for ways to desert the British cause and reintegrate themselves into their communities. American Loyalists were adept at exploiting the contradictions of their own society to find ways to reinsert themselves into its warp and weft. Using a combination of legal, political, economic, and social strategies, they set out to convince their fellow South Carolinians that as individuals they were trustworthy, honest, and useful citizens. Further they wanted to show that a state and nation that showed mercy to Loyalists was the kind of state and nation that would ultimately be a better place to live for all.

One caveat: the majority of this chapter deals with the experiences of white Loyalists. Black Loyalists were no less thoughtful or adroit in understanding the realities of their communities. Instead it was precisely because they did understand the fundamental realities of white South Carolina that they knew they had to leave. Savvy black Loyalists turned their attentions to how best to secure their freedom and prosperity outside of the United States. White British officials and Loyalist plantation owners all sought to secure as many enslaved people as possible to ship to Jamaica in order to enrich themselves. White Loyalists who were used to wealth as plantation owners in South Carolina wanted to secure that same prosperity and social status in a society they recognized—the plantation society of Jamaica. Poor white Loyalists were shell-shocked at the thought of moving to Nova Scotia, but black Loyalists reluctantly embraced it as a chance to achieve true freedom through the economic independence land ownership afforded. Black Loyalists in Charleston worked hard to avoid the slave catchers of all stripes who were determined to send them to Caribbean slave plantations or back to the rice fields of South Carolina.

From the beginning many white Loyalists stayed in the state even after being ordered out by the legislature. Porcher's shocking self-assurance in the face of legislative threats of the death penalty turns out to have been common. Loyalists were well aware of the Confiscation Act, as it had been published in the Charleston Loyalist newspaper. In response many Loyalists began an epistolary campaign to pave the way for their reentry into their home communities outside of occupied Charleston. While very few of these letters have been preserved, the evidence from those who failed suggests that while most Loyalists received encouragement, a few found their efforts to persuade their neighbors stirred up a hornet's nest. Those few received threats. Other Loyalists probably did not even try. In the end some four thousand white Loyalists evacuated Charleston with the British.[23]

The Loyalists who did stay strategized to evade the clear intent of the Confiscation Act to deprive them of their property and citizenship. Since possession is nine-tenths of the law, Loyalists reacted the same way as Porcher did—they plotted ways to maintain access to their property. Edward Rutledge fumed in 1782 that Loyalists were ignoring the clear decree of the act he had written. "Several of the Banished declare they are resolved to remain, of which neither the Lands or Policy of this State will admit." Across America proscribed Loyalists left their wives and minor children on the family estate in order to hold the family's claim. In South Carolina, Margaret Cunningham, a Loyalist widow, demonstrated the importance of squatter's rights when she strategically continued living in her home while appealing her husband's (and therefore her) confiscation. While she lost some of his land, the General Assembly relented and gave her "the Tract of Land on Rayburnes Creek Containing Two Hundred Acres, whereon she formerly lived." In her case a woman was able to hang onto family land even when a man could not. And the Cunningham family was an extreme example. Porcher's experience was far more common. He stayed on his own property and was offered legislative clemency in 1784.[24]

In response to the sheer number of determined Loyalists who stayed on their own properties, the legislature caved. In 1783 they passed legislation allowing Loyalists the de jure right to stay—since they had already claimed the de facto right. The legislature further recognized the onslaught of petitions they already received and for the first time granted Loyalists the right to a "trial at law" to determine the justness of their punishment. Trials and public hearings were the spoils of democratic citizenship—precisely what the Loyalists had lost in 1782. When Loyalists claimed the right to a hearing or the chance to present additional exculpatory evidence, they were claiming citizenship rights. In addition the 1783 assembly stayed all further sales of Loyalist property owned by those who had formally petitioned for clemency until "the final determination" on each man. In fact the legislature was merely putting their official stamp on the growing tendency of the commissioners of forfeited estates to avoid selling those estates. In particular the commissioners were loath to toss a woman out on the street, and so sales had already ground to a halt due to the Loyalists' successful tactics. In fairness the assembly extended this ad hoc understanding to all Loyalist petitioners. On the face of it, this rewarded people who had not played by the rules—people who had pushed the boundaries of the law by staying and petitioning for redress. In practice what it did was recognize that those who stayed and petitioned early were more likely to be men accepted by their neighbors, with stable communities and families wishing their return. Those lacking these essential protections and markers of good citizenship were less likely to have stayed.[25]

And while South Carolina was more generous to its former Loyalists than were most Americans, this distinction between those who left and those who insisted on staying was true throughout the states. In Massachusetts and Virginia, Loyalists who left the state early in the War for Independence never managed to reconcile with their former neighbors and were never welcomed back. In Virginia the only Loyalists who did manage to reintegrate were those who never left. Given these trends all over America, South Carolina's Loyalists were astute in moving heaven and earth to maintain their residency through-out the early postwar years. When the legislature decided to acquiesce to Loy-alist petitioners' insistence on claiming citizenship, it made a de facto decision to forgive the majority of them. For all the noise the General Assembly would make in 1784 while formally deciding to do that, they had cast the die in 1783. South Carolina Loyalists had already set themselves on the road to a rapid reintegration and reconciliation.

The same crowds that had turned out in the pre-Revolutionary Charles-ton streets to threaten stamp commissioners and tea merchants occasionally turned out in the two years immediately after the war—and when they did they targeted Loyalists who insisted on conducting themselves in public as if they were welcome citizens. At first glance those occasional riots, which dominated news coverage when they happened, seem like evidence of the proposition that ordinary people from the middling sorts, the working class and the artisan classes, were implacably hostile to the return and reintegration of former Loyalists. But in fact a closer look reveals that these crowd actions were rare and limited to protest against a small number of individuals—a safety valve for painful feelings, but one that worked quickly. Crowd actions may have attracted attention, but in fact they turn out to have been part and parcel of the delicate dance between former Loyalists and aggrieved former Patriots over how to reintegrate Loyalists—and whether there were Loyalists who were beyond reclamation. It is also striking how few crowd actions there really were—incidents in Charleston during Independence Day festivities in 1783 and 1784 and scattered incidents in the backcountry at Fishing Creek and Ninety Six in those years. Loyalists who found themselves targeted by these crowd actions had drawn attention by being "notorious" for their wartime conduct and had compounded the offense by failing to apologize adequately and make the difficult effort to pursue reconciliation. Taken together these incidents are not evidence of widespread resistance to Loyalist reintegration. Instead they show how open almost all South Carolinians really were to re-integrating many Loyalists—as long as they made that effort. People wanted the chance to get to decide on whether the former Loyalists who now lived in their community should be readmitted. What mattered to South Carolina politics—and to real life—was the perception that people's voices mattered.

When South Carolina celebrated its first truly independent celebration of Independence Day in 1783, on a day in which the war was finally over and all British troops had finally left Charleston, it might be expected that former Loyalists working to reintegrate themselves into the community would have laid low. Most clearly got the idea and stayed out of any public situation that might provoke an incident. So when less than a week later, a street confronta-tion did turn into several days of public brawling, the offender turned out to be a recent arrival to the state who seemingly neither knew nor cared about the unwritten rules governing the behavior of people who had not served the Patriot cause.[26]

Thomas Barron, who was not even a Loyalist but instead was a recently arrived British merchant, accosted a French soldier also walking down the street. They began by exchanging insults and ended up exchanging blows. Bystanders helped both men from the scene, but in the meantime the excited crowd spread rumors that the British merchant had killed the French soldier. Suddenly the crowd became convinced that Barron should pay for his crime, and so they hunted him down and publicly whipped him the same night. In case anyone doubted that Barron had overstepped the unwritten rules of behavior that governed anyone without convincing Patriot bona fides (including former Loyalists, recent immigrants, especially merchants, and the few people who practiced religions advocating pacifism) and had therefore attracted the anger of the crowd, the next day an editorial for the local paper crowed that "those who call themselves the friends of a particular description of people, are very ill advised when they attempt to irritate—the present temper of the people will not bear it." And yet while this incident suggests that former Loyalists did have to behave carefully as they worked to reestablish their social ties and their position of trust, it does not show widespread opposition to the reintegration of former Loyalists. Barron was a British merchant, not a Loyalist. He was one of a handful of men who had come during the British occupation of the state and profited directly from that occupation—and from the inability of good Patriot merchants to compete with him. He had further benefited from a controversial arrangement supported by the governor, but not by the people or the legislature, to allow these British merchants to remain (technically for twelve months but, practically speaking, indefinitely). So when one writer jubilantly celebrated the role of the riot in helping to "teach certain persons a little more civility," he might well have meant that the incident reined in the ambitions of former Loyalists.[27] But the crowd made it clear that British merchants were the focus.

By the middle of 1783, Loyalists had convinced the legislature to hold the trials called for in the 1783 law. They and their supporters had convinced the legislature through their overwhelming onslaught of petitions—and the fact that most of these Loyalists had in fact been living in the state the whole time and had never left. The hearings were advertised in the Charleston newspapers, which circulated widely throughout the state. Loyalists had plenty of advance warning with which to prepare their best case. On the other hand, foes had the chance to muster evidence against the petitioners. In a few cases, that negative evidence sank a Loyalist's chance of clemency. Originally the assembly intended to hold hearings at the local level. Had they done that, they would have guaranteed that Patriot neighbors would make the decision on each former Loyalist. However the unwieldiness of such a system convinced them to hold centralized hearings in Charleston and rely on the goodwill (or intense motivation) of people who lived in the backcountry to come testify. In practice this meant that while each hearing had a local legislator in attendance, the witnesses were all from the lowcountry. However since people could also submit letters as evidence against petitioning Loyalists, there was a limited outlet for backcountry people who wished to protest specific petitioners' efforts to gain legislative clemency.

What could Loyalists do to make their appeals successful? First and foremost they needed to show up. Time and time again, Loyalists made their best case for reintegration by showing their own willingness to do so even if it was awkward and difficult. Men who chose to stay throughout the appeal process had the upper hand, as it was easy for them simply to show up one night for their hearing. In fact this makes sense. Men such as Porcher had been able to stay precisely because they were able to convince their neighbors they were honorable men who would make reliable community members. They were already shown to be good risks. In contrast those Loyalists who had fled with the British in December 1782 were unlikely to be able to return quickly for a hearing, even if they had hired a lawyer to write a skillful petition on their behalf. Several times the hearing clerk noted about a petitioner (with some apparent irritation) that, "not attending agreeable to Advertisement nor any other persons for him, the Committee proceeded to form their Judgment." And that judgment was to deny the petition and refuse clemency.[28]

The next thing Loyalists could do to build a strong case for official state clemency was to produce positive character witnesses on their behalf. Just as petitioners tried to garner many supporting signatures on their petitions as a way to show that they already had substantial community support, so too did petitioners try to convince Patriot neighbors with good reputations to come and support them vocally at these hearings. Everyone understood that signing was easier than showing up to address an open committee hearing in Charleston, and therefore the act of being a character witness was a very persuasive argument in favor of offering legislative clemency. After all it would simply be a legislative rubber stamp on the decisions the locality had already made—the decision that made it possible for others to step forward and defend publicly the character of Loyalist petitioners. It is therefore unsurprising that when character witnesses did step forward and testify, their testimony was usually successful in persuading the legislature to lift punishments from the Loyalist. John Wigfall's character witness assured the committee that while he was in charge of a Loyalist militia, he was careful to "give Orders not to plunder" and that he "express[ed] his Abhorrence against Burning houses & plundering."

His supporters also argued he encouraged his militia to "take no Notice of anything to be molested"—in other words to turn a blind eye to anything and everything the locals were doing. Dr. James Clitherall's character witness was so supportive that he worried he had not offered sufficient aid in his previous testimony. He rectified this fault by writing the committee to give them "one Circumstance ... which escaped him last Night." The actual new evidence was not that impressive, but it does speak to how important character witnesses thought these testimonies were.[29]

Character witnesses were demonstrably eager to help persuade the legislature. Occasionally they were so eager to help that they seized on explanations that might get their friend off the hook but that also undermined their public reputations as citizens capable of self-control and discernment. Several witnesses protected John Wagoner by claiming he only took British protection because he "took to Drink & was scarcely ever Sober." It might have been true, but painting a man as a pathetic drunk hardly reassured anyone he was capable of wielding republican citizenship.[30]

As much as Loyalists could work to put forth a strong case, there was always the chance of a complication. The very nature of a publicly advertised open hearing was to invite public comment—and in a few cases witnesses surged forth to denigrate Loyalists' character rather than support their application. Three witnesses showed up to testify against Charleston cooper James Mackey, accusing him of deliberately spoiling meat put up before the British siege of Charleston. One of these witnesses insisted that Mackey (in better days) "bragged off" about it after "the British had possession of Town." James Rugge, another Charleston artisan, turned up at his hearing to face several determined adversaries who loudly protested and tried to interrupt him as he presented his case. The opposing witnesses carried the day. The committee recommended refusing clemency to Rugge, as the hearing showed he had "given undeniable proofs of his Preference of the British to the American Government" on "many Occasions." Further his persistent loyalism, which was shown by actions he took throughout the war, made him "a Subject very improper for the Support [of] a Republic." He was not relieved from confiscation in 1784.[31]

Any negative testimony was enough to damn Loyalist efforts at clemency and reintegration, but the worst-case scenario for a Loyalist petitioner was to attract negative commentary from an important, prominent Patriot. Even though Francis Marion was unusually supportive of former Loyalists, he had his limits. He testified on several days in isolated cases, suggesting that as a member of the legislature he made sure to hear all the cases and intervene when he felt it was important. One of James Gordon's witnesses argued that he took a British militia commission from "principle" in order to protect his neighbors from someone else getting it, but that argument failed when

Marion spoke up, testifying that Gordon had in fact led his Loyalist militia in operations that tied up significant Patriot forces for days. Marion rather bitterly remembered that Gordon "acted in Conjunction to keep the Little Pede [*sic*] men in arms against us."[32]

In the end Loyalists did what they could to shape their own stories and to make the best case they could to the legislature, but their fellow South Carolinians also chose who to support and who to reject. John Forsyth's experiences show how this delicate dance could play out in the semipublic forum of the legislative hearings. Forsyth brought several character witnesses with him to his hearing. James Smith testified that Forsyth was "an upright Dealer & honest man." Another witness tried to convince his listeners that Forsyth had only taken a position as the head of a Loyalist militia out of his desire to protect his Patriot neighbors—part of a local pact of collusion against all outside forces as a way to protect local property. Yet at least three hostile witnesses went out of their way to attend the hearing and destroy this line of defense. One hostile witness protested that Forsyth "was not solicited to take Commission, but offer'd himself to that Command." He had been energetic in organizing his militia and "had them [his troops] Drilled & offered the Commandant to march out" with his company at a time when some Loyalist militias had a reputation for arriving days late for every battle. In fact another hostile witness pointed out that Forsyth's militia company had been part of at least one British victory. Forysth tried to blunt this line of attack by coaching his supportive witnesses to suggest he would be content with partial legislative clemency. Whether or not he explicitly told his witnesses to hedge, they certainly did. They suggested an alternative to the legislature when they said he "would be happy to become a Citizen on any terms . . . without the Expectation of his Property being restor'd." In the end this was disingenuous, but it worked well as a strategy to deflect the full effects of such negative testimony.[33]

Loyalists working to convince their neighbors to accept them in the wake of war faced an increasingly optimistic society by early 1784—and one that would become even more welcoming to them over the next decade. While South Carolinians were scarred by their brutal experiences with war, they worked hard in the postwar years to reestablish their society and their own psyches. New Englanders such as John Adams and even highly literate southerners such as Thomas Jefferson turned their articulateness and roving self-examination into diary entries and letters full of self-incrimination, self-pity, and anxiety. In contrast most eighteenth-century South Carolinians spent little time in introspection. Perhaps that lack of self-introspection helped them heal faster from the wounds of war. Certainly they took practical steps toward rebuilding their society and their prewar economic vitality—and as those steps

Robert Edge Pine, "To Those, who wish to SHEATHE THE DESOLATING SWORD of War." Prints & Photographs Division, Library of Congress, LC-DIG-ppmsca-13642.

bore fruit by 1784, South Carolinians were prepared to be more generous to the Loyalists. Abandoned rice fields were replanted, and white planters rapidly imported new slaves to replace those who had joined the British during the Revolution. Balance sheets and tempers improved together.

By the time the legislature reconvened in January 1784, Loyalists had laid the groundwork for a conclusive reconsideration of their standing in South Carolina society. It had been less than two full years since British troops had finally left the state—but those two years had been crucial. The period gave Loyalists a chance to do the hard personal work of reconciling with their Patriot neighbors, and it gave those Patriot neighbors a chance to watch warily and observe those Loyalists and take their measure. Could they truly trust these men? Through time Loyalists could prove themselves and Patriots could convince themselves that full reintegration was possible and even desirable. Henry Laurens had observed in 1782 that "the Minds of the People are sore."[34] Yet by 1784 he had also come around to welcoming back and trusting at least some men who had chosen loyalism during the war.

✳ Success: Clemency and Reintegration

In many ways the question of Loyalist clemency had a preordained solution when the legislature reconvened for the 1784 session in January. Since the legislature had entertained hundreds of petitions, held several days of hearings, and solicited public input into the fates of individual Loyalists, it was likely that they would make official what had already happened—Loyalist reintegration and reconciliation. Those who had gotten scores of men to sign supporting petitions and had witnesses take time out of their schedule and stake their reputation in order to support them at public hearings had met the bar with their neighbors for reconciliation. Now the legislature's job was to lift official proscriptions and thereby make Loyalist reintegration secure.

Yet the uneasy acceptance of the general public, and the controversial nature of clemency for at least some of the Loyalists, made it less clear-cut at the time. While the logic of their previous actions made it seem a fait accompli, in fact the General Assembly fought over Loyalist clemency in the 1784 session. Legislators haphazardly started bills to relieve individual Loyalist petitioners (sometimes friends but sometimes simply men from their own district) of their punishment until it became clear that the growing collection of individual bills was clogging all legislative action. That haphazard collection that also made it clear to apprehensive legislators that they already had substantial support for comprehensive Loyalist clemency. Some of them were surprised by the widespread nature of that support, which gave them the courage to move forward. And while in the end they did offer clemency to the majority of Loyalist petitioners, they set a high bar for each individual, who had to survive individual consideration at both the committee and full house and senate level. Yet despite the vigorous discussion, in the end the result was the one that had already been set in motion. The General Assembly rubber-stamped the decisions of each locality—the decisions the Loyalists themselves had helped create—and lifted state punishments from most Loyalists a mere two years after inflicting such punishments on them to begin with.

Gov. Benjamin Guerard opened the 1784 session by urging the General Assembly to strengthen South Carolina by "forgiving and pitying our enemies." In Guerard's eyes "impartial justice" demanded that the state finally recognize that since many Loyalists subject to confiscation and amercement had merely taken British protection when the Patriots could no longer protect them, punishing them was illegitimate. Guerard used his official elected position to argue the same thing Aedanus Burke had—the legislature had treated people unequally, since proscribed Loyalists had in many cases only done what "many of their fellow Citizens were also constrained to do."[35] While Guerard meant to set the stage for rapid forgiveness and clemency, he probably simply set back his own cause. Many of the legislators already hated him, at least in part because they found him officious, bombastic, and utterly without the necessary politician's tool of politic speech. His speech certainly indicates that many elite South Carolinians were now convinced official clemency was in the state's best interests, even if the messenger was more likely to raise men's hackles than convince them.

Clemency legislation quickly became the major focus of the legislature's work in 1784. Legislators debated each Loyalist petition individually, giving them a final chance both to consider the evidence and to calibrate just how generous they wished to be. Loyalists tried to sway the debate further by testifying directly to the full legislature, but the legislature limited this opportunity. Edward Legge Jr. was lucky enough to get called into the house to "Answer to such Questions as may be ask'd." Of course this calibrated individual debate could also work against individual Loyalists and in favor of those who were still passionately opposed to clemency, even if only in a few cases. For instance when the legislature opened Edmund Ellis's case on February 13, 1784, they announced they had been informed of "several new & oppressive Acts [it] appeared he was guilty of." Someone also tried to derail John Gaillard's application with "a paper contain[ing] heavy Accusations." However a sympathetic legislator must have made Gaillard aware of the attack, as he came to his hearing prepared to answer each accusation point by point.[36]

In the end after vigorous debate the 1784 legislature moved to offer clemency to a majority of resident Loyalist petitioners. The act's title itself confirmed the intention to "restor[e]" estates and, more disingenuously, to "permit" people to return to the state—a permission most of them had simply assumed some time before. Even so the act mimicked the earlier 1782 Confiscation Act in creating gradations of treatment even for clemency. The bill offered the majority of petitioners either full legislative clemency (return of their citizenship and their property with no further restriction) or removal from confiscation and banishment with an accompanying imposition of a 12 percent amercement. Given that Patriot legislators continuously groused that they would have had a cheaper time if they had only had to pay 12 percent of their estates in the war, amercement was little to ask. A tiny but symbolic number of controversial Loyalist petitioners found themselves offered a less generous clemency consisting of the restoration of residency rights and their estates, an amercement, and a major restriction on their full inclusion in political life—they were denied the franchise and the ability to hold public office for another seven years. Certainly this speaks to some lingering distrust among the public and the legislators tasked with ameliorating the condition of former Loyalists. Voting was an important part of the duties and privileges that citizenship conferred, and so this was a significant imposition on the otherwise robust grant of citizenship. It certainly violated Burke's warnings about creating varieties of half citizenship that might degrade citizenship in the future. Yet even time-limited restrictions on voting and office holding were mild compared to the confiscation and banishment they had faced a mere two years before. Since even this disability was limited to a few years, and very few Loyalists even suffered from this restriction, the vast majority of formerly proscribed Loyalists seized this opportunity to move on and consolidate their political, economic, and social position in South Carolina. In practice even the seven-year voting restriction ultimately ended a year early.[37]

Who were those few Loyalists who found themselves singled out for limited citizenship? Those subject to the restriction were usually men who had served both the Patriot and Loyalist causes in substantial roles of public trust and responsibility. Apparently legislators believed that their word was not entirely trustworthy or that, having been badly burned once, South Carolinians should sparingly dole out increased levels of trust the second time. The restriction on office holding also suggests that a few Loyalists were singled out for this form of forgiveness with disapprobation because of political rivalries between the backcountry and the lowcountry. In a few cases such as Patrick Cunningham's, the former Loyalists subject to this ban on office holding were prominent backcountry leaders who were well respected in their own local community. Some hostile lowcountry leaders may have insisted on limiting backcountry Loyalists' ability to serve in the legislature in order to preserve their own power. Certainly it is telling that Cunningham's district sent him to represent them in the legislature as soon as the restriction expired.

Cleaning up the aftermath of confiscation was messy. Some former Loyalists who achieved clemency found that their estates had already been sold. Legislative clemency did not undo those deals. Loyalists received the revenues for their estates based on the valuations the commissioners of forfeited estates had estimated in 1782 when they sold property. In most cases people who purchased Loyalist properties had agreed to pay for those properties in yearly installments, so the income stream would simply be paid to the former estate owner. Loyalists in this situation joined the commissioners in complaining about purchasers who were recalcitrant in making their installment payments. Further some Loyalists felt they paid a de facto amercement of far more than 12 percent because the estates were often sold for pennies on the dollar. Yet plenty of men who purchased confiscated estates later thought they had overpaid and petitioned the General Assembly to be let out of their purchase contracts. In the end it took years to sort out the myriad financial details created by the rapid move from mass punishment to mass clemency.

Immediately after the people of South Carolina learned that the legislature was going to pass a generous clemency for former Loyalists, temporary trouble broke out again in Charleston's streets, although once again it was short and episodic, and only a few people found themselves in the crosshairs of the crowd. South Carolina's legislators were convinced that the majority of South Carolinians would support legislative clemency, seeing as it was based on substantial local support, but they nonetheless worried that some disgruntled people would resent amelioration for some individuals and take out their anger in publicly destructive ways. John Lewis Gervais, a member of the General Assembly, was worried that "in some cases we have been too lenient, some are permitted to return which I am afraid will not contribute to establish peace and good order among us." His words became prophetic when a secret committee circulated a handbill "warning off" thirteen men who the crowd believed were about to get clemency. (Twelve of them were recently pardoned Loyalists, while the thirteenth man was one of the hated British merchants who gained governmental clemency in order to protect the gentry's property in slaves at the end of the war.) In fact many of the men on this list were not able to gain enough support in their legislature and were not on the final list in the clemency act. Nonetheless they were threatened with violence and possible death if they refused to leave the state despite the legislature's offer of legal clemency. In many ways this was a continuation of the way in which pre-Revolutionary crowds had enforced political conformity through the threat of violence. But it also is a window into the ways in which aggrieved Patriots and former Loyalists had been negotiating the reintegration of those Loyalists into the community. Even before returning to their farms from Charleston, many Loyalists felt out the waters locally by writing to their neighbors. While most were given the nod to return (warmly or not), a few found themselves getting threatening letters in return warning them they were not welcome. In these interactions was the marriage of pre-Revolutionary tactics with the reconciliation dance Loyalists and Patriots performed after the war. It shows up most dramatically at this moment when a few Loyalists who had more friends in the legislature than they apparently had among the artisan class provoked a public pushback.[38]

In the end angry Charlestonians tried to drive out thirteen former Loyalists but focused their anger on only one of the thirteen: James Cook, a Charleston carpenter who had been an outspoken, ideological Loyalist throughout the war. The angry crowd gathered, "Lampooned" the General Assembly, and hanged Cook in effigy. They then set fire to the effigy and marched on Christopher Gadsden's wharf—presumably because Gadsden had become a noted public defender of Loyalist reintegration. Cook was probably singled out by the crowd, who otherwise accepted Loyalist reintegration, because he had gone far beyond garden-variety adherence to the British to an aggressive effort to hurt stalwart Patriots. He was widely credited with pushing a petition to the British occupying authorities calling for all tradesmen (artisans and merchants) who had not supported the British to be prohibited from pursuing their trade. The British wisely avoided enacting this policy, which would have bankrupted many. But people remembered Cook's mean-spirited desire to drive potential competitors out of business and refused to offer him the clemency they were willing to offer to so many. He in fact petitioned the General Assembly repeatedly to no avail in 1783 and 1784. His wife then petitioned to restore at least her traditional dower right as a last-gasp effort to hang on to whatever they could salvage of their South Carolina property. People became concerned that Cook might also be allowed to return. During their march with the effigy, the crowd lingered on Florence Cook's doorstep, yelling to her that her husband "should be hanged on his return as his effigy lately was." In the end Cook took the crowd's warning. His former community would never offer him reconciliation after his mean-spirited attack on them during the war. He never again set foot in South Carolina or tried to restore his property.[39]

In the next month, only one more former Loyalist found himself targeted by the crowd. The target was a backcountry Loyalist named William Rees, who had earned the enmity of Patriot militiamen for personally overseeing the hanging of a captured Patriot militia soldier. When the General Assembly removed him from confiscation (still requiring amercement) and he dared show his face in South Carolina, people reacted. Backcountry sympathizers in Charleston chased him through the streets and up to his roof, where they caught him and gave him fifty lashes. They threatened to whip him again and more severely if he did not leave the state forever. But many legislators were amused rather than worried by Rees's treatment. John Gervais thought the "the Juice of Hickory" was a fitting tribute to his cheek. In the end although Rees must have been embarrassed as well as left in considerable pain, he did go on to reestablish himself in South Carolina society and even to use the money he regained to help smooth his way.[40]

As unwilling as most South Carolinians were to live with James Cook, they were willing to live with a wide variety of former Loyalists. While it was the South Carolina gentry who got to make the formal decisions on which Loyalists were worthy of legislative clemency, the gentry made those decisions based on evidence that any particular Loyalist had wide support for reintegration. Gervais had been right when he reassured another political thinker that "the people in General are very well Satisfied with every part of [torn] to the return of those that were in opposition & oppressed them in their distresses."[41]

It cannot be emphasized strongly enough how generous this mass legislative clemency was. Two short years after the General Assembly publicly singled out and punished Loyalists, they welcomed their return and offered them restoration of all or the vast bulk of their property. Most Loyalists moved from distrusted outsiders stripped of everything to trusted full citizens with sizable assets—and all in two years. By any measure this was generous. South Carolina's Loyalists had worked to convince their neighbors to reconcile, and they succeeded.

✳ *Why South Carolinians Offered the Most Generous Clemency*

South Carolinians offered an inclusive reconciliation with former white Loyalists and made the terms generous. So the question remains—given the very limited research on this question, was South Carolina's experience of reintegration atypical? Previous generations of historians (who usually focused their research on other questions) have suggested that just as New York and the Carolinas suffered the worst civil warfare, that they also were harsher than other states in punishing their Loyalists. Yet the evidence does not bear this out. In fact Judith Van Buskirk's *Generous Enemies* suggests that New Yorkers empathized with Loyalists and were willing to reincorporate them into families, neighborhoods, and communities in the aftermath of the war—in large part because they had never left. And yet those New Yorkers who did come to legislative attention never were as successful as the South Carolinians. In the same year South Carolinians were offering mass clemency to former Loyalists, New York passed new anti-Loyalist legislation including a voting act that reiterated that former Loyalists were barred from voting. New Yorkers showed considerably more empathy and understanding on an individual level but never garnered the political backing to offer the mass clemency that South Carolina managed. Only thirty New York Loyalists were able to gain relief from confiscation by 1790—the year when South Carolina eliminated the last political prohibitions on the former Loyalists. The best New York ever offered was a 1792 act that guaranteed banished Loyalists the right to return but only if they accepted that their confiscated property was irretrievably lost to them and their families forever.[42] So what accounts for South Carolina's comparative generosity?

Mere class solidarity cannot explain South Carolina's generous and prompt reconciliation. But there is a subtler way in which class solidarity can help to make the actual process of reconciliation understandable. Gadsden's family certainly benefited financially from Loyalist clemency, but they were already comfortable. However, those shared social—and emotional—ties made it easier for elites to identify with each other and therefore forgive each other.

Class solidarity did not lead to reintegration, but it smoothed the way once Loyalists had begun the hard work of persuading their neighbors that they would once again be good community members.

People's instincts toward empathy were harnessed by the limited physical size of the state (one of the smaller American states). South Carolinians also benefited from a shared culture rooted in Charleston that held sway over the entire state. While there were ongoing tensions between the backcountry and the lowcountry, the backcountry elite was determined to integrate themselves into the lowcountry elite and to exert the same sway over their subordinates that the rice kings of the lowcountry held over everyone else. In the end Charleston's culture and elite pervaded the process and were able to shape a united decision in favor of reconciliation. Even ordinary people in the backcountry were influenced by the shared culture of the rest of the state, which meant that once a groundswell of support was built for reconciliation, it was easy for the people and their elected legislators to consolidate that reconciliatory urge into lasting legislation. Then any lingering resentments could be, and were, dealt with within the firm framework legislative reintegration had created.[43]

Timing is an important factor that illuminates the many ways in which South Carolinians were able to forgive each other because of their unique war experiences. In American areas where significant armed conflict came in the beginning of the war, Massachusetts and to a lesser extent other New England states, outspoken and vocal Loyalists found themselves pushed out quickly. These "early committer" Loyalists also tended to be the most ideologically motivated and the most outspoken, especially as compared to the South Carolinians, who were Patriots or neutrals until 1780. Other states outside of New England also drove out "early committers," but in areas that did not face a sizable British armed presence at the time (such as the Carolinas, Virginia, and Pennsylvania), very few people found themselves subject to legislative confiscation. When the "early committer" Massachusetts Loyalists sought reintegration after the war (typically in the years 1783–1786), they had been living abroad for almost a decade. In that time they had lost the ties of affection and trust that daily living brought. Massachusetts Patriots found it difficult to empathize with men they had not talked to in many years. And since early Americans imagined that women's political allegiances were subsumed under their husbands' allegiances, even when women had stayed, behind they were often unable to regain the family property after legal confiscation. After almost a decade, these early committer Loyalists could not go home again precisely because their former areas were no longer home.[44] By contrast southern states such as Virginia (as well as South Carolina) did not expel large numbers of Loyalists until 1782. Those Loyalists had either never actually left or returned quickly, which meant they still had existing (if tenuous) social ties to their neighbors and friends. Loyalists were able to build on these existing ties to claim legal clemency. In practice southern states offered more Loyalists some clemency precisely because the war had come to them last.

Timing mattered in another way as well. New York had suffered civil war throughout most of the Revolutionary War period—for years longer than South Carolina. When the war ended, New Yorkers were generous in offering clemency to some New Yorkers, but at the same time that the "generous enemies" chose to avoid adding many to the initial confiscations, they also avoided any further loosening over the years. New York's legislature allowed New Yorkers to avoid paying back their debts to former Loyalists by legally writing off the debts for pennies on the dollar. When former Loyalist militia soldiers went home again in South Carolina, they had never really stepped away from the community. They were accepted again. In contrast when some New York soldiers returned home, they found themselves whipped, abused, and kicked out. They were threatened with death if they dared show their faces again. Elderly and disabled Loyalist civilians found themselves subject to harsh beatings, even when they tried to demonstrate inoffensive, meek conduct. New Yorkers' long war may have made them understanding toward those who temporized within their own families, but after the legislature enacted a raft of anti-Loyalist legislation (including confiscation), New Yorkers were unwilling to offer generosity and clemency to those Loyalists who were now outside of the community. Many years of civil war took their toll on New Yorkers and made it difficult for them to choose to extend an olive branch. In contrast while South Carolinians experienced a vicious civil war, they only experienced those horrors for two years. They found it easier to forgive because they had only faced the horrors and pain of civil war for a short time. If anyone had experienced the terror of random militia enforcement of political thought and behavior in the South, it was the backcountry Loyalists rather than the Patriots. The backcountry Loyalists had seen the militia used against them for five years before the British even brought them substantive cover—but the Loyalists were in no position to harbor grudges in 1784.[45] These issues of timing certainly suggest why southern states would be more generous than northern states—but why was South Carolina so generous even in comparison?

Even other southern states, including those who had experienced less civil warfare, were much less generous than South Carolina. Georgia had a similar confiscation act to South Carolina's and also moved to halt sales of confiscated property in 1783 while debating offering mass clemency to their Loyalists. Yet South Carolina went on to normalize the status of most Loyalists in 1784, while Georgia never did. Virginia did not have many outspoken Loyalists by the 1780s. Patriot Virginians bitter in the wake of Governor Lord

Dunmore's decision to offer freedom to slaves in return for their military service in support of the king and against their former masters chose to drive out prominent Loyalists early in the war. By the time fighting returned in 1781, few Loyalists asserted themselves. Those who did come to the attention of the authorities were dealt with by the court system, not the legislature. North Carolina's legislature fought over the question of normalizing Loyalists' status starting in 1784, when South Carolina offered clemency, but never enacted a mass clemency. North Carolina Loyalists had to rely on being lucky enough and well-connected enough to benefit from the handful of bills in the 1780s that relieved single individuals from confiscation. North Carolinians finally regularized the status of the remaining former Loyalists when they decided that the new U.S. Constitution of 1787 required that they return Loyalist properties subject to the terms of the Treaty of Paris of 1783.[46]

So if timing suggests that despite the ferocity of the war in the South, southern states would still offer a more generous clemency than northern states, what explains South Carolina's generosity? With Virginia the answer seems to parallel the New York example—if Loyalists were pushed out early, it became almost impossible for them to return. And in Virginia's case a dependence on the court system did create a de facto clemency that allowed many Loyalists to enact a local process of reconciliation much like that in South Carolina. In order to prevail in district court decisions (both civil and criminal), Virginia's former Loyalists had to conduct the delicate face-to-face negotiations that worked so well for South Carolinians. Virginia courts were mild in their decisions, trying to reintegrate Loyalists whenever possible. In Adele Hast's words, "departure from Virginia seemed the one unforgiveable loyalist crime." So in both South Carolina and Virginia, Loyalists had to make an educated choice about the likelihood of achieving a peaceful reintegration with their neighbors. Those who felt that it was unlikely chose to take British transport out of America. Some 4,200 Loyalists from the southern colonies chose to leave the port of Charleston in the early winter of 1782. Yet the majority chose to stay. They made the correct bet that reintegration was possible and that their economic fortunes would be better by reclaiming their American property rather than relying on the generosity of the British government to make them whole for their losses. North Carolina's experience with courts also favored a process of local reintegration that was already happening on the ground, although the state also dragged it out for more than a decade after the end of the war.[47]

In the end the picture that emerges in all of the southern states is a locally driven, bottom-up process of local reintegration and reconciliation that required Loyalists to make their mea culpas to their community and build on personal ties in order to persuade their communities they would be trustworthy.

Loyalists found reconciliation by proving their ultimate loyalties lay with people and local communities rather than broad ideological categories such as nation and king. Despite the ferocity of the war in South Carolina, it had come late enough that most people had only been fighting for two years, and the Loyalists had remained a permanent part of their communities. This enabled a generous reconciliation. What finally set South Carolina apart from the other southern states was the decision to offer a de facto mass clemency at the legislative level despite the reliance on local decision making. The other southern states depended on the court system. When legislatures did step in, they operated as courts, passing individual acts of clemency rather than settling the issue once and for all. South Carolina stood alone among southern states in bypassing the court system as a method to adjudicate the status of former Loyalists. Further South Carolina's small size may have aided the people in their decision to settle the matter largely once and for all with an omnibus mass clemency bill in 1784. As will be seen, some former Loyalists continued to seek clemency in later years, but with a few exceptions the legislature had made their decision in 1784 and stuck to it. This set South Carolina apart and allowed them to consolidate a generous reconciliation, building the secure and prosperous white society that advocates of Loyalist reintegration had promised as the outcome.

It is certainly possible that if other scholars study Loyalist reintegration within the United States, they will come to find that South Carolina was not unusually generous but that in fact all American states offered a generous and prompt reconciliation to most, but not all, Loyalists. After all two careful and talented historians of New York City's Loyalist experience, who each have dedicated a chapter to the Loyalists' postwar situation, came to divergent conclusions about the experience of reintegration. Ruma Chopra suggests New York Loyalists were often unsuccessful at achieving personal and governmental reintegration, but Judith Van Buskirk argues that the "generous enemies" of her title were generous in peace as well as war. And the literature on reintegration across the United States is scarce and often depends on short unpublished works and chapters in longer works concerned with other questions.

In order to understand fully South Carolinians' reasons for pursuing reconciliation, it is necessary to consider some possible explanations that, in the end, fail. Politics is always a possible answer—but in the end it does not provide a convincing answer as to why South Carolinians embraced a generous mass clemency for Loyalists. Historians of the early Republic have noted how quickly partisan politics between political parties came to dominate public debate on cultural issues as well as on more conventional political issues. Since politics can explain everything and nothing, it is no surprise that historians have argued that the decisions both to deny and to extend clemency to

Loyalists were the result of partisan politics. Anne Osterhaut attributes Pennsylvania's reluctance to offer mass clemency to party politics in much the same way that David Maas does in his examination of Massachusetts. Both see the fact that one party adopted the cause of the Loyalists as the death knell for widespread clemency, since the other party then resisted what they saw as a factional issue. Yet Oscar Zeichner used political factionalism as part of his explanation of Connecticut's willingness to offer clemency to some Loyalists and to repeal wartime anti-Loyalist legislation as early as 1783. Factionalism seems to be the explanation to which anything can be attributed—which is ultimately unsatisfying. South Carolinians participated in the rise of political parties as did other Americans, but they muted their public disagreements in an effort to avoid openly airing white disagreement. As a slave society with a black majority in the lowcountry, South Carolina always favored expressions of white unity in order to discourage slave rebellion. Certainly South Carolina politicians differed on the fate of Loyalists, and this came to overlap other factional disputes, especially in Charleston's city politics. But those factional disputes were muted and brief. The only rabidly anti-Loyalist faction, Commander Gillon's supporters in Charleston, was quickly routed in its efforts to control government. By the time political parties (as opposed to factions) took root in South Carolina, the legislature had already passed mass clemency. And white South Carolinians continued to mute their political disagreements in order to preserve what became known in the nineteenth century as "the harmony we were famous for"—the culture of public agreeableness that a slave society created.[48]

Perhaps the realities of life in a slave society, and of the lowcountry's black majority, explain white South Carolinians' relative generosity toward defeated white Loyalists. White South Carolinians placed a high value on conformity in political culture. The "harmony we were famous for" depended on suppressing open white conflict in order to avoid giving slaves even the appearance of an opening for revolt. While everything in South Carolina's eighteenth-century existence was shaped by the presence of a restive enslaved underclass, that does not mean that slavery directly caused any particular action by whites. In this case slavery cannot be the sole or even main explanation. First if slave societies with large enslaved populations were driven to stifle open white dissent in cases such as punishing or offering clemency to Loyalists, then it would be expected that Virginia, Georgia, and to a lesser extent North Carolina would also have offered quick and generous clemencies to their Loyalists (or never punish Loyalists at all), just as South Carolina did. But in fact South Carolina went further than any other southern state. And the other state that experienced anything similar to South Carolina's more muted trend toward increased reintegration, or what one historian calls "cooling by degrees," was the one least dependent on slavery—North Carolina.[49]

Second if white solidarity had been so pressing, South Carolinians would certainly have gone about punishing Loyalists differently from the way they actually did. Logically they would have either made a lasting decision to eject most or all of the offending Loyalists in 1782 and then not reversed themselves as they did in 1784 or offered clemency to all (or almost all) of the offending Loyalists in 1782. Either would have preserved at least the public appearance of white solidarity and probably the reality of solidarity as well. Instead what they actually did—publicly punishing some white Loyalists in 1782 but allowing them to remain in the state and live openly for two years while they built legal cases for clemency and personal cases for reconciliation, all in the full view of a restive slave population—was a policy seemingly designed to broadcast serious ongoing white disunity. And so despite the reality that slavery shaped everything, it does not provide a convincing explanation of why white South Carolinians pursued such an awkward, bumbling two-year process of reintegration. South Carolina's winding path to governmental clemency and private reconciliation suggests that they used the healing passage of time to feel their way to a lasting, generous solution they could live with—but not one that made much sense within the context of a slave society.

Economics was posed then as well as now as a self-interested reason for Patriots to offer Loyalist clemency. There was the persistent national argument, most ably argued by Hamilton and echoed in South Carolina by Gadsden, that America's mercantile success demanded the reintegration of former Loyalists, since many of them were accomplished merchants who brought valuable international trading networks with them in an age where global trade still relied on individual ties across far-flung ports. In the early national period, these advocates for Loyalist reintegration also repeatedly reminded their fellow Americans that provisions in the Treaty of Paris of 1783 required that they readmit them and restore their property. However these were among the most hated and resisted requirements of the treaty and were widely ignored in every American state. Despite Hamilton's influence, Americans continued to pick and choose carefully which Loyalists they were willing to forgive—and outside of South Carolina, most Loyalists found that their pleas, and those of their allies, fell on deaf ears. When historian Kathy Roe Coker studied the occupational breakdown of South Carolina Loyalists who were offered clemency, she did not find significant differences between the treatment of the merchants and the treatment of others subject to confiscation.[50] If international mercantile ties were so important, there would have been more merchants restored relative to others—but there is no such pattern. On the other hand, merchants were not singled out for lasting punishment, either.

There were powerful economic reasons to drive out Loyalists as well as to try to keep them. Confiscated estates were valuable, and many rushed to buy them in order to improve their own bottom line. In fact some of them were prime land in large plots—the kind of plantations other South Carolinians were desperate to acquire. When South Carolinians originally enacted confiscation, legislators reportedly cried out, "A fat sheep—prick it! Prick it!" when the names of wealthy men were called out as candidates for confiscation. Edward Rutledge, the Speaker of the House of Representatives and the brother of the sitting governor during the 1782 confiscation debate, had been the major cheerleader for confiscation. At the same time he was shepherding the Confiscation Act through the General Assembly, he was organizing an investment circle dedicated to buying up the Loyalist estates he had helped legally confiscate. They began buying those estates at a fraction of their value and on the easy credit terms Rutledge had shaped in the legislation. Rutledge's cynical use of political power to enrich himself was hardly uncommon, as many men schemed to turn the sale of Loyalist property into personal advancement for themselves. By the depression of 1785, some purchasers were grateful to reverse their purchases of confiscated estates in a panic that they had overpaid and could not finish their installment payments with the required, yet scarce, specie. Therefore in the aftermath of mass legislative clemency, many investors cheerfully acquiesced to returning properties to former Loyalists in return for compensation from the state. But certainly in 1782 many individuals would have found it more personally profitable to buy well-located and well-tended Loyalist plantations at a discount and therefore to pursue harsh punishments against Loyalists.[51]

In fact historians were once optimistic that these confiscated estate sales might have been a ladder for upward mobility for men of modest background. However the best evidence suggests that in fact confiscated estate sales largely benefited those who were already comfortable—in particular because they were the people most likely to have ready cash to risk on what was, after all, a speculative investment that depended on the state maintaining Loyalist confiscation. In fact within a year of some South Carolina sales, the legislature carved out one-third dower shares of several estates that had already been sold. This action badly hurt investors in those estates, who received little compensation for the loss of value of their shares. Individual investors certainly salivated at the prospect of personally profiting from the Loyalists' losses, but so did the state. For years legislators used the confiscated estates fund as a slush fund for their pet projects that could not be easily funded out of regular revenue. More soberly the legislature also planned to use proceeds from the confiscated estates to build vital new infrastructure such as canals to expand the economic possibilities in the backcountry. Loyalist confiscation promised very real economic benefits to both Patriot individuals and the new state. Undoing Loyalist confiscation clearly hurt many financially.[52]

And hard on the heels of the 1784 Loyalist mass clemency came the devastating economic depression of 1785. If clemency had been driven by a belief that it would benefit South Carolina economically, then the experiment would almost certainly have been deemed a failure at that point. But instead of turning against reconciliation in 1785, South Carolinians continued to reconcile with former Loyalists, offering relief from amercements and social integration. So while there were some long-term economic advantages to readmitting the Loyalists, there were certainly powerful economic reasons not to do so as well. South Carolinians helped stabilize their economic situation long-term with Loyalist clemency, but there is no evidence this was the reason they did it. As much as Hamilton and Gadsden tried to push economics as the primary reason for reintegrating the Loyalists, there is no evidence that is what actually persuaded South Carolinians to act, and to act so generously.

Historians who have casually considered the question of Loyalist reconciliation have tended to attribute the reconciliatory instinct to the shared social class of those making the governmental decisions to offer clemency to well-known Loyalists. In other words the small wealthy elite of South Carolina (and other states) chose to forgive other members of the elite who had taken up the Loyalist cause. To put it even more bluntly, the elite scratched their own backs, as always. There is something to this argument. The majority of the legislators were from the lowcountry elite, and many of the Loyalists who received clemency were from the lowcountry. Even the backcountry legislators were drawn from an elite that increasingly married into the lowcountry elite. On the other hand, those lowcountry elites were disproportionately singled out for confiscation and amercement. Most backcountry Loyalists and most Loyalist men from the middling and lower sorts escaped official legislative notice and punishment from the beginning and therefore threw themselves on the mercy of their neighbors from the beginning. Most backcountry Loyalists who did have their farms confiscated were men who had already left the area at the time their estates were surveyed in 1783, and their absence after the war was over was the reason they were deemed worthy of confiscation and banishment. Therefore both backcountry and lowcountry Loyalists, and those with large estates and small farms, all ultimately had to pursue reconciliation the same way—through the hard work of renewing personal trust and personal relationships. Whatever reconciliation they did achieve, they achieved themselves.

Still there certainly was the appearance, if not the reality, of elite favoritism at work. Gadsden's public advocacy for Loyalist reintegration seems heartfelt, but it did not hurt that he also had multiple personal and emotional ties to proscribed Loyalists. His wife's father, merchant John Wragg, was on the confiscation list despite his connection to Gadsden. In 1783 Gadsden himself introduced Wragg's petition into the General Assembly, thereby throwing his weight behind it. Wragg was successful in achieving clemency, as he was reinstated in 1784 and only had to pay an amercement—an amercement that he almost certainly did not pay in full, as most amerced Loyalists ultimately paid less than they owed on paper. Gadsden benefited as well, since when his father-in-law died in 1796, his wife inherited her share of his 336 prime acres in Charleston, plantation with seventy-six slaves, and schooner complete with a slave crew. Gadsden also protected his children when he pursued clemency for Loyalists. His daughter Ann Gadsden Lord was the widow of a Loyalist merchant whose entire estate was confiscated in 1782. With her father's help, she eventually reclaimed property worth more than six thousand pounds sterling. Gadsden's son also stood to benefit from clemency for Loyalists since his wife came from a prominent Loyalist family and he would eventually inherit a portion of those reclaimed resources. Thus there is undeniably some truth to the argument that reconciliation was simply a way for the elite to scratch their own backs. The interconnected nature of the lowcountry elite certainly made reconciliation tempting for many families. Yet those same elites were the people buying up confiscated estates. In the backcountry the same pressures applied. As many people benefited from confiscation as were hurt by it. If class solidarity was so persuasive, then South Carolina's elite would never have enacted harsh confiscatory measures in the first place. In the end class solidarity may have made it possible to empathize with the choices others made, but it did not mean there were not reasons to ignore that pang of empathetic identification.[53]

Given the best historical work available today, South Carolinians do seem to have crafted the most generous and prompt reconciliation of any of the states. South Carolina Patriots and Loyalists waged a war so ferocious that both General Cornwallis and Gen. Nathaniel Greene despaired that whichever side could bring order and peace back to the lives of ordinary people would win the war. Yet those same people excelled at crafting a generous peace. As will be seen in the next chapter, they would guarantee that peace lasted by managing historical memory in order to avoid upsetting it, until after the generation that had known civil war had died.

✳ Making Reconciliation Sweeter and Stronger

Loyalists continued to try to improve their situation in the years after 1784's omnibus mass clemency legislation. While the legislature tried to hold the line in later years, they continued to be generous to former Loyalists and allowed them to chip away at their few remaining governmental impositions—individual by individual, debate by debate, bill by bill. They were often swayed by claims of equity or, as merchant Charles Atkins put it in his 1785 appeal, that former Loyalists had been "encouraged by the Humanity of the late Legislature, in restoring to their former happy Condition, several of his Country men in a similar situation with himself." Since few Loyalists were even still subject to confiscation after 1784, and even fewer of those interested in rebuilding their lives in South Carolina (as opposed to reclaiming their estate), the remaining Loyalist petitions for clemency over the years were less likely to be successful. Those later petitioners also were more controversial cases, which was why they had not petitioned in earlier years. For instance Edward Fenwicke was relieved from confiscation by a special act in 1785 after he secured help from Greene and other allies. He had trouble convincing a skeptical legislature that he had in fact worked for the Patriots as a spy. Given the common eighteenth-century understanding that spies were dishonorable men who operated for financial gain rather than the glory of country, Fenwicke's decision to use his spying activities as the central issue in his petition was risky. His application was even riskier because he was part of a spying ring run by John Laurens and had reported to him. Laurens had died in an engagement late in the war, leaving no obvious candidate to corroborate Fenwicke's story. So he is indicative of the efforts of later Loyalist petitioners who had weaker cases and therefore spent extra time trying to make them more attractive, with supporting witnesses, in order to prevail. Even Fenwicke had a rough time, as the legislature initially returned his property but not his citizenship. In the end only six living men (and a handful of estates) achieved later relief from confiscation, and each achieved it by an individual act. There would be no more omnibus relief for clemency.[54]

While very few former Loyalists would be readmitted to the full rights and privileges of citizenship after 1784, there was one form of relief that the legislature did generously grant in later years. Former Loyalists who had worked so hard to reconcile with their friends and neighbors and had built on that in order to achieve official legislative clemency chafed at the remaining restriction of amercement and were emboldened to try to remove that last, expensive reminder of their wartime behavior. Philip Porcher might have been pleased when in 1784 he was relieved from confiscation and merely asked to pay a 12 percent penalty off the top of his estate. But he was not. The same self-assurance that led him to stay despite banishment and to expect that he could craft a way to return to his former status drove him to keep expecting improvement in his situation. And once again he was an astute reader of his society and his elected legislature. In February 1785 he petitioned for relief for his amercement, complaining of "the scarcity of Coin" and the "General Calamity at Santee" (crop losses) making it impossible to pay "without reducing his Family to the greatest Distress." In effect he used the economic depression in 1785 as a way to avoid paying his obligations to the state—obligations that were intended to alleviate the state's shaky postwar finances by having Loyalists help defray wartime expenses they had declined to fund when the state was most vulnerable. Porcher parried this war-funding expectation, relying on his contributions to war bonds during the pre-1780 years when he was a Patriot. Once again his strategy worked, and he was relieved of his entire amercement.[55]

All sorts of Loyalists—even those who were lucky to have received clemency at all—were willing to try and try again to evade amercement. Many of these appeals have a cynical and opportunistic edge. Even as unlikely a figure as John Cunningham, a member of the infamous Loyalist family, petitioned to have his amercement dropped, arguing that his only "misfortune was, that he was Brother to and nearly related to several men of the same name, who were very active against this country." Robert Murrell Jr. tried the same tactics that had worked to save him from confiscation when he delivered a supporting petition signed by forty-eight supporters hoping the assembly would not "let the Innocent suffer with the Guilty." James Clitherall waged a decade-long campaign to drop his amercement, using stratagems as varied as trying to substitute a required duty on slave imports (in other words substituting a payment he had to make anyway for his amercement debt) and reassessing the value of his properties.[56]

In the end most Loyalists were also relieved of amercement. Of the individuals originally punished with only amercement in 1782, 30 percent (sixteen) of them appealed their confiscation in the next year. After the General Assembly passed the 1784 mass clemency, they also relieved 38 percent (eighteen) of the amerced Loyalists from that punishment. In 1785 the legislature came close to passing a bill designed for further equity and to fulfill the generous spirit they already showed to Loyalists. The bill itself would have lifted all amercements from those who had been amerced in the 1782 legislation, under the premise that there was no difference between the eighteen who had been relieved and the thirty-one who had not except some had been "more fortunate." In that spirit the committee read aloud the names of the thirty-one men still subject to amercement. After the reading the House of Representatives rejected the committee's decision by a 66–39 vote—a dramatic victory for those who still wished to punish Loyalists. Yet in practice more and more Loyalists were relieved as the 1780s wore on, regardless of whether they had originally been subject to amercement or confiscation.[57]

Former Loyalists had learned well that it was better simply to evade the intent of the law and then challenge it. Just as Philip Porcher and others had evaded the banishment, so too did they evade the requirement to pay their amercement. Despite the fact that the law required all Loyalists to finish paying by 1785, the deal making and avoidance went on for years. William Valentine, who was moved from confiscation to amercement in 1784, was quite taken aback to be arrested in December 1787 for nonpayment. His surprise suggests that while the General Assembly left the amercement law on the books, many Loyalists felt free not to pay. In 1787 the assembly also appointed a member to investigate whether anyone was still paying their amercement, but the investigation was later dropped without any action to resolve the widespread nonpayments. In the end former Loyalists were able to craft a way to avoid both confiscation and amercement. The state was generous indeed.[58]

Even when South Carolinians focused on self-aggrandizement in the postwar years, it at least is evidence that they felt sufficiently secure with the return of the Loyalists to worry about other issues. In one sadly comic example, the legislature diverted from dealing with an economic recession, a loss of tax revenues, and their inability to support disabled Revolutionary veterans in order to approve the purchase of several fine mahogany chairs for themselves in 1785. Clearly they thought the legislature needed the prestige of just the right kind of seating. On one hand, it seems like a spectacular waste of money at a time the state was short. On the other, a legislature concerned with the quality of wood on which they place their behinds is a legislature not concerned with fears of instability.

For the rest of the decade of the 1780s, South Carolinians continued to focus on rebuilding a harmonious white society that would offer the stability that their Revolutionary experiences had taught them to protect. Many lowcountry South Carolinians had thought they lived in a stable world only to have the rug pulled out from under them in the Revolution. (Backcountry citizens had been disabused of that notion of stability again and again, most recently in the Regulator crisis.) After the Revolution all white South Carolinians worked to create stability. This meant creating a stable political culture and a prosperous economic future. It also meant ruthlessly suppressing South Carolina's black near majority and the few Native American sources of power left after the war. White South Carolinians turned to philanthropy as a way to build a more attractive and stable place. Tellingly the founders of the Camden Orphan Society, meant to provide a better way to deal with the orphans of the Revolution as well as those children who continued to find themselves alone in the world, held their inaugural meeting on Independence Day, 1786. The spirit of the Revolution would live on in philanthropy.[59]

The Scottish-heritage St. Andrew's Society found their organization unpopular and suspected after the war due to suspicions that most of its prewar members were Loyalists. (There was something to this accusation.) Yet by 1787 the society had overcome this discouraging problem. Former Patriots and former Loyalists joined together to elect Revolutionary military hero William Moultrie as president. The recorder of their minutes was moved to observe that Moultrie's election was proof that "'the thickness of Scottish blood had overcome the tenuity of the bitter waters of civil strife.'" But it was not Scottish blood at all but rather a determined American effort at reconciliation that swept through all manner of secular philanthropic efforts. And this impulse did not limit itself to secular concerns but also made itself felt in church affairs.[60]

South Carolinians also turned to the fertile glue of religion to knit themselves together further. Before the Revolution religion had been a source of division as Methodists and Baptists struggled for legitimacy and self-determination against a lowcountry-dominated and state-established Anglican Church. In the aftermath of the Revolution, South Carolina joined the movement of other American states to disestablish Anglicanism and open the religious marketplace to all Protestants. The Anglican Church was in disarray as it was associated with loyalism; many Church of England clergy of South Carolina had fled to England despite the general trend to offer clemency. As Baptists and Methodists gained legitimacy and social power, these emerging churches became another place in which former Loyalists and former Patriots could find healing.

Building a new church was a tremendous investment in social trust and in the community. When Anglicans in the High Hills of the Santee (on the boundary between the lowcountry and the backcountry) built a new church in 1788, they built on land donated by Patriot militia leader and hero Gen. Thomas Sumter. Yet among the prestigious roster of Revolutionary leaders who sat on the vestry board was William Rees, a former Loyalist who had been subject to confiscation in 1782, been publicly threatened and whipped by a Charleston mob in 1784, and then been relieved of confiscation in 1784. In addition to sitting on the vestry board, he held a place of honor in a centrally placed pew near the minister and in front of most of the congregation. (To be fair Sumter had an even better pew.)[61]

Having laid the groundwork for a more lasting peace in the 1780s, South Carolinians cemented their handiwork with a new constitution in 1790. The 1790 constitution finally removed all remaining legal constraints on those Loyalists who had found at least partial governmental clemency. While a few Loyalists never had their confiscation lifted, in the end the constitution made it clear that Loyalist reconciliation had happened by 1790 and was even uncontroversial. In particular this post–Constitutional Convention document swept away all voting restrictions on former Loyalists. Several districts, especially in the backcountry, quickly elected formerly proscribed Loyalists to represent them in the 1790s. The civil war of the American Revolution was finally well and truly over.

FIVE ✳ *(Mis)Remembering the Founding Moment*

We Are All Patriots Now

To this day South Carolinians excel at deliberately forgetting inconvenient memories of the reality of their first civil war—the American Revolution. Tradition-minded women in South Carolina's capital city who want to burnish their own white upper-middle class bona fides can join the local chapter of the Daughters of the American Revolution. That chapter is named in honor of Ann Pamela Cunningham, an antebellum South Carolinian who founded the Mount Vernon Ladies Association to save George Washington's home from both the "polluted shades" of northern tourists who seemingly failed to understand true southern virtue and an increasingly industrialized and diverse America that some elite Americans found threateningly far away from Revolutionary-era virtue. At first glance this assertion of southern nationalism through a studied appropriation of Revolutionary-era nostalgia seems like an incredible irony. Cunningham was certainly the grandchild of South Carolinians who had fought in the American Revolution. However they had fought for the British cause as American Loyalists. She was well aware of her own ties to loyalism. Her sense of some quiet lasting aspersion on her own character through her family's Loyalist past led her to seek societal approval through historic preservation. In the twentieth century, a local chapter of the Daughters of the American Revolution was named for her in honor of her efforts at historic preservation—and without any mention, or seemingly any knowledge, of her ancestors' significant contributions to efforts to defeat American independence.

Cunningham's actions seem willfully blind to context, and her desire to redeem herself through the preservation of the legacy of the Revolution her grandparents' generation fought to stop seems ironic or even inexplicable. It turns out that what first appear to be her own glaring inconsistencies are actually indicative of society-wide decisions to manage public conversations about the war and its combatants carefully and ultimately to manage historical memory in order to secure a long-term reconciliation between Loyalists and

Patriots. South Carolinians created a public culture of war commemoration that deliberately made loyalism unmentionable. Certainly they created a useable past in which all Americans became Patriots and the legacy of civil war was erased from civic memory—even as former Loyalists successfully reintegrated themselves so thoroughly into the bonds of community that they and their families would become inseparable from their fellow citizens. Cunningham was unnecessarily self-conscious about her family's Loyalist past. No one seems to have mentioned it to her, and her social prominence was undiminished. She was roommates with one of John C. Calhoun's daughters when she attended boarding school. Their relationship soured quickly, but because of Miss Cunningham's prickly moodiness, not her ancestry. Yet despite her self-consciousness, she understood well the bargain South Carolinians had made. If she were truly afraid of stirring up social disapprobation, she would have stayed far away from public conversations about the American Revolution. She would never have delved into publishing on the subject, as she did, and then into public efforts at national historic preservation. Her self-confidence in pursuing historic preservation shows just how successful South Carolinians were in healing the wounds of civil war through deliberate silence. Yet even this fortunate reconciliation came with a price. South Carolinians' creation of a public culture that effaced the reality of their first civil war helped lead people to be far too optimistic when faced with the looming possibility of another civil war—the American Civil War.[1]

South Carolinians, and Americans generally, were not the first or last people in the world to realize that historical memory is a powerful tool for either encouraging old grudges (often in an effort to bolster the economic and political goals of a currently ascendant group) or, more rarely but hopefully, for tamping down anger in an effort to build a more stable society. Bosnia has stood out in modern history as an example of ascendant ethnic groups cynically manipulating popular historical memory of things that happened centuries before in an effort to stir up current hatreds and incite ethnic war. In the Balkans Serbs used politicized memories of five-hundred-year-old conflicts to help incite the local population to fight over more recent aggravations.[2] More positively South Africa's Truth and Reconciliation Commission is an effort to remove the stings of memory by airing those memories. Participants in the Truth and Reconciliation Commission efforts publicly acknowledge painful experiences in an effort to make sure those memories make it into the historical record—and by so doing have helped South Africans forge a more positive future. Even in the South African example, however, publicly airing painful and divisive memories is controversial and does not always lead to greater unity. While people have long recognized the importance of historical memory, they have often used it to maintain or create disunity. South Carolinians were unusual in using historical memory to promote healing and unity from a violent and disunited past.

Historical memory has been a hot topic in the academy for some time and has led to important new insights in American history. David Blight's masterful *Race and Reunion* taught American historians how central changing cultural uses of historical memory can be for understanding deep changes in American life. After the pain of the American Civil War, both northerners and southerners committed to knitting the nation back together. In order to do so, they changed the way in which both sides publicly and privately remembered the war in order to turn it from a nation-splitting conflict over slavery and the place of black people in American life into a heroic war of masculine accomplishment fought over nothing. Slavery, the real cause of the war, was ruthlessly written out of the American saga of the Civil War so that white Americans could create a past that suited their need for unity. This very telling example certainly has relevance for the way in which South Carolinians constructed a version of Revolutionary memory that promoted unity at the expense of the reality of principled and armed opposition to the creation of an independent state in an independent nation.

Other historians of early American history have recognized the way in which memories of the American Revolution were shaped and reshaped to cement changing political and social alliances in the first decades of the new United States. New Americans manipulated public memory to create a national identity that could knit disparate communities and regions into a true nation. For example in David Waldstreicher's *In the Midst of Perpetual Fetes*, Independence Day orations and festivals became a place for conflicting political parties each to claim the mantle of unity through carefully constructed memories of the Revolution. In Sarah Purcell's *Sealed with Blood*, Americans carefully constructed narratives of military heroism and sacrifice in the Revolution to create a narrative of national identity that excluded women and blacks while valorizing military bloodshed. She argues that in displaying a public memory culture of the military aspects of the war, Americans "transformed the bloodshed, division, and violence of war into beautiful symbols of unity and national cohesion." Of course now, as then, if one looked closely one can see the cracks under the efforts to create a masterful shared public narrative of national identity that created unity out of bloodshed, partisan divisions, and ethnic and racial hatreds.[3]

But people did not peer deeply under the surface. Instead they enthusiastically participated in creating the bricolage of public memory—the odd mélange of public orations, local commemorations, shared readings in newspapers and pamphlets, plays (often of dubious artistic merit), poems, epitaphs, and all the other media in which individuals helped create a shared public memory of the Revolution. And while everybody had their own ax to grind in the effort to burnish their own position in the community, out of these varied contributions came a remarkably consistent public memory of the American Revolution in South Carolina.

The Revolutionary generation and the two generations immediately after them were convinced of the vitality of memories of the Revolution for the good of the nation and for the good of each individual soul. The importance of memories of the Revolution was understood—which is why Mason Weems raced to publish a heroic image of George Washington to burnish the heroic fiber of a new generation of young men. The fact that he made up the infamous story that George Washington was so virtuous that he could not tell a lie about cutting down his father's favorite cherry tree speaks to how deeply felt was this impulse to memorialize. When South Carolinians tapped into public memory making to write out the Loyalist past in order to preserve the fragile reintegration of former Loyalists and their descendants, they were using powerful tools. Even the public architects of historical memory—the first generation of American historical preservationists—helped create a public narrative of the Carolina Revolutionary experience that excised Loyalists and turned attention away from their descendants. Many of these historical preservationists were themselves the children and grandchildren of Loyalist families. In the end Loyalist descendants were able to write themselves into the warp and weft of South Carolina's aristocratic elite by writing their forbears out of history. All in all it was a great deal.

Since this work deals with the culture of the creation and maintenance of public memory (which means activities with some public function and public sanction), the evidence focuses on areas in which South Carolinians publicly grappled with issues of remembering the American Revolution. Clearly part of the work of historical memory must have taken place in more intimate settings—for instance when parents and grandparents told children tales of the Revolution. Certainly such tall tales existed and influenced the culture into which younger generations were socialized. One visitor recalled that around 1800 he visited Charleston and heard "frightful tales of woe" as he circulated, many of which focused on "pillage, fire, & sword." William Gilmore Simms grew up listening to his grandmother tell him tall tales of violence between Loyalists and Patriots during the Revolution. But most of these tales seem to have been stripped of their specific perpetrators and simply were told to highlight the heroism of South Carolinians against a faceless and nameless enemy designed to frighten children. In contrast among the Ball family of the lowcountry, cordial, and even close, relations between the Loyalist and Patriot sides of the family continued, even though one Loyalist family member

Letter from Elias Ball (Wambaw) from Limerick, 1784. Courtesy of the
South Carolina Historical Society, Charleston.

("Wambaw" Elias Ball) fled to England with the British and never returned to the United States. In much later generations Wambaw Elias became a story told to children in the clan to scare them. Wambaw Elias was a "mean fella" who captured his own runaway slaves and sold them before departing for England. His portrayal as the family Tory lived on, coming to match late nineteenth-century portrayals of Loyalists as especially cruel, hard people. Only after the American Civil War did his descendants forget the history of warm relations. And today Wambaw Elias Ball is a brief colorful figure in an otherwise sad tale of one man's efforts to reestablish the uncomfortable history of his white and black family's tortured heritage of slavery.[4]

✳ Forgetting as Fast as Possible

Americans were acutely attuned to the importance of collective memory. As the first generation of a new, independent American Republic (and one that considered itself the only one in the eighteenth-century world), they were concerned with ensuring the continuation of their experiment in human liberty. Shared public commemorative culture was vital in reminding adults of the rightness of their novel experiment. Such public commemorative culture was also essential for raising the next generation of democratic citizens to support and embrace fully their vital role in this fragile new Republic. Public festivities took on important new roles in the creation of a stable American nationalism. In so doing Americans embraced public memories of the Revolution that privileged unity over conflict. Public events may have been bound up in current ugly political struggles, but the rhetoric claimed agreement and unity over open admissions of difference. Additionally the heat of post-Revolutionary political divisions frightened Americans. In the tempestuous fight over how to govern the fragile new nation, they found value in avoiding other sources of conflict. They turned their back on memories of internal conflict and publicly celebrated a vision of the American past in which all had been united in the pursuit of the Revolution. This shared public historical memory was a crucial part of the nation's vital public education project—to inculcate the rising generation with an unquenchable fire for American liberty. Eventually most young South Carolinians came to believe that almost all colonial residents had supported the Patriot cause. Even though they were intellectually aware of loyalism, they did not associate it with their own history.[5]

In addition South Carolinians shied away from public conflict for fear that open disunity among the white population would encourage clear-eyed slaves to believe white conflict gave them an opening for revolt. Having chosen to offer clemency and reconciliation to former Loyalists, South Carolinians were obliged to tamp down lingering Revolutionary conflicts between whites.

Federalists and Anti-Federalists could and did openly jockey for power in Charleston's public festivities, but speakers and crowds quickly learned to be silent about the presence of former Loyalists in the audience. One open source of white conflict at a time was more than enough for the nervous white minority of the lowcountry. In order to mitigate simmering conflict, they created a shared and usable Revolutionary past, albeit a past that was silent about the fact of loyalism.[6]

Charlestonians, like other Americans, began to celebrate Independence Day during the Revolutionary War. From the very beginning, these celebrations signaled an imagined unity. While their rhetoric praised a unified Patriot cause, Charlestonians actually used the cover of public celebration to threaten suspected Tories with property violence (like broken windows) if they did not participate in the ritual of public illuminations by lighting candles in their windows to signal their adherence to the new Revolutionary regime. Public commemoration served to force Loyalists into either supporting this imagined unity (which was the path most people took) or openly identifying themselves as Loyalists (which put their business arrangements, property, and personal safety at risk).

South Carolinians were determined to be in forefront of creating national rituals to bind the nation together. David Ramsay, who later wrote an early history of the Revolution in South Carolina, was sure he gave the first Independence Day oration in the new nation when he spoke in June 1778 in between a thirteen-gun salute and a cheerful round of toasting. This was despite the intolerable summer heat in South Carolina by July—a heat that made the eighteenth- and nineteenth-century tradition of hours-long public orations painful. South Carolinians also began to celebrate a local holiday celebrating the state's heroic contributions to the war effort. Palmetto Day, or Carolina Day, as it came to be known by the middle of the nineteenth century, celebrated the minor victory of South Carolina Patriots at the Battle of Sullivan's Island (1776), where Patriots managed to hold Fort Moultrie against a small British invasion party. When the British occupied Charleston in 1781–82, Independence Day and Palmetto Day were understandably dropped as public celebrations.[7]

One group of South Carolinians never bought into the fiction that public celebrations of the American Revolution should avoid any association with the reality of wartime disunity. No white person asked slaves what they thought about the yearly commemorations of Independence Day in South Carolina. But actions speak louder than words. In 1798, 1819, and 1820, arsonists struck during Independence Day celebrations. Nervous South Carolina whites blamed the recent immigration of slaves who had been exposed to the 1791 Santa Domingo insurrection for the 1798 arsons, but throughout the early national and antebellum period, white celebrants betrayed themselves with their repeated letters and newspaper reports on the "work of incendiaries." Slaves were prosecuted for several of the arsons. Black people were integral to public celebrations of independence despite the bitter irony that South Carolina blacks did not share in the freedom whites celebrated. Visiting northerner Edward Hooker was horrified by the "incongruity" of slaves serving "an independence dinner" while being deprived of their own freedom. Charleston's free black population was openly excluded from Independent Day festivities, as a public advertisement for 1799's festivities made clear: "No admittance for people of Color."[8]

David Ramsay was an important orator and public figure in early national South Carolina. He was a prominent Charleston doctor (although not a South Carolina native) and wrote several histories of the state, including a long history of its role in the Revolution. He worked tirelessly to promote a vision of South Carolina's Revolutionary experiences that erased the real strength Loyalists had during the Revolution while playing up the brutality that the British committed against the Patriots. He was concerned with the future of the American experiment and sought to use his writing and speaking to shape a unified America. In his Independence Day oration of 1820 in Charleston, he emphasized the unity of patriotic South Carolinians against the despotic British foe. In Ramsay's public memory, South Carolinians' prosecution of the war was noted for "our countrymen['s] . . . magnanimity" in the face of British inhumanity: "no barbarity which she did not exercise. . . . Husks and offals would have attested British mercy to conquered rebels." When he played up British bad war behavior, he therefore made his own Patriots in the audience feel they had been true heroes who stood up to horrors and then were able to uphold standards of wartime behavior despite the enemy sinking to low levels. It was complete balderdash, of course, but effective rhetoric to unite the audience. As long as the focus was on the British (and not their Loyalist allies), South Carolinians could publicly celebrate together.[9]

Ramsay did address the reality of Loyalist armed opposition once during his multihour oration. And he was the only early national era orator to do so, despite the likely presence of former Loyalists in the audience and the realities of the civil war still present in the living memories of many South Carolinians in the late 1790s and early 1800s. Ramsay laid the blame for internal division at the feet of the British: "There was a time when the heart of the patriot sunk within him and when Britain hoped to regain, by *our division,* what we had rescued from her by unanimity. She exulted with fiend-like ecstasy at the *scenes of anarchy and civil war,* which the embarrassed finances, and feeble powers of the confederacy too awfully portended" (emphasis added).[10]

Loyalists could not have been genuinely attached to Britain or genuinely afraid of putting unlimited power in the hands of the South Carolina plantation gentry. Instead the undeniable chaos of the war in the backcountry was sold as a deliberate British plan rather than an expression of disunity—even hatred. Despite the acknowledgment of South Carolina's not-so-distant past of committed loyalism and civil warfare, Ramsay painted a picture of largely united South Carolinians against a brutal British foe who showed none of the finer feelings of enlightened men. Ramsay was the most articulate and sophisticated of the Independence Day orators.

South Carolinians may in fact have been motivated to bury the recent chaotic, brutal, and disunited past in favor of a carefully burnished memory of British barbarities and American unity in order to heal the wounds they felt not only from the actual past but from the unsettling emotions stirred up by increasingly heated political partisanship in the early national period. Early Americans generally felt threatened by the rise of party politics, despite James Madison's eloquent arguments in the *Federalist Papers* that the clash of factions could actually make the polity stronger. Predisposed to distaste for factionalism, South Carolinians were especially concerned about the rise of faction in a state that depended on white unity in the face of a restive, sizable slave population. Therefore in his oration Ramsay cautioned South Carolinians that the "nation of freemen . . . pay no unhallowed devotion at the altar of faction." Further his oration ended with a plea that Americans, "while celebrating the acquisition of our common inheritance, meet like *a band of brothers;* and, *forgetting the circumstance of occasional division,* let us present to the world the noble spectacle of a nation of freemen—pure in patriotism—with but one mind, and one soul, IN DEVOTION TO OUR COUNTRY" (italic emphasis added).[11] Undoubtedly partisan tension between Federalists and Democratic Republicans was uppermost in his mind when composing these lines, but it is likely that he also meant to include the Loyalist past as one more "circumstance of occasional division."

New political events only increased South Carolinians' general tendencies to downplay the realities of the Loyalist past in their rush to forget systematically (and conveniently). While a tiny minority of Americans actually served in the War of 1812, the war was very popular. Historian Nicole Eustace has argued that Americans utilized public culture making (especially literary production) during the war in order to create a national identity for the first time. Southerners experienced the relief of being genuinely united on the question of the war, leaving disuniting partisan bickering to the New Englanders. South Carolinians used Independence Day to encourage unity in the face of the new British aggression and accordingly downplayed anything that smacked of disunity, including "party feeling." Paradoxically the cathartic climax of the Battle of New Orleans also reinvigorated discussions of military heroism, as jubilant Americans celebrated their military victories in both wars against the British. Of course such orations usually ignored painful and humiliating losses and therefore continued the widespread practice of carefully shaping public memory.[12]

✳ New Generations, New Memories of Loyalism

In the first quarter century after the Revolution, Independence Day was the main way that South Carolinians publicly celebrated their Revolutionary experience. As the past grew more comfortably distant, and even the landscape healed from the wounds of war, a new generation of South Carolinians broadened the variety of public commemorations that sought to preserve the virtuous Revolution for the rising new generation of Americans who could never claim their blood had secured American liberty. The new generation would work to build fruitfully on the willful forgetting of their forefathers in order to shape a useful past. It would take half a century to defang the reality of loyalism enough to allow open discussion of Loyalist military activities in the Revolution. When the grandchildren of the Revolutionary generation finally openly discussed the Loyalist past, they did it in service of the new project of a militant southern nationalism seeking armed confrontation within the United States. Only with that new emphasis on unity through a strident southern nationalism could South Carolina's Loyalist military past reemerge.

Palmetto Day (now Carolina Day) became increasingly popular since it allowed antebellum South Carolinians to solidify a shared public memory of Revolutionary unity. In many ways it was an ideal holiday for antebellum South Carolinians as it celebrates the successful defense of Fort Moultrie from British (not Loyalist) invasion in 1776 and is celebrated a scant week before Independence Day. Palmetto Day allowed a new generation of South Carolinians who had never seen military service in either the Revolution or the War of 1812 to lash themselves to a glorious military defense. Military commemorations became important at the exact moment few Americans had even served. It was not paradoxical so much as convenient: Palmetto Day was a convenient choice for South Carolinians interested in celebrating their military history without upsetting the de facto agreement to avoid talking about the reality of sizable numbers of returned Loyalists and their contributions to the Revolution. Because Palmetto Day celebrated a moment before brutal civil war emerged in South Carolina, its elevation as a holiday allowed South Carolinians to extol a moment when they were mostly united against the British foe in valiantly and heroically defending their homeland.

Palmetto Day was the only battle commemoration that South Carolinians chose to memorialize for more than three decades—precisely because publicly celebrating battles led to the problematic question of who actually fought in them. Local almanacs included only a few specific Revolutionary battles, and very few of them were local. For example *The Carolina and Georgia Almanack* of 1783 included Tarleton's defeat but also the battles of Trenton and Bunker Hill. Almanac writers conspicuously avoided battles in which the majority of the combatants had been militia members, since the militia members on the British side would all have been Loyalists—and in many cases their children and grandchildren were valued members of the community. For example the almanacs never mentioned Kings Mountain or the Battle of Huck's Defeat. This silence is particularly telling because generally Americans chose to commemorate battles that Americans had actually won. Some of the most decisive victories in South Carolina's Revolutionary experiences came from backcountry battles in which Loyalist militias fought Patriot militias, yet almanacs and public commemorations avoided these completely.[13]

South Carolinians were not alone in being slow to commemorate battlefields. Historian Thomas A. Chambers has pointed out that all Americans waited a half century before beginning to embrace battlefield commemoration. Southern states were even further behind. In Chambers's telling, this is because there was little to nothing left of the physical remains of the battlefields in the South, and many of the (potentially) most interesting ones, such as the dramatic American victories at Camden and Kings Mountain, were in isolated rural areas served by poor, unpaved roads. In response the romantic visitors who pioneered battlefield tourism did not want to seek out such disappointing and difficult to access sites. Even Virginia's Revolutionary crown jewel battlefield—Yorktown—did not attract tourists until the 1850s when it was finally served by a steamboat that brought people in from the District of Columbia. When tourists finally began to venture onto southern battlefields, they continued in the path laid out by tourists to other regions in that they were more interested in communing with the physicality of the site rather than the oratory preferred by elites who organized other kinds of celebrations. Yet it is hard not to believe that southern battlefields were deliberately forgotten for so long not only because of their access problems but also because of their terrible legacy of blood-soaked conflict. Chambers points out that many of them had no burying grounds because no one had the time or inclination to bury all the bodies. Given this grim reality, South Carolinians understandably did not rush out to put up plaques on these sites in order to attract a tourist trade that was only beginning to emerge in the antebellum period.[14]

The first time South Carolinians actually commemorated a notable battle involving Loyalist militias was well into the antebellum period. In 1839 they celebrated a one-time commemoration of the Battle of Huck's Defeat.[15] Huck's Defeat offered a tempting prospect for any orator, as the fighting was vicious and personal. The Loyalists and Patriots in the battle had known each other personally. The battle itself was triumphantly named by the victorious Patriots in mocking tribute to Capt. Christian Huck, an American Loyalist officer in Banastre Tarleton's legion, who was already hated because of widely repeated accusations of wartime atrocities. Before the battle he and his men surprised the family of locally prominent militia leader Col. William Bratton. Bratton's wife, Martha, and their children were imprisoned for the night, and the Loyalists threatened to hang the sons in the morning. At the same time, the Patriot militia leaders were hiding in the area and received intelligence of where the Loyalist troops were encamped. When the battle commenced just after dawn the next day, Huck was killed in the first round of fire, and only fifty Loyalist militiamen managed to escape. The battle was an overwhelming Patriot victory and therefore one well worth celebrating in later years.

The Bratton family, whose nineteenth-century members saw this as an ideal way to burnish their family's reputation, spearheaded the 1839 events. Dr. John Bratton, one of the sons of William and Martha, still owned the battle-field and chose to open his land to the public for the ceremony. He undoubt-edly hoped that publicly celebrating his father's military exploits would help his own rising profile as an increasingly important cotton planter in South Carolina's prosperous antebellum economy. On a stifling, hot summer day some 1,500 people, including four aged Revolutionary soldiers, turned out to hear hours of high-flying oratory, watch a procession of badly trained militia parade, and enjoy lengthy toasts in return for the bribe of a free luncheon.[16]

For the first time, orators at a public commemoration explicitly recog-nized South Carolina's Loyalist past. At the Huck's Defeat celebration, the main orator admitted that some South Carolinians "joined the standard of the enemy, and committed frequently the most horrid and revolting deeds." The horror of civil war simply made the victorious Patriots "like David of old, with a sling and a stone, against the Goliath of British might." Logically this would make Loyalists an overwhelming presence as the giant Goliath, but in-stead they seemed to exist in the story merely as a way to turn Patriot ancestors into biblical heroes. Further the orator argued that "the inhabitants of York District [the local county], to their imperishable honor were never paroled as prisoners, nor took protection as British subjects—preferring rather exile and resistance, than lame submission and a dishonorable peace."[17] So despite frankly admitting South Carolina's sizable number of Loyalists who were will-ing to fight for the British cause, the speaker reassured the audience that no locals needed to worry that their fathers or grandfathers had been Loyalists. The Loyalist past was acknowledged, only to be flushed from local history. It was a complete fabrication but a very convenient one. It is hard to tell whether the speaker even realized he was engaged in selective memory making or whether five decades of silence had been so effective that he did not realize

MONUMENT TO LEFT WAS THE FIRST ERECTED ON THE FIELD. IN 1815. BY DR. WILLIAM McLEAN OF LINCOLNTON. N. C.
THE MONUMENT TO THE RIGHT WAS ERECTED AND INSCRIBED TO PRESERVE THE INSCRIPTION ON THE "OLD MONUMENT"

Kings Mountain Monuments, Postcard. North Carolina Collection,
University of North Carolina at Chapel Hill Library

he was promulgating a shared vision of York County's past that was not even true.

Certainly this selective memory allowed the speaker and the audience to revel in a bloody vision of Revolutionary heroism. An aged Revolutionary soldier who was credited with killing the hated Captain Huck was feted for being "a whig from the first, a whig to the last, he didn't believe in the tories, and he made the tories believe in him." Men were encouraged to take up the mantle of military heroism from that past with an off-putting emphasis on how once "the waters of the spring below us, that now gush forth so clear and transparent, were on that occasion completely crimsoned with the blood of tories and British soldiery."[18] The commemorators showed a certain bloodlust that was perhaps the single best indicator that they no longer feared, or even saw, their own tortured past of repeated civil conflict.

Later antebellum battlefield commemorations followed this pattern of acknowledging the fact of Loyalist feeling only to dismiss it as limited, without sizable support, and merely a rhetorical device for reveling in bloodlust. By the 1850s South Carolinians had refined this strategy to use Revolutionary War memories to promote a strident southern nationalism willing to court bloodshed in war rather than avoid it. They repeated this sudden rediscovery of the Loyalist military contributions to the American Revolution, stripped of any acknowledgment that those Loyalists came from the area, when they publicly commemorated another nearby battle in 1855. Prominent local citizens planned for more than a year to host a grand celebration of the Battle of Kings Mountain on its seventy-fifth anniversary. By this time South Carolinians engaged in a new use for selective historical memory. The legacy of the American Revolution could be used to inculcate southern nationalism for a generation of southerners who increasingly felt themselves called to defend their region. South Carolinians began to imagine their forefathers as the original defenders of southern independence and state's rights. This narrative thrived by inculcating listeners with the heroism of standing against a fearsome enemy. Loyalist and British soldiers could serve interchangeable goals as stock-character bloodthirsty antagonists, because South Carolinians no longer paid attention to the differences. Loyalists had been so thoroughly reincorporated that no one was worried about offending—because they did not remember there was anyone they might offend. The Kings Mountain planning committee chose to invite all the states that they considered to be "children of the same family, as joint possessors of the same heritage of fame." Tellingly they invited South Carolinians, North Carolinians, Virginians, Tennesseans, and Kentuckians. Practically speaking these states had all sent Patriot militiamen who had fought at the Battle of Kings Mountain. On a deeper level, the imagined understanding of Kings Mountain as a southern battle for America made it imperative that it become a shared southern national experience.[19]

An air of martial romanticism pervaded the celebration. Various volunteer militia companies enthusiastically paraded along the route while listening to the "inspiriting strains of martial music." An animated reenactment of the battle was marred by an accident in which one reenactor shattered his right arm by accidently shooting himself. He was carried off the field for a thoroughly unromantic immediate amputation. Perhaps this should have served as a reminder of the very real hazards of war that a generation who had largely not seen military service had forgotten, but nobody took it in that vein. The tragedy of the American Civil War was still a few years away. They encouraged themselves to consider a lack of human compassion as the marker of real martial masculinity. One orator celebrated the imagined brutality of the Overmountain men who "turn[ed] aside for nothing, save now and then to shoot a tory, as a bear hunter shoots a snake, merely to kill the vermin." Revolutionary War memory became a way for South Carolinians to talk themselves into another civil war.[20]

George Bancroft, America's famous and nationalistic historian, was the keynote speaker. Bancroft's own interesting intellectual evolution was on display that day. He was descended from Loyalists, yet he fundamentally disdained the Loyalists and passionately identified with the democratic promise of America. Despite his northern birth, he also came to side with rising southern self-promotion, and he sought to burnish the South's contribution to the nation including those of the American Revolution. For Bancroft, Kings Mountain was an inspiring example of southern bravery in the face of overwhelming odds. "All honor must be awarded to the south, since she was left to herself in the hour of her utmost distress." Bancroft played up regional hostilities by emphasizing that the South had honored the Revolutionary contributions of the North but not vice versa. Those who offered to toast picked up the theme of united southerners standing firmly against internal and external enemies with a toast to "Virginia, North Carolina and South Carolina: Firmly united in the days of 1780, may they ever be found, side by side, battling in defense of their constitutional rights and liberties against a common foe." If all of this was too subtle a call to southern nationalism for some in the audience, the reading of a congratulatory letter from Missouri spelled it out. A Missourian in the midst of the Bleeding Kansas insurrection asserted that "we have a similar foe to encounter in Kansas." Border Ruffians bringing homegrown terrorism down on the heads of their fellow Americans had become the natural (and virtuous) inheritors of Patriots who fought in the American Revolution. Toasts to John C. Calhoun, the patron saint of southern nationalism, were slipped in with the illustrious Revolutionary company of George Washington, Francis Marion (the Swamp Fox), Andrew Pickens, and Thomas Sumter (the Gamecock). Then again they were slaveholders all.[21]

Loyalism could serve its place in this noxious self-congratulatory brew of southern nationalism. Once again celebrants were reassured that the region was "filled . . . with whigs, and now with their descendants." Wherever those Loyalists had come from, memory making demanded it was not nearby. In fact the area had produced plenty of Loyalists, but at both the celebration at Huck's Defeat and Kings Mountain people needed to believe that no one in the audience could possibly be tarred with loyalism. Tories themselves were painted in colorful but subhuman terms—mere stock figures in the greater celebration of southern nationalism.[22]

In conclusion Tories reemerged in public commemoration after the Revolutionary generation had long passed, and at a time when their grandchildren were taking their place in public life. Public discussion reemerged in the context of a new aggressiveness about the South's military contributions to the war. Such contributions were touted not for themselves but for the assertion of southern honor in the face of growing sectional conflict. The exploits of the Revolution served to call a new generation of southerners to arm for battle to preserve southern free white liberties. Despite these new purposes, these memories were still carefully shaped to shield Loyalist descendants from any difficulties. Public memory making had worked so well that even seventy-five years after the Battle of Kings Mountain, local descendants did not publicly acknowledge the reality of substantial Loyalist support in their region. After so long perhaps they did not even know. Did such an adroit use of public historical memory mean that after more than half a century, people had truly come to forget the Loyalist past and the presence of the descendants of Loyalists?

❋ Historic Preservation and the Children and Grandchildren of Loyalists

Loyalist William Blake complained that his amercement would carry a lasting "stigma" that would unfairly penalize "the rising generation."[23] Many other Loyalists must have worried about what the future would hold for their children and grandchildren even as they were convinced that reintegration was the wisest move. The prompt and generous reconciliation white Loyalists were able to shape certainly suggested that their descendants would be able to build comfortable lives free from the shadow of discrimination against them for their Loyalist families. But, of course, they did not know that for sure. Blake's worry about a lasting stigma for his children was perceptive in its understanding that hard feelings might linger long after people had outwardly resolved their differences. Certainly some Loyalists' children did indeed worry about their reception in society as they sought to find marriage partners, run for office, establish new business relationships, and build their own position in white society. As it turns out, Blake had nothing to worry about. The children and grandchildren of Loyalists went on to occupy the status of their parents or even to rise above their parents' position. A few Loyalist descendants such as the Cunninghams believed that people might whisper about their families' past, but there is no evidence that these few thin-skinned individuals were right. Tellingly most Loyalists and their children disappeared back into the fabric of South Carolina society and achieved the social status that others of their talents and wealth achieved. Reconciliation efforts between Loyalists and Patriots were so successful that there ceased to be any distinctions made or felt by the descendants of those who had fought for and against American independence.

In fact the majority of Loyalists who stayed and reintegrated themselves across the United States were well accepted, allowing their family members to claim their identities as full-blooded Americans. In one postwar example, Charleston Loyalist Philip Porcher's son joined one of Gen. Francis Marion's relatives in founding a library. His Loyalist ancestry did not matter at all as he rose through the ranks. He also served in the state house for eight terms, which shows that his Loyalist ancestry was no bar to the support of the electorate. Limited evidence suggests this easy reintegration was not limited to South Carolina. One striking example is the Key family of Maryland. Philip Barton

Key of Maryland left Maryland in the wake of his Loyalist military activities and even filed a claim with the British in 1785 to get reimbursement for his losses as a Loyalist. Yet he quickly returned to Maryland and opened a successful law practice, regaining his former wealth despite never overturning the official confiscation of his property. He was elected to the U.S. House of Representatives in 1806, despite a campaign against him on the grounds of his past loyalism. With self-satisfaction he reflected that he "returned to my country like a prodigal to his father, felt as an American should feel, was received and forgiven, of which the most convincing proof is my election." His nephew Francis Scott Key (whose father was a Patriot veteran) was so integrated into America that his War of 1812 poem became the American national anthem—fittingly the anthem is the product of a man with both Loyalist and Patriot family members.[24]

Even infamous Loyalist families found that their children and grandchildren were able to shake free of any stigma. For South Carolinians of the Revolutionary generation, the surname Cunningham was notorious. The entire Cunningham clan of Ninety-Six were Loyalist militia leaders in the Revolution. Worse, they recruited many of the lesser men of the area to follow them into effective Loyalist militias that wreaked havoc on Patriot civilians and militias alike. William Cunningham became embittered by his treatment as a Loyalist at the hands of vengeful Patriots and stepped up his campaign of strategic harassment, which led to heated allegations of atrocities against him. Patriots began to refer to him as "Bloody Bill." His brothers and cousins had better reputations for upright conduct but were tarred with his brand of unrepentant Loyalist action. While "Bloody Bill" Cunningham fled to Florida in the wake of the Revolution, his brothers and cousins stayed and reintegrated themselves into society. Patrick Cunningham, for example, left the state at the end of the war but took the legislature's mass clemency act of 1784 as an invitation to return. He successfully appealed his confiscation in 1785 but was still subject to the disapprobation of legal amercement and a seven-year restriction on voting. When the new state constitution restored his voting rights in 1790, his neighbors sent him to represent them in the General Assembly. His young son Robert must have been proud of that achievement and the warm endorsement from all their neighbors it implied. Yet family legend held that Cunningham refused to serve more than a single term because the lowcountry legislators were hostile and rude to him—pointedly passing him over for committee assignments. He was convinced he was targeted for social ridicule due to his Loyalist past. It is certainly possible that when he entered the legislature less than a decade after the end of the war, his fellow legislators saw this as a willful assertion of potentially dangerous political sympathies and sought to limit his power until they felt they could trust him. His exclusion from committee memberships could also have been as much about the lingering hostilities between the lowcountry and the backcountry in this period before upcountry cotton fortunes finally knit together those regions in a shared aristocracy. It could also be that his fellow legislators just did not feel that a first-term legislator should serve on influential committees. Cunningham may well have simply misunderstood. The Cunninghams had been well-regarded military leaders, but some of them also turned out to be touchy and even neurotic, their fears of social disapprobation leading them to look for insults that were not intended. Cunningham's anger influenced his young son to take quick offense as an adult, but even this overly sensitive man had a hard time finding things he could construe as insults over the years.[25]

Robert Cunningham was born in 1786, just after his father returned to South Carolina. Growing up in the 1790s and 1800s, he came of age in a time when Loyalists were integrated back into the community and little was said about them publicly. Yet he grew up with a thin skin on the subject, which suggests that he and his family believed they did come under increased scrutiny. And South Carolina was changing in other ways at the time. His father had been a moderately successful mixed-crop farmer, but Robert's generation always knew the affluence of being prosperous cotton planters. His family's rising affluence gave him self-assurance as he entered his place in the state's elite despite the potential drawback of his father's wartime loyalism. He studied law under John C. Calhoun, becoming friends in the process. At the outbreak of the War of 1812, he rushed to volunteer, "burning with the desire to wipe out forever the popular stigma" of his family's association with Bloody Bill. The district voters in Laurens County, stirred by his reputation as a war hero in the popular war, sent him to represent them in the legislature in the election of 1820. Stories differ on what happened next. A family supporter claimed Cunningham heard whispers against another man with the same name and stood up to defend him against charges of Tory descent, admitting in a "manly avowal" that he was of the Tory Cunningham family. People outside his network of supporters suggested that Cunningham overheard others discussing his fundamental untrustworthiness (despite his own military service) because of his Tory ancestry. In any case accounts all agree on what happened next. He quit politics in disgust and refused ever to hold another public office. Perhaps he really did find that despite widespread integration, he was still viewed suspiciously. He also followed his father's example by refusing to stick around long enough to discover whether opposition to his rise rested on his wartime Loyalist ties or on distaste for his personal qualities. However much family legends emphasized Cunningham's own understanding of the situation as a case of stigma against him due to his Loyalist ancestry, here is the case of a man who was duly elected by the voters and was friends with many other powerful and influential South Carolinians yet gave up office because he thought people were whispering mean things about him. His thin skin, not his ancestry, was his greatest political weakness.[26]

In South Carolina's 1830 nullification controversy, Cunningham was a Unionist. While admirers attributed his insistence on union to his military service, it is certainly tempting to suspect that as someone smeared with disunity and even disloyalty his whole life, he clung to national unity for himself. Whatever the emotional basis for his unionism, his thin skin gave him away again in South Carolina's heated debates on nullification. An impassioned orator standing on Columbia's courthouse steps bandied about the opprobrious epithet *Tory* repeatedly, in such a way that suggested he intended to target Cunningham. Or at least that is the way the ever-sensitive Cunningham took it. He challenged the orator to a duel but was saved from having actually to risk his life by the kind intervention of several mutual friends.[27]

Perhaps there was some lingering resentment against the children of Loyalists—or at least against the Cunninghams. But again they might have attracted resentment as much for their upwardly mobile cotton fortunes as for their eighteenth-century loyalism. Patrick's son John complained to John C. Calhoun after the publication of accounts of his ancestors' war behavior of his "peculiar" position in his own neighborhood of Abbeville. He reflected on his difficulties when his "family in this State has against it many strong prejudices associated with the Revolution" and concluded that those reservations were likely to stand in his way in trying for political position. As an ambitious young man, he asked Calhoun, a family friend, whether he should leave for Memphis or New Orleans, where he could make a name for himself without the constant quiet resentment of his family's past. Calhoun provided him the letter of recommendation he requested to use on his travels. His reservations about his place in South Carolina society were genuine, but the mere fact that multiple members of his family sought and obtained political office and other honors suggests that they possessed the self-confidence born of a deep assurance that their family's past was not held against them.[28]

Even in private life, Robert Cunningham's aggravations continued. In an effort to clear the air, he set out to find and publish historical proof of his ancestors' honor. He resented the widespread, blunt antebellum characterization of Loyalists as brutal men bent on committing atrocities for blood sport—men who were lacking in some crucial features of humanity and civilization—in other words archetypal "others." In his apologia he hoped to place his ancestors' acknowledged loyalism in a better light. In so doing he also placed himself in a burgeoning field of semiprofessional historical research and writing. Robert involved his invalid daughter, Ann Pamela Cunningham, in the project, hoping that he could get her to stop moping by giving her an outlet for her energies. It worked better than he hoped, and the granddaughter of a Loyalist became determined to change the way people saw all Loyalists. She resented the way early national and antebellum historians had been too hasty to condemn Loyalists as unprincipled men looking for personal spoils, given that plenty of Patriots were also motivated primarily by the possibility for plunder. She certainly believed her own forebears were motivated by loftier goals. While she was sensitive about her family's past, she also showed great self-confidence that her position in society was such that she could not be hurt by frankness about her Loyalist ties. This confidence in choosing to write about her own family's loyalism speaks loudly about the successful reintegration of the Loyalists and their descendants without stigma.[29]

In 1845 Cunningham anonymously published a defense of her forebears in an appendix to a compilation of New England Loyalist papers. She hoped to show that they had behaved decently, while many Patriots had simply sought self-advancement. Unfortunately she went too far when she tried to rescue William Cunningham from his appellation "Bloody Bill." At one point she argued that he was warped by persecution, which "speedily changed a kind and affectionate tempered man into a vengeful and unsparing partisan." Instead of clearing her relatives' reputation, she inspired the ire of a prominent and far more articulate writer—William Gilmore Simms, the Charleston novelist, historian, and prominent southern intellectual.[30]

Simms was an ardent historian, if a biased one. He exhaustively gathered oral histories from the last surviving Revolutionary soldiers and used those resources in writing histories and novels of the American Revolution in the South. He was angry when he read Cunningham's revisionist history. He responded with five articles in the *Southern Literary Messenger* in 1846 debunking her inept historical writing. While three articles dealt with the general role of the Loyalists in the Revolution, two cut to the jugular and demolished her efforts to find anything good to say about William Cunningham. In Simms's words Cunningham would not "leave at rest a memory, which nothing but a diseased and mistaken judgment could have wished to summon." Simms was especially vicious because he was convinced (and not without reason) that her "Bloody Bill" defense impugned Patriot heroes. He demolished Cunningham's argument paragraph by paragraph, and the only good thing he could find to say about her ancestor was he was a "bold, bad man." Since she had published anonymously, Simms could only deduce that the writer must be a person with "a blind and stubborn attachment, whether of *kindred* or sympathy" (emphasis added).[31]

Cunningham began an angry, tit-for-tat exchange in the pages of *Literary Messenger*. While she continued to hide her identity as both a woman and the grandchild of the subjects of the piece, her tone gave her away to emotionally astute readers. James Henry Hammond, the South Carolina politician and a friend of Simms, was perceptive when he warned Simms to back away from the continued confrontation: "You were very severe on the 'Cunningham Family' & it strikes me that this answer does not probably come from the North, but from much nearer home." Hammond did not know who the author was, but he did reflect that the "Cunninghams here are extremely sensitive and always on the qui vive for insults on their ancestry." Hammond seems to confirm that while everyone was aware of their ancestry, nobody dwelled on it the way the family did. Still it must have been easier for people who did not live with tall tales of "Bloody Bill" hanging over their head to dismiss such talk as oversensitivity.[32]

Simms eventually discovered the author of the tainted histories and apologized to her for giving "pain to such a creature so delicately constituted." His opinion did not change, but the southern code of manners made it ungallant to argue with an ill woman. Ironically Simms also refused to believe a woman had really written such a work, and he continued to speculate on what man might be pulling the strings behind the scene. He refused to back down, warning the Cunningham family that while they were currently free from any sanction "identified with his infamy & name" (obviously, the Cunningham family vociferously disagreed), they ran the risk that trying to defend Bloody Bill would "only incur the danger, in the vulgar mind," of connecting the Cunningham descendants with him. Simms threatened that if they did not back off from their revisionist histories, their work "will greatly endanger their own position." He warned them that the implicit bargain of Loyalist reintegration had always required that Loyalist families maintain a decorous silence. Simms did seem to have the historians' knack for separating his professional judgment from his feelings about living people, and he certainly believed the Cunninghams were being overly sensitive. But in an age of rising interest in history, he was faithful to a view of the American Revolution that emphasized the worst attributes of the Loyalists when they were admitted as historical actors at all.[33]

The entire controversy makes it clear that while loyalism was largely excluded from public memory at commemorative events, it was still part of a shared oral history of the Revolution. In that semiprivate history, most former Loyalists were acknowledged to have chosen the wrong side but with the benefit of healing time had come to be considered honorable citizens. John C. Calhoun, whose own father, Patrick, had served as a Patriot leader, remembered that his father had never said "aught against either" of the Cunningham ancestors besides Bloody Bill that might "impeach their humanity, or conduct." Instead the elder Calhoun spoke "favorably" of Patrick Cunningham. Yet despite personal appeals, John Calhoun made it clear that he had grown up hearing highly embellished stories about William Cunningham. Just like in public commemoration, in private conversation loyalism reentered the conversation with a few stock villains such as "Bloody Bill" filling in for the all the Loyalists. Loyalism could finally be addressed publicly in the late antebellum period so long as no one living was identified with it.[34]

Ann Pamela Cunningham and her father should have left well enough alone. In trying to clear their name from the stigma they perceived, they instead reminded people of their ancestry without convincing anyone of their cause. Their efforts to rehabilitate the historical memory of their ancestors violated the expectation that all sides would cease to talk publicly about the reality of wartime loyalism. Originally this compromise was easy for Loyalist families since they had everything to lose by violating this norm. But with the passing of time, reintegration and reconciliation had worked so well that the descendants of the Loyalists began to question the need to abide by the unspoken compact of silence. The Cunningham family's supreme confidence about their established place in society allowed them to charge into efforts to restore their Loyalist ancestors to an imagined pantheon of Revolutionary heroes. They were genuinely surprised and hurt by the ferocity of resistance to their efforts to redeem the historical record, but their surprise marks them as unsophisticated recipients of a successful society-wide reconciliation. Nevertheless, while this is evidence that there was some lingering hostility to Loyalist families in South Carolina, it is also seemingly the only extent case of even perceived discrimination.

Cunningham finally found a more effective outlet for her burning desire to clear her family name. She turned from trying to place her Loyalist forbears in the pantheon of honorable Revolutionary war heroes to burnishing the history of the Patriot leaders already part of the canon. She began by joining another female historian in compiling materials on female Patriots in the Revolution, leading to a three-volume history. Fueled by her early success, she sought further to preserve the architecture of the Revolutionary past—the past that people could visit rather than only read about. In 1853 she anonymously published "An Appeal to the Ladies of the South" in the *Charleston Mercury* and then in other southern newspapers. Signing herself "a southern matron," she started a patriotic appeal to raise money to purchase Mount Vernon, the homestead of George Washington. While her efforts to preserve Mount Vernon certainly helped support the Patriot vision of the Revolution, she also pitched her appeals to a southern sense of superiority. She suggested that if her fellow southern women did not raise enough money to buy the property that the "sacred" Mount Vernon would be defiled as "the seat of manufactures and manufacturers" with the "noise and smoke" characteristic of the Yankee North destroying its pastoral repose. It was a southern plantation, a reminder to all Americans that the father of the country had been a southern gentleman.

Cunningham meant to suggest that Mount Vernon's spacious vistas, unspoiled by factories, represented the best of the antebellum southern way of life. Her defense of Mount Vernon was therefore also a defense of what she saw as an ideal way of life that was unjustly under attack. Historic preservation allowed her to defend that culture just as surely as intellectuals could through their pens. The ever-sensitive Cunningham family could fully inscribe themselves in the American story by finding a new common enemy and then cementing their allegiance to the United States through a shared adulation of the Patriot past.[35]

Cunningham's efforts to resolve her own lingering sense of societal stigma put her in a growing late antebellum movement for historical preservation in response to Americans' newfound interest in touring an ever-wider range of historic sites. The rise of leisure travel in the United States fueled an interest in historical tourism. Early travelers enjoyed getting a walking history lesson rather than listening to an orator drone on. When Americans reported that they walked among crumbling sites of the past, they inspired the urge to preserve those "sacred places" for future generations. Americans feared that the Revolutionary past might disappear with the Revolutionary generation. But when they toured historical sites, they metaphysically connected with their history. If each new generation could rediscover the past through historical tourism, then the Anglo-American virtues of the Revolution could be preserved. Cunningham may have seen herself as a defender of southern honor through her historical endeavors, but she certainly also found a way to bypass her own tainted Revolutionary ancestry and write herself into the fabric of American patriotism.[36]

Mount Vernon was already a popular tourist attraction, but the financially troubled Washington family was tired of nonpaying tour groups picnicking on their lawn. In 1858 they happily sold the property to Cunningham's new organization: the Mount Vernon Ladies Society. This granddaughter of Tories found herself surrounded by women chosen for their distinguished Revolutionary ancestry. Cunningham headed the organization and ran the property for many years. Her astute management put it on a solid financial foundation and made it a model of nineteenth-century historic preservation. She truly found her personal outlet in historical preservation work.

If one scratches the surface of the early history of American historic preservation, a surprising number of Loyalist descendants are revealed. Cunningham's savvy urge to write herself into the seemingly unsullied Patriot Revolutionary past was widely shared. In Massachusetts several Loyalist returnees (men who fled by 1776 and came back in the 1780s) were early members of historical societies, including the Massachusetts Historical Society and the American Antiquarian Society. William Paine, one such Loyalist, became the vice president of the American Antiquarian Society and was chosen to speak for the organization at a patriotic occasion in 1815. In South Carolina, Cunningham was not the only grandchild of Loyalists to turn to historic preservation. Frederick Augustus Porcher, the founder of the South Carolina Historical Society, was the grandson of Loyalist Philip Porcher of Charleston.[37]

Frederick Porcher had an academic temperament. Despite inheriting a sizable plantation, he never was a very good planter and became a professor at the College of Charleston. Trained at Yale, he pursued history as an avocation and wrote several pieces on the lowcountry's Revolutionary history. He did all of this even though he was well aware that his grandfather had been punished for Loyalist activity. In his memoir he openly cataloged the fact that his grandfather "had been amerced by the Jacksonboro Convention." Of course he wrote his memoir after the Civil War, so the troubles of the Revolution seemed far away to a man shell-shocked by the South's loss in the war. He did not stop with publishing on the Revolutionary War. He also founded the South Carolina Historical Society in 1856 to "collect, preserve and publish such historical matter . . . as should seem desirable." The institution collected extensive materials on the Patriot cause, highlighting its virtues and guaranteeing that future generations would know of South Carolina's past. Like Cunningham, in addition to founding the organization, he served as president for a long stretch, gaining personal and family honor through his pursuit of historic preservation. The Porcher family had negotiated their reintegration and reconciliation so effectively over three generations that the grandson of a Loyalist could become the long-serving and respected head of a historical society dedicated to sharing the virtues of the people who had beaten the family more than fifty years before.[38]

While there were lingering whispers about some Loyalist clans, the paucity of such evidence suggests that Loyalist children and grandchildren were remarkably well integrated into South Carolina society. Porcher's memoirs indicate no sense of personal social stigma. Instead he remembered how he was able to look down on distant kinsmen in town who had become Methodists. In the Porcher experience, loyalism was a brief stigma that was not handed down to later generations. Rather in two cases Loyalist grandchildren became prominent and influential historic preservationists, chiefly memorializing a Whiggish view of the Revolution. Temperament clearly played a role, but it is telling that both of these famous nineteenth-century South Carolina preservationists had a Loyalist in the closet. Again and again Americans used lingering memories of loyalism to create a rosy view of the "unified" past.[39]

Both confident and well-integrated grandchildren of Loyalists also personify the devil's bargain at the heart of the way public memory was deliberately distorted to allow memories of disunity in the Revolution to die. These descendants of Loyalists were so confident in their own inclusion in society that they pursued historical memory making itself. While Cunningham flirted with rehabilitating the memory of the Loyalists themselves, she quickly retreated to the shared project of promulgating a vision of a unified Revolutionary war past. Both Loyalist descendants also found in their attraction to history a way to attach themselves to, and serve, an increasingly aggressive southern nationalist vision that honored the dead Founding Fathers while advocating for the end of union. Out of the disunity of the past, Loyalist descendants helped shape an imagined past unity. But they bent this vision of a unified past toward the goal of fostering armed disunion once again. All of this forgetting meant that South Carolinians healed the wounds of the civil war of the Revolution in a way that relied on deliberately forgetting how terrible civil war can be. When southerners began to flirt with the idea of civil war again and then court such a war, their own previous chastening experiences did them no good—for they had effectively erased those experiences from their collective memory. That which was forgotten had allowed them to reincorporate the Loyalists with generosity and build a wealthy and confident white society. But that which was forgotten also made them too confident in their ability to wage a civil war again.

✳ Fiction Is Safer

Even when South Carolinians began to admit to the internecine violence of their Revolutionary past late in the antebellum period, they chiefly did it through the seemingly safer grounds of fiction. Like many painful social realities, loyalism turned out to have a franker (and more vivid) life in antebellum novels rather than in oratory at public events. The stock Tories of Kings Mountain's seventy-fifth anniversary migrated into the novels of leading southern writer and intellectual William Gilmore Simms. The safe emotional distance of fiction gave South Carolinians room to discuss and even revel in their brutal history of civil war through a lens that did not implicate living individuals.

Simms was a leading novelist, historian, and public intellectual of the antebellum South. Today his novels molder in historical obscurity, read occasionally by college and graduate students. People who do read him today generally read novels from his colonial settlement series such as *The Cassique of Kiawah* (1859), which literary scholars regard as his least formulaic and therefore best novel. Yet in Simms's own day South Carolinians embraced his Revolutionary history writing enthusiastically. And historians to this day grant that he undertook extensive research into the American Revolution, using both copious available written materials as well as undertaking a large project to gather oral histories from the last survivors of the period. Simms's insistence on vigorous historical research was unusual for an antebellum writer, as most history writers used little source-based evidence until the late nineteenth century.

Simms's bent for history came from his grandmother, who filled his youthful ears with colorful (and sometimes exaggerated) stories of the American Revolution. She ignored South Carolina society's de facto rule that they should practice studied silence on the subject of loyalism. Her stories painted a black-and-white world of "Patriot heroism and Tory depravity" for young Simms. These influenced his interest in the Revolutionary War, especially as it played out in his beloved lowcountry. His biographies of generals Francis Marion and Nathanael Greene, two of the most famous and influential military leaders of the American Revolution in the South, gave him a template for an admiring exploration of the role of partisan warfare. But in the nineteenth century, writers who wanted to influence a wide audience needed to write novels, since other than the Bible they were the primary fare for average readers. Simms became a prolific novelist in the romantic tradition. He modeled himself on James Fenimore Cooper and Sir Walter Scott, using the genre of the romantic novel to delve into detail-oriented historical tales. His most famous novel, *The Partisan* (1835), began his seven-volume series chronologically moving through the entire Revolution in South Carolina. *The Partisan* has had lasting influence in how Americans understand the Revolution, since it is also the template for the popular Hollywood film *The Patriot* (2000).[40]

Simms's novels brought South Carolina's Loyalist legacy back into the open through a safer fictionalized world. While battlefield commemorations still seemed like a risky place to discuss Loyalist wartime actions, novels offered a safe space for the real terrors of civil war to reemerge. Simms shared the bloodthirstiness of his fellow South Carolinians when it came to imagining the blood-soaked lands of the war, but he occasionally tempered it with a wary sympathy for some Loyalists and for the civilians, Loyalist and Patriot, who were swept up into the fury of civil war. Still when northern historian Lorenzo Sabine, the first to write about American Loyalists, argued in print that South Carolina had more active Loyalist support than any other area of America, Simms was outraged. It did not help matters that Sabine also suggested that Charleston, Simms's beloved hometown, had surrendered without even trying to defend the city. In fact Sabine was being a responsible historian in pointing out the depth of Loyalist support in South Carolina. Simms responded by going on a northern lecture tour to defend South Carolina's Revolutionary contributions. The tour itself failed miserably, which fueled Simms's southern nationalistic pride in the Revolution.[41]

Throughout his work Simms portrayed the brutality and violence of the American Revolution in the Carolinas. Rather than shrinking from the nature of the warfare as brutal and internecine, he romanticized and celebrated it.

The Patriot hero of *Mellichampe* spoke for Simms when he says that the war "is a strife between brothers, all of whom have learned to hate as I do, and to seek to destroy with an appetite of far greater anxiety. The terms between Whig and Tory, now, are death only. No quarter is demanded—none is given." A party in *Woodcraft* wanders by the evidence of all this hatred: a field where "no coffin or shroud enwrapped the forms of those who had cast themselves off." Clearly civil conflict had reentered South Carolina's public conversations about the American Revolution. Simms took South Carolinians from silence to admitting and even reveling in their violently conflicted past. Yet because it was safely sanitized as fiction, they could reject any intimation that civil wars caused unnecessary suffering.[42]

Yet a contradiction lay at the heart of Simms's historical imagination. He was willing, even eager, to electrify his audiences with scenes of wartime brutality. And while orators at public events had laid those brutal acts at the feet of the British (ignoring Loyalists altogether), Simms put most of the blame at the feet of the Loyalists. Yet Simms had denied Sabine's argument that a sizable number of South Carolinians had been Loyalists in the war. Logically if there were so many instances of violence and hatred, would there not have been many Loyalists? Simms was in fact well aware that there were South Carolinians in his time whose forebears had fought for the British cause. He knew Ann Pamela Cunningham's ancestry, after all.

Perhaps the best clue is the way in which his most merciless portraits of Loyalists and their wartime conduct seem most overwrought when he attributes Toryism to lower-class men without morals or good breeding. His lower-class Loyalists are the scum of the earth, although they provide much of the humor and pathos of his novels. In *The Partisan* Loyalists are motivated by "a profligate lust for plunder" to participate in "that saturnalia of crime." In *Woodcraft* the Loyalist character Goggle steals a gold watch and always collects payment for his spying. Another Loyalist joins the British cause because "the right side with him . . . is that which promises most plunder." Most of the time Simms painted Loyalists as stick figures—evil Tories incapable of redemption. In *The Partisan* he describes a group of Loyalist prisoners as "generally of the very lowest class, and just the sort of men to fight, according to the necessity of the case, on either side. Such, indeed, were the Tories throughout the state, with very few exceptions." Rarely Simms painted a more sympathetic portrait of Loyalists, and when he did those Loyalists are from the upper class. For instance in *Mellichampe* he created a character modeled on the real-life Col. Thomas "Burnfoot" Brown, who became a Loyalist leader after barely surviving "ruthless torture at the hands of Patriots." Walton, a character in several of the books, follows what was actually a typical path for lowcountry plantation owners at the time. He was a Patriot until the British occupied the lowcountry.

At that time he took British protection and became a reluctant Loyalist. Unlike most real-life South Carolinians, the fictional Walton feels terribly about it and switches back to the Patriot cause shortly after the British cracked down on wavering Loyalists. He rallies to the Patriot cause once more and raises a militia unit that fights valiantly. In the end his loyalism catches up with him, and the British execute him for violating his promise to remain neutral. Overall Simms painted a picture of loyalism in which poor people with no morals were Loyalists and elite men avoided it. The very few who briefly elected loyalism then rejected it.[43]

Interestingly Simms's portrayals of Tories in his novels became less, rather than more, sympathetic over his writing career. During the 1830s and 1840s, he wanted to establish himself as a writer in the romantic tradition. He blamed loyalism on the lower sorts, but he was far more interested in portraying battlefield scenes than in understanding ideology. In fact his Patriot characters are remarkably devoid of ideology as well. In Simms's hands the British became merely foreign invaders, and the Patriots were good men who naturally rushed to defend their beloved homeland from the ravages of the invading foe. Loyalists simply seized on the chaos to make a profit. It was only as he began self-consciously to use his writing to promote southern nationalism that he chose to pillory Loyalists.

By the 1850s Simms, like many other southern intellectuals, had become convinced that the South was under attack. His own sectionalism hardened, and he used his public writing to defend the South he loved and to advocate for all measures necessary to defend it in the face of what he understood to be an increasingly hostile national culture. It was in this period that he penned a history of South Carolina in the Revolution with the intent to defend the state's Revolutionary history against those attackers (such as Sabine). In his later Revolutionary war novels, Simms used his retelling of South Carolinian heroism in militia fighting to defend the South's honor and the southern way of life. His Loyalist characters became more engaging and comic, yet less and less realistic or sympathetic. In the end he backed away from even acknowledging that South Carolina produced its own Loyalists. With the prospect of civil war looming on the horizon, he changed his tune in the late 1850s. He attacked another novelist's work, arguing that South Carolina's Loyalists had not even been natives of the state. Instead they were somehow "refugees previously expelled from other states" who entered the state under British protection in the 1780s. And while a previous novel had made a thinly veiled version of Thomas "Burnfoot" Brown a sympathetic character, when he revisited the character in his 1867 novel *Joscelyn*, he made him an exemplar of great evil. Historical memory, even in the hands of an accomplished researcher, swayed with the winds of the changing times.[44]

White South Carolinians successfully used control of public memory for more than seventy-five years to guarantee the lasting inclusion of former Loyalists and their children and grandchildren. These efforts to shape the public memory of the American Revolution worked well—so well, in fact, that the children and grandchildren of the Loyalists felt not only confident in asserting themselves in their society but also empowered to pursue the making of a shared societal historical memory themselves. This shared culture of public silence on the subject of loyalism and the creation of a remembered war in which all South Carolinians chose Patriotism worked so well that most people genuinely forgot the reality. When novelists and orators finally began to address South Carolina's vivid history of Revolutionary militia warfare, they did it with stock Tories so horrible that they could only exist in the pages of a novel. While Loyalists in the 1780s had been worried that the "stigma" of Loyalist behavior and the resulting legislative censure would affect their children and grandchildren, that turned out not to be the case. White South Carolinians made common cause with each other in creating "the harmony we were famous for"—the nineteenth-century political and social climate of conformity that allowed them to live peacefully with each other, all while sitting on the cauldron of a slave society in which a majority of South Carolinians were oppressed slaves. They may have been morally blind in their adherence to slavery, but they were wise in their realization that controlling how they talked about loyalism and the resulting civil war of the American Revolution could help them avoid igniting another conflagration. Their efforts to control the uses and abuses of historical memory worked well and ensured the stability of their society for decades.

This adroit use of studied silence about the reality of the past was a double-edged sword. People genuinely forgot about the civil war their parents and grandparents had fought, and so they also forgot to be chastened at the prospect of civil war. Ann Pamela Cunningham and William Gilmore Simms briefly antagonized each other as they each worked to shape a historical narrative they could be proud of. They came together, however, in their conviction that the memory of the American Revolutionary War was a useful tool in promoting a strident sectional appeal that would give way to southern nationalism, which could only end in southern independence. The white descendants of Loyalists and Patriots agreed that South Carolina's best choice was to embrace the prospect of civil war in order to achieve a perfect southern society.

At least when the conflagration came, they finally found unity. They left the nation and founded the Confederacy together. America's second revolution would not really be a civil war for white South Carolinians—they finally found themselves all on the same side.

✳ *Epilogue*

A Walk through Historic Charleston

Tourists in Charleston today often stroll down Archdale Street past the pale pink Victorian confection known as the Mills House Hotel. Perhaps they are looking for the award-wining she-crab soup around the corner at 82 Queen. But as they wander on, they amble by a late eighteenth-century home tastefully painted gray with muted blue hurricane shutters protecting the historic windows. The Philip Porcher house, once a statement that the Porcher family had truly arrived in the cosmopolitan transatlantic elite, is now a bed and breakfast for tourists who want to step back in time and experience a world they imagine as somehow both more elegant and more simple than theirs.

In order to protect his new showplace home, Philip Porcher chose public loyalism when it was politically convenient. When it turned out he had made a bad bet, he abased himself to his former friends who chose the Patriot cause. His Patriot brother-in-law had correctly read the tea leaves when he predicted that Porcher's many friends would come to his aid. His strategy of harnessing his continued residence in the state (despite the confiscation law) and his willingness to make humble personal apologies was the beginning of a viable strategy to save his recently built home and the sizable lands and funds that went with it. Porcher capitalized on his willingness to do the hard work to reinvigorate his social connections, and that work paid off in his sizable collection of signatories supporting his petition to the legislature for clemency. In 1784 the legislature returned all of his property, including the Charleston home—and, most important, his citizenship.

Visitors who stay at the bed and breakfast can read about the American Revolution, but nowhere in the marketing materials for the property or the information in tourist guidebooks is there any mention of the fact that Porcher was a Loyalist who was subject to confiscation and banishment. Once again all concerned have chosen to perpetuate a now two-century project to erase the reality of the American Revolution as a civil war.

South Carolinians worked so hard and were so effective in shaping a public culture of commemoration that they stayed silent about the reality of their civil war, all the while hoping it would be enough to guarantee a peaceful reconciliation. They succeeded beyond their hopes. Porcher's anxious son

Philip Porcher House, Charleston (front view). Photograph by Alec Grossman.

Peter inherited his share of his father's estate in due time. For the Porcher family, confiscation and banishment was an anxious and unpleasant moment in long lives of privilege. Peter Porcher went on to enjoy prosperity and honor as an eight-time member of the South Carolina General Assembly. And Philip's grandson Frederick later established the South Carolina Historical Society to preserve the nation's founding history for later generations—a version that privileged the Patriot side and preserved the studied silence on the complex reality of America's first civil war. Historic preservation was just another method in the tool kit of reconciliation, and surprisingly often it was spearheaded by the grandchildren of Loyalists. The former Loyalist who had worried that his children and grandchildren might face a lingering stigma was mercifully proved wrong. In fact former Loyalists and Patriots so thoroughly erased the past in order to smooth over the reincorporation of former Loyalists into the state, that their grandchildren faced no stigma at all.[1]

White South Carolinians did a thorough (perhaps too thorough) job of burying the past in order to give themselves a more stable and enjoyable future—at least until the trials of the Civil War rewrote southerners' perceptions of internecine conflict. White southerners who focused on their belief that the Revolution was a dispute over constitutional principles that protected property absolutely—even property in human beings—conveniently failed to remember how ideologically muddy and personally devastating any war could be, including the vaunted Revolution of their memory. The devil's bargain of selective memory had allowed Patriot and Loyalist neighbors to live together in peace and encourage their children to marry each other. Smug certitude about having created a nonviolent political culture led Americans to let their guard down by the antebellum period, believing that they could selectively forget anything that threatened that peace. Certainly this flawed memory made it easy to do what white southerners wanted to do anyway: secede from the Union and defend that choice, even if it meant war. Both sides were overly optimistic, but southerners had especially inflated views of their own abilities as soldiers and the brutal realities of war. Sadly it seems as if white South Carolinians' skill in crafting a lasting reconciliation from one war allowed them to skip merrily into another war without due regard for the possible consequences. Perhaps it is true that no good deed goes unpunished.

In the bitterness and loss of the Civil War, the South's Revolutionary past faded from public and private thought and memory. The latter war makes for an easier narrative for white southerners as it offers the comforting image of a united populace against a common enemy (at least if one ignores the continued presence of African American descendants of slaves). When the Rockefeller family "discovered" Williamsburg, Virginia, in the first decades of the twentieth century, they found that the white southerners who lived in Williamsburg had to be convinced that the Revolution was "their" war. For the inhabitants of Williamsburg, their war was the Civil War. White South Carolinians felt—and often still feel—the same way. When you travel to Charleston, the Revolutionary past is a footnote to the many historic sites that showcase the Civil War and the many gift shops selling upscale Confederate paraphernalia. The large mansions on the Battery bought with the back-breaking labor of enslaved African Americans in the antebellum cotton fields of upcountry South Carolina dominate the landscape and the historic home tour. Yet the Revolutionary past is still all around, largely disregarded by tourists and locals alike.[2]

With the rise of the nation-state, nationalism made forgiveness and reconciliation harder, even as it made it more necessary. And to this day we have not moved beyond the nation-state and its reliance on, and encouragement of, a passionate nationalism that punishes and even exterminates its own minorities to give lip service to the fantasy of one ethnic nation, undivided. Around the world societies have struggled with the need for reconciliation and the crushing reality humans have long known: forgiving and moving on is very difficult. Today a growing body of political science literature studies efforts around the world in damaged societies trying to recover from everything from state-sanctioned apartheid to state-encouraged genocide. What unites these studies is that they try to quantify what cannot be nailed down—the creative, varied, and society-specific methods that actually work to help people reunite and heal and, by so doing, create more stable and reassuring societies for ordinary people to actually live in. South Africa's effort at state-sanctioned reconciliation, the now famous Truth and Reconciliation Commission, cannot be easily replicated in other societies. Arguably by encouraging people to relive long-ago traumas, these commissions can reinvigorate the power of those experiences. For individuals seeking healing, remembrance can serve as therapy, allowing someone finally to feel heard. But what heals individuals can poison societal efforts at reconciliation.

At a moment when nationalism was still gaining strength as a new way to organize society, Americans cast off a national identity as Englishmen, the freest people in the world. They found themselves trying to create a new national identity strong enough to unite a postcolonial, multiethnic, democratic republic. And in temporarily solving the problem of a cohesive national identity, they found a persuasive way to heal their society from the wounds of revolutionary civil war. Americans' long-standing love for the idea that our Revolution was uniquely nonviolent was created in the crucible of that vital moment immediately after the war. Americans could have enjoyed their triumph over those former neighbors who lay tantalizingly in their power. Yet in the majority of cases, they chose to seek reintegration and reconciliation rather than revenge. In order to do so, they worked hard to forget the reality of their civil war as quickly as possible. And so American exceptionalism grew out of, and was aided and abetted by, a deliberate strategy to reincorporate white people by shutting out the painful memories of civil war. Those memories that could not be shut out were displaced onto the British in order to create a unified public culture of commemoration that represented the Revolution as a battle between nations rather than a war for the soul of America waged between its own people. American exceptionalism may have yielded bitter fruit over the intervening two centuries, but at the time it was an ambitious project to create a more generous and inclusive society by deliberately choosing to forget some painful memories.

When tourists to Charleston stay in the Revolutionary-era Porcher House and ignore the reality of America's Loyalist past, all while imagining an idyll of antebellum white prosperity and an honorable Civil War, they are reinscribing the American decision to forget that the Revolution was a civil war—no matter what evidence may remain. Reconciliation is possible, but societies need to work at it. Americans embraced Christopher Gadsden's charge that "he that forgets and forgives most ... is the best citizen."[3] At the heart of the founding of the United States was a concomitant commitment to subvert deliberately the way the nation remembers the past in order to create a more inclusive and vibrant future. Gadsden was right—choosing to obscure the reality of civil war did lead the United States into a prosperous and stable future. But it also allowed Americans to forget the lessons of the Revolution and thereby fail to temper the instinct to resort to violence and war.

Our propensity for self-healing and looking always to the future has indeed made American society more generous and our understanding of democratic citizenship more expansive and robust. Americans justly deserve praise for choosing the difficult path of reintegration and reconciliation over continuing the divisions of civil war from generation to generation. Yet even commendable choices can have unfortunate consequences, as silver linings come with clouds. No reconciliation is without cost. The project of reconciliation was worth it and was well executed. American exceptionalism, and the relentless focus on the future at the expense of honesty about the nation's past, arises from the same instincts that made Americans willing to embrace both difficult neighbors and the painful constraints of moving forward together.

Notes

Introduction

1. Henry Laurens to John Owen, London, Aug. 9, 1783; Laurens to Elias Ball, London, Sept. 11, 1783, in Hamer, Rogers, and Chesnutt, *Laurens Papers,* 16:260, 336.

2. Ball, *Slaves in the Family,* 8–9.

3. Shy, *People Numerous and Armed,* 23.

4. Aedanus Burke to Arthur Middleton, Jacksonborough, Jan. 25, 1782, in Barnwell, "Middleton Correspondence 1," 192–93. On evolutionary psychology research on this point, see Rosenbaum, *Payback,* 110–11; Carlsmith, Wilson, and Gilbert, "Paradoxical Consequences," esp. 1323.

5. Jasanoff, *Liberty's Exiles;* Frey, *Water from the Rock.*

6. Ball, *Slaves in the Family,* 238–39. Historians have long tried to establish exactly how many people had to flee the United States after the Revolution. The most contemporary source is the appendix "Measuring the Exodus" in Jasanoff, *Liberty's Exiles,* 351–58. Other useful and authoritative sources include Calhoon, *Loyalists in Revolutionary America,* and P. H. Smith, "American Loyalists."

7. No. 5 William Blake (on Amercement), Free Conference Comm. Meeting, SCDAH.

8. Walsh, *Gadsden Writings,* 197.

Chapter One: The American Revolution

1. Draper, *King's Mountain,* 265–66.

2. Chopra, *Unnatural Rebellion,* 62; Van Buskirk, *Generous Enemies.*

3. I am borrowing the telling phrase "uncivil war" from Hoffman, Tate, and Albert, *Uncivil War.*

4. For a persuasive account of the growing sophistication of Charleston's economy and society, see Hart, *Building Charleston.* For more on the backcountry and the Regulator movement, see R. M. Brown, *South Carolina Regulators;* Kars, *Breaking Loose Together;* Klein, *Unification of a Slave State.*

5. Gregory Palmer, *Biographical Sketches,* 93. For more on the South Carolina Loyalists as a group, see Lambert, *South Carolina Loyalists.* For more on the Loyalists in general, start with the following: Jasanoff, *Liberty's Exiles;* Norton, *British-Americans;* Potter, *Liberty We Seek.*

6. Oliver Hart and William Drayton qtd. in Krawczynski, *William Henry Drayton,* 158–82.

7. Maj. James Wemyss qtd. in Edgar, *Partisans and Redcoats,* 62–63.

8. Borick, *Gallant Defense,* 252; Sir Henry Clinton to William Phillips, May 25, 1780, Clinton Papers, William Clements Library; Pancake, *This Destructive War,* 66–69.

9. Ewald qtd. in *Gallant Defense,* 230–32.

10. Borick, *Gallant Defense,* 237–38; Lord Rawdon to Lord Cornwallis, July 7, 1780, as reprinted in Scoggins, *Day It Rained Militia,* 196–97.

11. Jim Piecuch, *Three Peoples One King,* xxvi–xxix.

12. Rawlins Lowndes qtd. in Borick, *Gallant Defense,* 232

13. Borick, *Gallant Defense,* 252; Samuel Carne qtd. in Piecuch, *Three Peoples One King,* 184.

14. Frey, *Water from the Rock,* 173–74; Nadelhaft, *Disorders of War,* 62; Gary Nash qtd. in Piecuch, *Three Peoples One King,* 8.

15. John Adams qtd. in Piecuch, *Three Peoples One King,* 43; Maj. James Wemyss qtd. in Piecuch, *Three Peoples One King,* 197.

16. Ibid., 216–22.

17. Ibid., 161.

18. Henry Laurens to William Manning, Feb. 27, 1776, in Hamer, Rogers, and Chesnutt, *Laurens Papers,* 11: 123–24; Piecuch, *Three Peoples One King,* 63–76, 150–51.

19. Van Buskirk, *Generous Enemies,* 1–2; Edgar, *Partisans and Redcoats,* 80; George Neely, Federal Pension Application S4613, as excerpted in Scoggins, *Day It Rained Militia,* 174–75.

20. Buchanan, *Road to Guilford Courthouse,* 9–16; Kelly, "Branded as a Rebel"; H. F. Rankin, "Moore's Creek Bridge." The historical literature on the military campaigns in the Revolutionary South is voluminous. Here are a few importance places to start: Buchanan, *Road to Guilford Courthouse;* Gordon, *Battlefield History;* Nadelhaft, *Disorders of War;* Pancake, *This Destructive War;* Babits, *Devil of a Whipping;* D. K. Wilson, *Southern Strategy;* Lumpkin, *From Savannah to Yorktown;* Cashin, *King's Ranger.*

21. W. Brown, *Good Americans,* 37; Act no. 1017, "An Act to Prevent Sedition and Punish Insurgents and Disturbers of the Public Peace," in Cooper and McCord, *Statutes of S.C.,* 1: 343–46; Alexander Innes to the Earl of Dartmouth, Charles Town, May 16, 1775, in Bargar, "Charles Town Loyalism," 129; Mr. Timothy to Mr. Drayton, Charlestown, Aug. 13, 1775, in Gibbes, *Documentary History,* 1:139.

22. "Act Enforcing an Assurance of Allegiance and Fidelity to the State," in Cooper and McCord, *Statutes of S.C.,* 1:147–51; Act no. 1101, "An Act for Enlarging the Time for Taking the Oath of Allegiance and Fidelity; and for Other Purposes Therein Mentioned," in ibid., 1:450–52; Act no. 1117, "An Act to Give Further Time for Taking the Oath of Affirmation of Fidelity and Allegiance to this State," in ibid., 1:468–69.

23. Moses Hall, Veteran's Pension Application, in Dann, *Revolution Remembered,* 199. For more on the experience of living through the war, see Crow and Tise, *Southern Experience;* Hoffman, Tate, and Albert, *Uncivil War;* Higginbotham, "Reflections on the War of Independence." Edgar, *Partisans and Redcoats.*

24. Borick, *Gallant Defense,* 60, 99–100; Gen. Francis Marion to Gen. Horatio Gates, Oct. 7, 1780, Gates Papers, qtd. in Piecuch, *Three Peoples One King,* 196.

25. Borick, *Gallant Defense*, 98, 152; Diary of Lt. Anthony Allaire, March 24, 1780; Draper, *King's Mountain*, 488; John Lewis Gervais to Henry Laurens, Santee, S.C., May 13, 1780, in Hamer, Rogers, and Chesnutt, *Laurens Papers*, 15:292.

26. Ferguson, "Partisan-Militia"; Edgar, *Partisans and Redcoats*, 71; Buchanan, *Road to Guilford Courthouse*, 378–83; Collins, "Autobiography," 270–72; Pancake, *This Destructive War*, 202.

27. James Creswell to W. H. Drayton, Ninety Six, S.C., Aug. 22, 1776, in Gibbes, *Documentary History*, 30–31; Gen. Greene to Samuel Huntington, Camp on the Cheraws, Dec. 28, 1780, in Showman, *Greene Papers*, 7:9; Greene to Gen. Robert Howe, Camp on the Pedee, Dec. 29, 1780, in ibid., 7:17.

28. James Simpson to Germain, New York, Aug. 28, 1779, in A. S. Brown, "Simpson's Reports," 514–18.

29. Ibid., 516–18.

30. William Gipson's Pension Application, in Dann, *Revolution Remembered*, 186–87.

31. Lee, *Crowds and Soldiers*, 176–77. Lee depends on the use of the phrase "law of retaliation" from Selesky, "Colonial America."

32. Power, "'Virtue of Humanity,'" 9–10; Pancake, *This Destructive War*, 70–71.

33. Lee, *Crowds and Soldiers*, 389; William Davie qtd. in Pancake, *This Destructive War*, 83–85; Nadelhaft, *Disorders of War*, 67.

34. Moses Hall, Veterans Pension Application, in Dann, *Revolution Remembered*, 202; Edgar, *Partisans and Redcoats*, 62–63.

35. Dann, *Revolution Remembered*, 188.

36. Draper, *King's Mountain*, 265–66. Draper did have an ear for the romantic, and some stories of King's Mountain are undoubtedly embellished. Even the embellished ones, however, are evidence of the enthusiasm with which people told stories of callousness and hatred to the other side. Hesseltine, "Lyman Draper."

37. James Collins later remembered the families searching for the dead Loyalist soldiers in "great numbers" who had been "thrown into convenient piles" and were being eaten by animals. Collins, "Autobiography," 261; Buchanan, *Road to Guilford Courthouse*, 234.

38. I rely on Jerome Nadelhaft's best estimates of casualties. Nadelhaft, *Disorders of War*, 61. Nadelhaft used Peckham, *Toll of Independence*. Henry Laurens to Mary Laurens, Paris, Dec. 30, 1782, in Hamer, Rogers, and Chesnutt, *Laurens Papers*, 16:111.

39. Pancake, *This Destructive War*, 60–62; Edgar, *Partisans and Redcoats*, 62–63; Krawczynski, "William Drayton's Journal," 190.

40. Francis Richardson and Archibald Simpson qtd. in Frey, *Water from the Rock*, 206–7.

41. Maj. William Pierce qtd. in Piecuch, *Three Peoples One King*, 274.

Chapter Two: 1782

1. John Lewis Gervais to Henry Laurens, Philadelphia, Sept. 27, 1781, in Hamer, Rogers, and Chesnutt, *Laurens Papers*, 16:16, 31, esp. n. 13.

2. Henry Laurens to Richard Champion, Nantes, Aug. 10, 1782, in ibid., 15:561; Salley, *House J. 1782*, 13.

3. Lambert, *South Carolina Loyalists*, 195; John Matthews to Arthur Middleton, Uxbridge, S.C., Aug. 25, 1782; Ralph Izard to Middleton, Philadelphia, May 30, 1783, in Barnwell, "Middleton Correspondence 3," 71, 78.

4. Aedanus Burke to Arthur Middleton, Jacksonborough, Jan. 25, 1782; Burke to Middleton, Camp before York, Oct. 16, 1781, in Barnwell, "Middleton Correspondence 1," 187–93, 208. On evolutionary psychology research on this point, see Rosenbaum, *Payback*, 110–11; and Carlsmith, Wilson, and Gilbert, "Paradoxical Consequences," esp. 1323. Historians have increasingly considered the complex ways in which emotions and difficulties in emotional self-regulation have shaped epochal events such as the American Revolution. See especially Eustace, *Passion Is the Gale;* Stearns and Stearns, *Anger.*

5. Henry Laurens to John Davies, London, Feb. 2, 1782, in Hamer, Rogers, and Chesnutt, *Laurens Papers,* 15:466; Laurens to George Appleby, Bath, Feb. 18, 1783, in ibid., 16:150.

6. Henry Laurens to John Davies, London, Feb. 2, 1782; Laurens to William Manning, Nantes, Aug. 3, 1782; Laurens to Edward Bridgen, Nantes, Aug. 10, 1782, in ibid., 15:466, 545–55.

7. Edward Rutledge to Arthur Middleton, Dec. 12, 1781, in Barnwell, "Middleton Correspondence 1," 187–93, 208; Walsh, *Gadsden Writings,* 195n3.

8. Carlsmith, Wilson, and Gilbert, "Paradoxical Consequences."

9. Edward Rutledge to Arthur Middleton, Apr. 14, 1782, Edward Rutledge Papers 1749–1800, 43/506, South Carolina Historical Society, Charleston; Charles Cotesworth Pinckney to Middleton, Camp near Bacon's Bridge, Apr. 24, 1782, in Barnwell, "Middleton Correspondence 3," 61; Kelman, "Reconciliation from a Social-Psychological Perspective"; Henry Laurens to Edward Bridgen, Nantes, Aug. 10, 1782, in Hamer, Rogers, and Chesnutt, *Laurens Papers,* 15:554–55.

10. Walsh, *Gadsden Writings,* 196.

11. Barnwell, "Middleton Correspondence 1," 200.

12. Haw, *John and Edward Rutledge,* 159. Rutledge instructed Marion and others to see that the proclamation was "properly circulated." Gov. Rutledge to General Marion, Sept. 26, 1781, in Gibbes, *Documentary History,* 175.

13. Salley, *Senate J. 1782,* 7, 21.

14. Aedanus Burke to Arthur Middleton, Petersburgh, Nov. 18, 1781; Burke to Middleton, Jacksonborough, Jan. 25, 1782, in Barnwell, "Middleton Correspondence 1," 191.

15. Burke to Middleton, Jacksonborough, Jan. 25, 1782.

16. Act no. 1157, "An Act for Pardoning the Persons Therein Described, on the Conditions Therein Mentioned," in Cooper and McCord, *Statutes of S.C.,* 4:526–28. The act specifically pardoned persons who had taken the December 17, 1781, or the September 22, 1781, offers from Governor Rutledge.

17. Haw, *John and Edward Rutledge,* 160; C. F. Lee, "Transformation of the Executive"; Weir, "Violent Spirit."

18. Nadelhaft, "'Snarls of Invidious Animals,'" 72.

19. Ibid. In an effort to preserve some lowcountry legislative power, the governor arranged for polling places for lowcountry voters in the Patriot-controlled areas in the interior. In practice this was not likely to bring in many additional voters, but it did

preserve the ability of men in the military to vote and therefore gave legitimacy to the placement of lowcountry representatives.

20. Burke to Middleton, Jacksonborough, Jan. 25, 1782, in Barnwell, "Middleton Correspondence 1," 192.

21. Edward Rutledge to Arthur Middleton, Jacksonborough, Jan. 23, 1782; Burke to Middleton, Jacksonborough, Jan. 25, 1782, in ibid., 193, 210.

22. Burke to Middleton, Jacksonborough, Jan. 25, 1782, in ibid., 192–93.

23. Ibid.; Salley, *House J. 1782,* 74–80, 89, 110, 122; Edward Rutledge to Middleton, Jacksonborough, Feb. 14, 1782, and Feb. 26, 1782, in Barnwell, "Middleton Correspondence 2," 4–7.

24. Burke to Middleton, Jacksonborough, Jan. 25, 1782, in Barnwell, "Middleton Correspondence 1," 192–93; Garden, *Anecdotes of the Revolutionary War,* 179.

25. Charles Drayton was a brother-in-law to both Arthur Middleton (who served as South Carolina's representative to Congress in 1781) and Charles Cotesworth Pinckney. Edward Rutledge to Arthur Middleton, Jacksonborough, Feb. 14, 1782, in Barnwell, "Middleton Correspondence 2," 5; Salley, *Senate J. 1782,* 103–5.

26. Rutledge to Middleton, Jacksonborough, Feb. 14, 1782, in Barnwell, "Middleton Correspondence 2," 5; Salley, *Senate J. 1782,* 94, 97–98, 111–13.

27. Henry Laurens to Alice Delancey Izard, Paris, June 5, 1783, in Hamer, Rogers, and Chesnutt, *Laurens Papers,* 16:204–5.

28. Salley, *House J. 1782,* 12. There is also a version in the Governor's Messages (Rutledge Administration, Jan. 18, 1782), Executive Papers Collection, South Carolina Department of Archives and History (hereinafter SCDAH).

29. Cooper and McCord, *Statutes of S.C.,* 6:629–32, 4:518.

30. Lambert, *South Carolina Loyalists,* 95.

31. Ditz, "Shipwrecked," 68; Bloch, "Gendered Meanings," 43. For work on the importance of the denial of self-interest in properly regulated masculinity, see Kann, *Republic of Men,* 45–47.

32. Charles Cotesworth Pinckney on behalf of Mrs. Burn, Widow of John Burn, Feb. 26, 1783, Petitions Received by Commissioners of Forfeited Estates, folder 5, box 5, Misc. Papers Relating to Claims on Estates, Commissioners of Forfeited Estates, Comptroller General Papers, S 126170, SCDAH; Pass for William Blake, Henry Laurens, London, May 6, 1782, in Hamer, Rogers, and Chesnutt, *Laurens Papers,* 15:498.

33. Burke to Middleton, Jacksonborough, Jan. 25, 1782, in Barnwell, "Middleton Correspondence 1," 192–93.

34. W. Brown, *Good Americans,* 129; Hast, *Loyalism in Revolutionary Virginia,* 128–31; DeMond, *Loyalists in North Carolina,* 158–59.

35. Cooper and McCord, *Statutes of S.C.,* 4: 521–22. North Carolina revised its confiscation law several times to make payment terms more generous, including letting people pay in soldiers' certificates and state currency. DeMond, *Loyalists in North Carolina,* 168; Lambert, "Confiscation of Loyalist Property," 82; Jameson, *American Revolution;* Reilly, "Confiscation and Sale"; Yoshpe, *Disposition of Loyalist Estates;* R. D. Brown, "Confiscation and Disposition."

36. Coker, "Punishment of Loyalists," appendix A.

37. Returns are still extant only from a few districts, but there is reason to believe the commissioners did indeed survey all areas at the time. Officer's Returns from Ninety Six District, June 1, 1783, box 5, folder 7, Miscellaneous Papers of the Forfeited Estates, Comptroller General Papers S 126170.

38. Act no. 1157, "An Act for Pardoning the Persons Therein Described, on the Conditions Therein Mentioned," in Cooper and McCord, *Statutes of S.C.*, 4:526–28; Hast, *Loyalism in Revolutionary Virginia*, 123–24. For Margaret Balfour's letter to her sister-in-law, see DeMond, *Loyalists in North Carolina*, 123.

39. Aedanus Burke to Arthur Middleton, May 14, 1782; Burke to Middleton, July 6, 1782, in Barnwell, "Middleton Correspondence 1," 201, 205–6.

40. Burke to Middleton, July 6, 1782; Justice Aedanus Burke to Gov. Benjamin Guerard, Dec. 14, 1784, Aedanus Burke Papers, South Caroliniana Library, University of South Carolina.

41. Salley, *House J. 1782*, 62.

42. Ibid., 124–27; Rutledge to Middleton, Jacksonborough, Feb. 26, 1782, in Barnwell, "Middleton Correspondence 2," 7–8; Thompson and Lumpkin, *House J. 1783–1784*, 221; Act no. 1157, "An Act for Pardoning the Persons Therein Described, on the Conditions Therein Mentioned," in Cooper and McCord, *Statutes of S.C.*, 4:526–28.

43. Act no. 1147, "An Act for Settling the Qualification of the Electors and Elected, in the Next General Assembly," in Cooper and McCord, *Statutes of S.C.*, 4:510–11; Burke to Middleton, Jacksonborough, Jan. 25, 1782, in Barnwell, "Middleton Correspondence 1," 193.

44. Burke to Middleton, Jacksonborough, Jan. 25, 1782, in Barnwell, "Middleton Correspondence 1," 193; Kruman, *Between Authority and Liberty*, 88–103. For contrasts in other states, see DeMond, *Loyalists in North Carolina*, 156; Ousterhout, *State Divided*, 161–62; Zeichner, "Loyalist Problem in New York"; Zeichner, "Rehabilitiation of Loyalists."

Chapter Three: Hope for Reconciliation

1. Barnwell, "Middleton Correspondence 1," 197; Edward Rutledge to Arthur Middleton, Jacksonborough, Cane Acre, Apr. 23, 1782, in Barnwell, "Middleton Correspondence 2," 14.

2. *Royal Gazette*, Apr. 30, 1782, July 9, 1782, Aug. 13, 1782, Sept. 10, 1782; 99/Secret Correspondent to General Marion, Charlestown, Nov. 13, 1782, Peter Horry Collection Letterbook, Peter Force Papers 1683–1789, David Library of the American Revolution.

3. Bailey, *Popular Influence*, 23, 68–84, 166; Higginson, "Short History," 157.

4. Higginson, "Right to Petition," 143–48; Bailey, *Popular Influence*, 31; Maurice Simmons, in Salley, *House J. 1782*, 135. Another version of Simmons's petition can be found in the Senate Journal (engrossed manuscript), Feb. 15, 1783, SCDAH.

5. Bailey, *Popular Influence*, 6.

6. Bogin, "Petitioning," 420–21.

7. Henry Laurens to Edward Bridgen, Bath, Oct. 11, 1782, in Hamer, Rogers, and Chesnutt, *Laurens Papers*, 16: 36.

8. This figure contains only Loyalist petitions that can easily be located in the legislative records in full, as opposed to those petitions that are recorded as existing in the legislative journals (but there is no extant copy). This figure also excludes Loyalists who were later pardoned but for whom there is no petition still extent. I also checked my data against appendix C in Coker, "Punishment of Loyalists," 503–7; Edward Rutledge to Arthur Middleton, Aug. 1782, in Barnwell, "Middleton Correspondence 2," 21.

9. Klepp, *Revolutionary Conceptions;* Zagarri, *Revolutionary Backlash.*

10. For more on the traditionally strong legal protections for dower rights (which the 1782 South Carolina legislature deliberately stripped from Loyalists), see Salmon, *Women and Property,* 156–72.

11. Margaret Cunningham, 1785–86, Petitions to the General Assembly, South Carolina Department of Archives and History (hereinafter GA Petitions); Adams and Lumpkin, *House J. 1785–1786,* 78, 167–68, 188; Andrew Cunningham Plat for 1,000 acres in Berkeley County, Colonial Plat Books (Copy Series), 9:208; Andrew Cunningham Plat for 100 acres in Berkeley County, Colonial Plat Books (Copy Series), 11:373; Andrew Cunningham, File no. 1686B, Reel 29, Frames 488– , Accounts Audited of Claims Growing out of the Revolution in South Carolina, 1775–1856, SCDAH.

12. Henry Laurens to Richard Champion, Nantes, Aug. 10, 1782, in Hamer, Rogers, and Chesnutt, *Laurens Papers,* 15:561; Laurens to Anne Burn, London, Aug. 8, 1783, in ibid., 16:247.

13. Thompson and Lumpkin, *House J. 1783–1784,* 382; Act. no. 1177, "An Act to Amend an Act Entitled 'An Act for disposing of certain estates, and banishing certain persons, therein mentioned,'" March 16, 1783, in Cooper and McCord, *Statutes of S. C.,* 1:555–57. On the value of women's "moveables," see Ulrich, "Hannah Barnard's Cupboard," 256–63.

14. Arthur Middleton to Aedanus Burke, Apr. 7, 1783, in Barnwell, "Middleton Correspondence 2," 29.

15. Mary Cape, 1783–263; Sarah Scott, 1783–186, GA Petitions. Ann Legge, Jan. 22, 1783; Ann McGillivray, Jan. 28, 1783, in Thompson and Lumpkin, *House J. 1783–1784,* 15, 53.

16. Ann Legge, 1783–336, GA Petitions.

17. Note that original sources alternate between Mackie and Mackey. James Mackie, no. 122, Testimonies and Notes, Petitions for Relief from Confiscation 1783–1784, General Assembly Free Conference Committee, S 165035, Papers of the General Assembly, South Carolina Department of Archives and History (hereinafter Free Conference Comm. Hearings); Eleanor Mackey, Jan. 29, 1784, in Thompson and Lumpkin, *House J. 1783–1784,* 387–88.

18. Mary Beth Norton disagrees with Linda Kerber's perspective, arguing that Loyalist women had embraced traditional ideals of appropriate female roles. Norton, "Eighteenth-Century American Women"; Florence Cook, Jan. 23, 1783, in Thompson and Lumpkin, *House J. 1783–1784,* 22; Kerber, *Women of the Republic,* 127–29; *South Carolina Gazette and General Advertiser,* Apr. 29, 1784; Hamer, Rogers, and Chesnutt, *Laurens Papers,* 16:431.

19. Margaret Brisbane, 1783–261, GA Petitions; Edwards, *Privy Council Journals,* 11–12, 127–28; Kerber, *Women of the Republic,* 416–17.

20. Benjamin Quark for John Wigfall, Testimonies and Notes, General Assembly Free Conference Committee Petitions for Relief from Confiscation 1783–1784, S 165035 (hereinafter "Hearing Testimony"), SCDAH.

21. Supporters of Richard Wayne, 1783–369, GA Petitions.

22. Zubly and Hawes, *Journal of Zubly*, Dec. 31, 1778, 75.

23. Henry Laurens to William Manning, Parish, Dec. 4, 1782, in Hamer, Rogers, and Chesnutt, *Laurens Papers*, 16:67–68.

24. Henry Laurens to Elias Ball, London, Sept. 11, 1783, in ibid., 16:336.

25. Henry Laurens to John Owen, London, August 9, 1783, in ibid., 16:260.

26. John Wagner, in Thompson and Lumpkin, *House J. 1783–1784*, 15–16. This petition is also found in the Senate engrossed manuscript, but the original is not in the GA Petition series. William Glen, 1783–53, GA Petitions.

27. Edward Fenwick, Accounts Audited of Claims Arising from the American Revolution, Account no. 2345, excerpted in Adams and Lumpkin, *House J. 1785–1786*, 24.

28. Aaron Loocock, 1783–273; Thomas Buckle, 1783–350, GA Petitions.

29. William Burt, 1783–7; Andrew Hibben, 1783–34, GA Petitions.

30. William Cameron, Jan. 24, 1783; James Mackey, Jan. 23, 1783, in Thompson and Lumpkin, *House J. 1783–1784*, 25, 35. For more on the paranoid style in eighteenth-century politics, see Wood, "Conspiracy"; Pasley, "Conspiracy Theory"; Richard Hofstadter, *Paranoid Style*.

31. Thomas Eustace, in Thompson and Lumpkin, *House J. 1783–1784*, 35; John Walter Gibbs, 1783–19, GA Petitions.

32. Alexander Rose, petition excerpted in Thompson and Lumpkin, *House J. 1783–1784*, 15; Jacob Deveaux, 1783–86; James Brisbane, 1783–70, GA Petitions; Palmer, *Biographical Sketches*, 93.

33. John Wigfall, 1783–370, GA Petitions; Report of the Commissioners on the Petition of John Deas, Esq., enclosed with Oct. 1783 letter to Commissioners, Box 4, Miscellaneous Papers Relating to Claims on Estates, Commissioners of Forfeited Estates, Comptroller General Papers, S 126170, SCDAH.

34. Freeman, "Dueling as Politics," 295–96 n19.

35. Charles Johnston, 1783–95, GA Petitions; Benjamin Villeponteax on behalf of Charles Johnston, 1783–335, GA Petitions; Petition of Sarah Clark, Ann Smith, and Sarah Clement on behalf of John Hartz, excerpted in Thompson and Lumpkin, *House J. 1783–1784*, 20. For more on the grim realities of disease and death on British prisoner-of-war ships, see Borick, *Relieve Us of This Burthen*.

36. John Scott, Jan. 24, 1783; Sarah Scott, Feb. 1, 1783, in Thompson and Lumpkin, *House J. 1783–1784*, 35, 76–77, and in *Senate J. 1783*, Feb. 3, 1783, Senate Journal, SCDAH. For more on the execution of Isaac Hayne, see Bowden, *Execution of Hayne*.

37. Edward Fenwick, June 26, 1785, in Adams and Lumpkin, *House J. 1785–1786*, 24.

38. John Adamson, 1783–40, GA Petitions; Supporters of John Adamson, Jan. 28, 1783, in Thompson and Lumpkin, *House J. 1783–1784*, 53–54.

39. Joseph Seabrook, 1783–240; James Cassells, 1784–36, GA Petitions; Coker, "Punishment of Loyalists," 214–16.

40. Patrick Muckle Murray, Feb. 3, 1783, in Thompson and Lumpkin, *House J. 1783–1784*, 81–82.

41. John Harth, 1783–15; Christopher Williman, Jan. 22, 1783, in Thompson and Lumpkin, *House J. 1783–1784*, 13–14; Inhabitants of S.C. in behalf of James Lynah, 1783–394, GA Petitions.

42. Kettner, *Development of American Citizenship*, 122–27. For some different angles on citizenship, see Holland, *Body Politic*, and Wyatt-Brown, *Honor and Violence*.

43. Inhabitants of St. Stephens Parish on behalf of Philip Porcher, 1783–10; Isaac Delyon, 1783–359, GA Petitions.

44. Murrin, "Roof without Walls." For a different view, see Blassingame, "American Nationalism," and Varg, "Advent of Nationalism."

45. Gilbert Chalmers, Jan. 22, 1783, in Thompson and Lumpkin, *House J. 1783–1784*, 14; Inhabitants of St. Stephens Parish on behalf of Philip Porcher, 1783–10, GA Petitions.

46. Edward Rutledge to Arthur Middleton, Cane Acre, Apr. 23, 1782, in Barnwell, "Middleton Correspondence 2," 14.

47. James Gordon, 1783–54, GA Petitions; Maurice Simmons, in Salley, *House J. 1782*, 135; Henry Laurens to Edward Bridgen, Bath, Oct. 11, 1782, in Hamer, Rogers, and Chesnutt, *Laurens Papers*, 16:37.

48. Weir, "Violent Spirit," 96–97.

49. Krawczynski, "William Drayton's Journal," 190.

50. Ibid.

Chapter Four: Uneasy Neighbors to Trusted Friends

1. Stephen Mazyck to Peter Porcher, Charlestown, June 14, 1783, 49/509, Porcher Family Papers, South Carolina Historical Society, Charleston.

2. Philip Porcher, Apr. 1782, 1782–3, GA Petitions; Edgar and Bailey, *Directory S.C. House Rep.*, 2:534; Inhabitants of St. Stephen's Parish in Support of Philip Porcher, 1783–10, GA Petitions.

3. Inhabitants of St. Stephen's Parish and Others, 1783–59; Philip Porcher, 1785–39, 1785–29, 1788–62, GA Petitions.

4. Edgar and Bailey, *Directory S.C. House Rep.*, 3:568–69; Philip Porcher Inn, http: //bbonline.com/sc/porcher/; Porter and Prince, *Frommer's Portable Charleston*, 54–56.

5. Report of the Commissioners on the Petition of John Deas, Esq., enclosed with Oct. 1783 letter to Commissioners, Box 4, Miscellaneous Papers Relating to Claims on Estates, Commissioners of Forfeited Estates, Comptroller General Papers, S 126170, SCDAH.

6. Ibid.

7. Trish Loughran argued that the print culture of early America was not national but local and regional. If so, Charleston would still support a statewide print culture that allowed opinion makers to shape a cultural consensus in favoring governmental and community reconciliation. Loughran, *Republic in Print*; Holton, *Forced Founders*.

8. Christopher Gadsden to Gen. Francis Marion, Nov. 17, 1782, in Walsh, *Gadsden Writings*, xxv, 194–97; Godbold and Woody, *Christopher Gadsden*.

9. Aedanus Burke to Arthur Middleton, May 14, 1782, in Barnwell, "Middleton Corr. 1," 200.

10. Gadsden and Burke both attributed anti-Loyalist sentiments to a conspiracy involving Rutledge and his brother Edward, although Gadsden thought they manipulated politics in order to make money while Burke thought they simply were willing to wring every cent they could out of their offices. Burke, *Address*, 16–17, 24.

11. Ibid., 7.

12. Ibid., 28–32.

13. Aedanus Burke, Charge to the Grand Jury of Ninety Six District, Nov. 26, 1783, *South Carolina Gazette and General Advertiser*, Dec. 18, 1783 (hereinafter 96 Grand Jury); Burke, *Address*, 25.

14. Burke, 96 Grand Jury; Barnwell, "Middleton Correspondence 1," 200.

15. Burke, 96 Grand Jury; Aedanus Burke's Charge to the Grand Jury, June 9, 1783, *South Carolina Gazette and General Advertiser*, June 10, 1783; Walsh, *Gadsden Writings*, 197.

16. Grubb, "Growth of Literacy," 454; Murray, "Family, Literacy Training," esp. 782–83.

17. Jacobs, "Treaty and the Tories," 62–68; *South Carolina Gazette and General Advertiser*, July 12, 1783, July 29, 1783; Walsh, *Charleston's Sons*, 113–17; Nadelhaft, *Disorders of War*, 97–110.

18. *South Carolina Gazette and General Advertiser*. See also July 19, 1783, and May 18, 1784.

19. *South Carolina Gazette and General Advertiser*, May 4, 1784.

20. Crary, *Price of Loyalty*, 391–92.

21. Henry Laurens to Countess of Huntingdon, Charleston, March 31, 1785, in Hamer, Rogers, and Chesnutt, *Laurens Papers*, 16:548; Olwell, *Masters, Slaves, and Subjects*, 262.

22. Krawczynski, "William Drayton's Journal," 202; Camden Orphan Society, Camden Records 1786–1812, South Caroliniana Library, University of South Carolina; Edgar and Bailey, *Directory S.C. House Rep.*, 2:375. Charlestonians also founded an orphan society at the same time, although they seem to have regarded it as a way to teach working-class children to behave more like the elite. Thomas Jefferson, Elementary Education Act, 1817, as reprinted in James Bryant Conant, *Thomas Jefferson and the Development of American Public Education* (Berkeley: University of California Press, 1962), 125.

23. I am relying on Robert Lambert's estimates that 4,200 white Loyalists registered to leave with the convoys by the middle of August 1782, according to British military records and the correspondence of British commanders in Charleston. Lambert, *South Carolina Loyalists*, 254.

24. Edward Rutledge to Arthur Middleton, Cane Acre, April 23, 1782, in Barnwell, "Middleton Correspondence 2," 14. Virginia and Pennsylvania Loyalists used the same strategy of "parking" their families on the lands to create a stronger claim. Hast, *Loyalism in Revolutionary Virginia*, 127–31; Ousterhout, *State Divided*, 218–20; Margaret Cunningham, 1785–6, GA Petitions; Adams and Lumpkin, *House J. 1785–1786*, 78, 167–68; Andrew Cunningham, File no. 1686B, Reel 29, Frames 488– , Accounts Audited

of Claims Growing out of the Revolution in South Carolina, 1775–1856, SCDAH.

25. Act no. 1176, "An Act to Alter and Amend an Act Entitled 'An Act for disposing of certain Estates and banishing certain persons therein mentioned,'" in Cooper and McCord, *Statutes of S.C.*, 1:553–54; Act no. 1189, "An Ordinance for Disposing of the Estates of Certain Persons, Subjects and Adherents of the British Government; and for Other Purposes Therein Mentioned," March 17, 1783, in ibid., 1:568–70.

26. Travers, *Celebrating the Fourth*, 39–41; *South Carolina Gazette and General Advertiser*, July 5, 1783.

27. *South Carolina Gazette and General Advertiser*, July 8, 1783.

28. Some telling examples include no. 54, Edith Rose; no. 53, Mary Philip; no. 58, Elizabeth Atkins; no. 55, Nicholas Laffilie; no. 61, McBeth [probably Alexander MacBeth], Testimonies and Notes, Petitions for Relief from Confiscation 1783–1784, General Assembly Free Conference Committee, S 165035, Papers of the General Assembly, SCDAH (hereinafter Free Conference Comm. Hearings).

29. No. 40, John Wigfall, Free Conference Comm. Hearings. Fraser testimony in support of Dr. Clitherall, in Fraser to Gibbs, Feb. 15, 1783, Box 4, Misc. Papers Relating to Claims on Estates, Commissioners of Forfeited Estates, Comptroller General Papers, S 126170, SCDAH; and John Floyd to Honorable Gibbes, Feb. 14, 1783, Folder: Forfeited Estates, Miscellaneous, Box 4, Miscellaneous Papers Relating to Claims on Estates, Commissioners of Forfeited Estates, Series 126170, Comptroller General Papers, SCDAH.

30. No. 123, John Wagoner recommitted, Free Conference Comm. Hearings.

31. Walsh, *Sons of Liberty*, 97–98. No. 59, James Mackie; no. 122, David Sayler recommitted; no. 104, William McKinney; no. 70, James Rugge, Free Conference Comm. Hearings; Thompson and Lumpkin, *House J. 1783–1784*, 221.

32. No. 68, John Forsyth; no. 71, James Gordon; no. 66, Robert Muncrief Jun., Free Conference Comm. Hearings.

33. No. 68, John Forsyth, Free Conference Comm. Hearings.

34. Henry Laurens to William Manning, Paris, Dec. 4, 1782, in Hamer, Rogers, and Chesnutt, *Laurens Papers*, 16:67.

35. Thompson and Lumpkin, *House J. 1783–1784*, 400–402.

36. No. 50, Edmund Ellis Reconsidered, Feb. 13, Feb. 14, 1784; John Gaillard, Feb. 14, Feb. 23, Feb. 24, 1784, Testimonies and Notes, Petitions for Relief from Confiscation 1783-1784, General Assembly Free Conference Committee, S 165035, Papers of the General Assembly, South Carolina Department of Archives and History (hereinafter Free Conference Comm. Meeting).

37. Act no. 1299, "An Act for Restoring to Certain Persons, Therein Mentioned, Their Estates, Both Real and Personal, and for Permitting The Said Persons to Return to this State," March 26, 1783, in Cooper and McCord, *Statutes of S.C.*, 1:624–26; Edgar and Bailey, *Directory S.C. House Rep.*, 4:139–40.

38. For example John Champneys, the Loyalist merchant who was warned off in 1784, was not relieved of confiscation until 1789. James Cook never gained traction for clemency—only relief for his wife generated any serious discussion. Act no. 1435, in Cooper and McCord, *Statutes of S.C.*, 5:94; John Lewis Gervais to Henry Laurens,

Charleston, Apr. 15, 1784, in Chesnutt and Taylor, *Laurens Papers,* 16:430; *South Carolina Gazette and General Advertiser,* Apr. 29, 1784.

39. John Lewis Gervais to Henry Laurens, Charleston, Apr. 15, 1784, in Hamer, Rogers, and Chesnutt, *Laurens Papers,* 16:431; *South Carolina Gazette and General Advertiser,* Apr. 29, 1784; Walsh, *Sons of Liberty,* 120; Edwards, *Privy Council Journals,* 117.

40. John Lewis Gervais to Henry Laurens, Charleston, May 5, 1784, in Hamer, Rogers, and Chesnutt, *Laurens Papers,* 16:450; *Gazette of the State of South Carolina,* Apr. 29, 1784; Nadelhaft, *Disorders of War,* 11; *South Carolina Gazette and General Advertiser,* May 11, 1784.

41. Gervais to Laurens, Charleston, May 5, 1784, in Hamer, Rogers, and Chesnutt, *Laurens Papers,* 16:450.

42. Van Buskirk, *Generous Enemies;* Tiedemann, "Patriots, Loyalists," 80; Zeichner, "Loyalist Problem in New York," esp. 298. In New York treatment of Loyalists became a major issue between rising political factions, which made it difficult for those promoting Loyalist rehabilitation to prevail.

43. Rachel Klein has convincingly argued that South Carolina's backcountry elite solidified their control during the Regulator movement before the American Revolution. Klein, *Unification of a Slave State.*

44. One caveat: David E. Maas suggests that while Massachusetts drew an increasingly hard line against the Loyalists in the 1780s, they were able to do this in part because they had actually confiscated very few estates. He estimates that 87 percent of Loyalist estates were left unmolested. Of course South Carolina also did not confiscate the estate of every Loyalist, either. Maas, "Massachusetts Loyalists"; Maas, *Return of the Massachusetts Loyalists,* 318.

45. Van Buskirk, *Generous Enemies,* esp. 210–11; Chopra, *Unnatural Rebellion,* 211–15.

46. W. Brown, *Good Americans,* 228–29; Lambert, "Confiscation of Loyalist Property," 84; DeMond, *Loyalists in North Carolina,* 166–68; Harrell, *Loyalism in Virginia.*

47. Hast, *Loyalism in Revolutionary Virginia,* esp. 168–69. Alfred Fabian Young has pointed out that a majority of all Loyalists, not just southern Loyalists, chose to stay after the American Revolution. Young, *Democratic Republicans,* 66. I originally found his estimate of these numbers in Chopra, *Unnatural Rebellion,* 220n162. For a recent survey of the situation in North Carolina, see Lucas, "Cooling by Degrees," esp. chap. 3.

48. Ousterhout, *State Divided,* 217–19; Siebert, *Loyalists of Pennsylvania,* 86–90. Oscar Zeichner did not emphasize (or even recognize) how unusual Connecticut's experience was compared to the states that surrounded it. Zeichner, "Rehabilitiation of Loyalists," 319–28; Weir, "'Harmony We Were Famous For.'"

49. It may seem contradictory to assert that North Carolina's reconciliation was both harsher and more limited than South Carolina's and that it did happen. Jeffrey Lucas has argued that North Carolinians did gradually reintegrate Loyalists, but he agrees with earlier historians that they proceeded legislatively case by case instead of using an omnibus bill. In fact because of the individual nature of the reintegration, North Carolina's example shows how rare South Carolina's experience was. Lucas, "Cooling by Degrees."

50. Coker, "Punishment of Loyalists," 459–61.

51. Barnwell, "Middleton Correspondence 1"; Garden, *Anecdotes of the Revolutionary War in America,* 179.

52. Reilly, "Confiscation and Sale"; R. D. Brown, "Confiscation and Disposition"; Yoshpe, *Disposition of Loyalist Estates.*

53. Godbold and Woody, *Christopher Gadsden,* 227–28; Coker, "Punishment of Loyalists," 298; Walsh, *Gadsden Writings,* 195–96.

54. Charles Atkins, 1785–34, GA Petitions; Adams and Lumpkin, *House J. 1785–1786,* 135–36. Kathy Roe Coker's research indicates that Atkins was relieved of confiscation in 1785, but I did not find persuasive evidence to that effect. Coker, "Punishment of Loyalists."

Edward Fenwicke petitioned in 1785 and 1786 in order to gain the right to return to South Carolina eventually and secure his estate. I have found no evidence that he formally regained his citizenship until the 1790 constitution swept away the last of the anti-Loyalist restrictions. Feb. 5 and 9, 1785, Governor's Messages, Records of the General Assembly, SCDAH; Edward Fenwicke, 1786–54, GA Petitions; Committee Report on Edward Fenwicke's Petition, 1786–11, GA Petitions.

Kathy Roe Coker's research found fifty-one new Loyalist petitioners after 1784, and she indicates that 45 percent of those were successful. My research only uncovered six men who found relief based on the official legislative acts before 1790. She used relief after 1790 as well, which may be part of the difference. I did not use post-1790 material because the constitution regularized the status of former Loyalists. Coker, "Punishment of Loyalists," 452.

55. Adams and Lumpkin, *House J. 1785–1786,* 107–8, 134; Stevens and Allen, *House J. 1787–1788,* 487.

56. John Cunningham, 1787–51, 1786–25, 1786–27, 1789–19, 1791–99, GA Petitions; Adams and Lumpkin, *House J. 1785–1786,* 106–7, 228, 235, 436; Stevens and Allen, *House J. 1787–1788,* 153, 458. John Cunningham had appealed to the South Carolina legislature and the British Loyalist Claims Commission simultaneously. Lorenzo Sabine, *American Loyalists,* 235; Palmer, *Biographical Sketches,* 195; James Clitherall, 1783–189, 1785–66, 1785–75, 1785–47, 1786–34, 1787–34, 1791–92, 1792–185, 1793–67, 1794–22, 1794–137, 1794–111, 1798–30, GA Petitions.

57. Sixteen Loyalist petitions were found, while eighteen Loyalists were offered relief. The "missing" petitioners may have submitted petitions that are now lost. Alternatively they may have pursued relief through back channels, including soliciting friends. Adams and Lumpkin, *House J. 1785–1786,* 186–88.

58. Stevens and Allen, *House J. 1787–1788,* 196, 324–25; William Valentine, 1788–17, GA Petitions.

59. Rules of the Camden Orphan Society, July 4, 1786, Camden Orphan Society, Camden Records 1786–1812, South Caroliniana Library, University of South Carolina.

60. Bragg, *Crescent Moon over Carolina,* 224–25.

61. Edgar and Bailey, *Directory S.C. House Rep.,* 2: 698–99; Church of the Holy Cross Vestry Minutes (including a pew chart), SCDAH.

Chapter Five: (Mis)Remembering the Founding Moment

1. David Moltke-Hansen, "Why History Mattered: The Background of Ann Pamela Cunningham's Interest in the Preservation of Mt. Vernon," *Furman Studies* 26 (December 1980): 34–42.

2. Glenny, *Fall of Yugoslavia;* Wingfield, *Flag Wars and Stone Saints.*

3. Waldstreicher, *Midst of Perpetual Fetes;* Purcell, *Sealed with Blood,* 3.

4. Charles Caleb Cotton qtd. in Travers, *Celebrating the Fourth,* 38; Ball, *Slaves in the Family,* 8–9.

5. For a full discussion of the importance of public commemoration in the new Republic, see Waldstreicher, *Midst of Perpetual Fetes;* Travers, *Celebrating the Fourth;* Purcell, *Sealed with Blood.*

6. Waldstreicher, *Midst of Perpetual Fetes,* 9.

7. Huff, "Nationalism in 4th of July"; Travers, *Celebrating the Fourth,* 62–65.

8. Edward Hooker qtd. in *Celebrating the Fourth,* 145–48; Waldstreicher, *Midst of Perpetual Fetes,* 314.

9. Ramsay, *1820 Independence Day Oration,* 3, 24; Newton, "Three Patterns," 145–46.

10. Ramsay, *1820 Independence Day Oration,* 24. I searched all of the published orations in the South Carolina newspapers and published separately and have found no other mention of loyalism. See W. Smith, *Oration,* 4–8; Tucker, *Oration;* Desaussure, *Oration.*

11. Ramsay, *1820 Independence Day Oration,* 32.

12. Eustace, *1812.*

13. *The Carolina and Georgia Almanack or Ephemeris for the Year of Our Lord 1783, Being the Third after Leap-Year, and the Seventh of American Independence* (Charlestown, 1783). Representative almanacs include *S. C. Almanack; S.C. and Georgia Almanack 1784; Carolina Almanack; S.C. and Georgia Almanack 1793; Carolina and Georgia Almanac 1796; Mirror Almanac.* All of these can be found in the Book Division of the South Caroliniana Library.

14. Chambers, *Memories of War.*

15. I searched all of the South Carolina archival repositories as well as published sources. There does not seem to be any earlier battlefield commemorations other than Palmetto Day. I suppose it is possible that another commemoration will turn up at some point in some other archive, but there are no references in any secondary sources, either. There is a historical marker at King's Mountain dated to 1819, but there are no records of when and how it was placed.

16. *Proceedings of a Celebration of Huck's Defeat.*

17. Ibid., 2.

18. Ibid., 4–5.

19. Preston, *King's Mountain,* 2, 4.

20. Ibid., 4, 26–27, 36–37, 46, 51.

21. D.R. Atchinson letter to King's Mountain memorial celebrants, Platte City, Missouri, Sept. 12, 1855, in Preston, *King's Mountain,* 88. For the celebratory toasts and

boasts, see John Preston's address in Preston, *King's Mountain*, 49 and 56. For evidence from George Bancroft's speech to the crowd, see Preston, *King's Mountain*, 76-80.

22. Preston, *King's Mountain*, 16.

23. No. 5, William Blake (on Amercement), Free Conference Comm. Meeting.

24. The evidence on multigenerational integration and acceptance is limited in large part because almost no one has considered the issue at length. Recent dissertations and theses suggest the evidence is out there. See Palfreyman, "Peace Process"; Lucas, "Cooling by Degrees"; Coleman, "Loyalists in War"; Stoney, "Frederick Porcher Memoirs," 142–44; New, *Maryland Loyalists*, xi, 121–22.

25. Edgar and Bailey, *Directory S.C. House Rep.*, 4:139–40; appendix on Cunningham family in Ward, *Samuel Curwen Papers*, 618–38.

26. O'Neall, *Biographical Sketches*, 395–96; William Gilmore Simms to Benjamin Franklin Perry, Woodlands, Oct. 30, 1846, in Oliphant, Odell, and Eaves, *Simms Letters*, 2:202.

27. O'Neall, *Biographical Sketches*, 399–400.

28. John Cunningham to John C. Calhoun, Abbeville Court House, Oct. 15, 1846, in Meriwether, Hemphill, and Wilson, *Calhoun Papers*, 23:492–94. Calhoun did provide John with a letter of introduction to a former Louisiana governor. Calhoun to Alexander Mouton, Nov. 8, 1846, in ibid., 23:532.

29. Moltke-Hansen, "Why History Mattered," 36–38.

30. Ward, *Samuel Curwen Papers*, 634–38.

31. Moltke-Hansen, "Why History Mattered," 38; Simms, "Civil Warfare," pts. 1–3; "Biographical Sketch," pts. 1–2, 513, 516.

32. James Henry Hammond to William Gilmore Simms, Jan. 28, 1847, in Oliphant, Odell, and Eaves, *Simms Letters*, 2:260n27.

33. Ann Pamela Cunningham's brother John even challenged Simms to a duel in defense of his sister's honor. Simms to Benjamin Franklin Perry, Oct. 30, 1846 in Oliphant, Odell, and Eaves, *Simms Letters*, 2:200–203; Simms to Perry, May 20, 1847, in ibid., 317–18.

34. Robert Cunningham to John C. Calhoun, Laurens District, Nov. 19, 1846; Calhoun to Cunningham, Nov. 25, 1846, in Meriwether, Hemphill, and Wilson, *Calhoun Papers*, 23: 543–51.

35. Ellet, *Women of the Revolution;* West, *Domesticating History*, 1–15; Hosmer, *Presence of the Past*, 41–49; Howe, "Ann Pamela Cunningham's Legacy."

36. Chambers, *Memories of War;* Sears, *Sacred Places*.

37. Kermes, "'I Wish for Nothing,'" 48; Coker, "Punishment of Loyalists," 195–203; *Charleston Year Book* (Charleston, 1884), 166.

38. Stoney, "Frederick Porcher Memoirs," 65–67.

39. Ibid., 142–44.

40. Simms's seven Revolutionary novels, ordered by the events they portray, are *The Partisan* (1835), *Mellichampe* (1836), *Katherine Walton* (1851), *The Kinsmen* (1841, later renamed *The Scout*), *The Forayers* (1855), *Eutaw* (1856), and *The Sword and the Distaff* (1852, renamed *Woodcraft*). For more on the literary influences on Simms, see Wimsatt, *Major Fiction*, 64; Holman, "Influence of Scott"; Holman, "Simms' Picture," 443–47.

Mel Gibson's performance in *The Patriot* has become the way today's Americans understand the American Revolution in the South.

41. Sabine, *American Loyalists;* Busick, *Sober Desire for History,* 82–87.

42. *Mellichampe* qtd. in Busick, *Sober Desire for History,* 73–74; Simms, *Woodcraft,* 211.

43. Sean R. Busick disagrees with this assessment of Simms, arguing instead that he was sympathetic to Loyalists. Yet he agrees that they are almost always drawn from the lower classes and painted as driven by class-based revenge against the lowcountry elite. Busick, *Sober Desire for History,* 73–74; Brichford, "That National Story," 75; Simms, *Partisan,* 2:129–32.

44. Holman, "Simms's Changing Views."

Epilogue

1. No. 5 William Blake (on Amercement), Free Conference Comm. Meeting, SCDAH.

2. Handler and Gable, *New History in an Old Museum.*

3. Christopher Gadsden to General Francis Marion, Nov. 17, 1782, in Walsh, *Gadsden Writings,* 197.

Bibliography

Archival Materials

DAVID LIBRARY OF THE AMERICAN REVOLUTION

American Loyalist Claims, Great Britain, Treasury
Thomas Burke Papers, 1763–1852
Byles Family Papers, 1757–1837
Dartmouth Collection
Sol Feinstone Collection
John Floyd Letters, 1775–1786
Peter Horry Collection (Peter Force Papers 1683–1789)
Gideon Dupont Bundle
Arthur Middleton Papers, 1767–1783
Misc. Docs Relating to Refugees, 1780–1836, Great Britain, Treasury
Parker Family Papers 1760–1795
Charles Cotesworth Pinckney Papers, 1775–1817
Papers of the American Loyalist Claims Commission, 1780–1835, Great Britain, Audit
    Office
Revolutionary War Pension and Bounty-Land-Warrant Application Files, United
    States
John Rutledge Letters, 1780–1782

SOUTH CAROLINA DEPARTMENT OF ARCHIVES AND HISTORY

Accounts Audited of Claims Growing out of the Revolution in South Carolina, 1775–
    1856
American Loyalist Claims (Public Records Office, SCDAH microfilm)
Cane Creek Monthly Meeting Society of Friends
Commissioners of Forfeited Estates, Comptroller General Papers
Comptroller General, Committee to Adjust Public Accounts Letterbook
Comptroller General, Forfeited Estates Plats
Comptroller General Papers, Commissioners of Forfeited Estates
Comptroller General Papers, Papers Relating to Claims on Estates
Comptroller General Papers, Plats
Colonial Plat Books (Copy Series)
Executive Journals of South Carolina, 1800–1802

General Assembly Free Conference Committee Concerned with Petitions from Relief from the Confiscation Act of 1782
General Assembly, Petitions
Governor's Letterbooks
Governor's Messages
Pacolet (Skull Shoals) Baptist Church
Records, Bush River Monthly Meeting
South Carolina Commissioners of the Treasury, Letters
South Carolina Court of Common Pleas, Judgment Rolls (Charleston)
South Carolina General Assembly Papers
South Carolina Governor Received Correspondence
South Carolina Petitions to the General Assembly
South Carolina Senate Journals (rough and engrossed journals)
South Carolina Tax Returns, 1783–87
Stoney Creek Independent Baptist Church
Stoney Creek Independent Presbyterian Church
York County, Minutes of the Proceedings of the County and Intermediate Court, Journals, WPA Transcripts

SOUTH CAROLINA HISTORICAL SOCIETY

Ball Family Documents Series
Samuel Bonsall Petition
Edward Fenwick Letter, 1783
Gibbes Family Papers
Memorial of Isabella MacLaurin, 1784
Material Relating to America from the Ogilvie-Forbes of Boyndlie Papers
Richard Pearis Loyalist Claims
Pinckney Family Papers
Porcher Family Papers
Rugeley Papers
Edward Rutledge Papers
James Simpson Papers

SOUTH CAROLINIANA LIBRARY

William Ancrum Papers
Nisbet Balfour Papers
Bethabara Baptist Church
Black Creek Baptist Church
Bush River Baptist Church
Padgett's Creek Baptist Church
Thomas Bee Letters
Samuel Boykin Affidavit
Calhoun Family Papers, 1758–1843
Camden Orphan Society Records, 1786–1876

Alexander Chesney Journal
Christopher Gadsden Papers
Mordecai Gist/Margaret Adams Gist Papers
Oliver Hart Papers
John Jeffries Papers
Kings Mountain Centennial Association Records
Francis Marion Papers
Samuel Mathis Journal
Methodist Church Records
Lynch's Creek Circuit, Darlington County Methodist Church
William Moultrie Papers
Moultrie-Montague Letters
Mount Sion Society, 1783–1784
William Murrell Papers
Bethesda, York County Presbyterian Church
Fairfield County, Mt. Olivet Presbyterian Church
Salem, Black River Presbyterian Church
John Rutledge Papers
John Simpson Papers
Matthew Singleton Papers
South Carolina Royalist Troops Muster Rolls
Stone Family Papers
William Tennent III Papers

Published Primary Sources

The Gentleman's Compleat Military Dictionary, Containing the Military Art. Boston, 1759.
The South Carolina and Georgia Almanack or Ephemeris for the Year of Our Lord 1783, Being the Third after Leap-Year, and the Seventh of American Independence. Charlestown, S.C., 1783.
South Carolina and Georgia Almanack. Charleston, S.C., 1784.
The Carolina and Georgia Almanack or Astronomical Diary. Charleston, S.C., 1787.
South Carolina and Georgia Almanack. Charleston, S.C., 1793.
South Carolina and Georgia Almanac. Charleston, S.C., 1795.
The Palladium of Knowledge, or the Carolina and Georgia Almanac. Charleston, S.C., 1796.
The Mirror or Carolina and Georgia Almanac. Charleston, S.C., 1804.
Proceedings of a Celebration of Huck's Defeat, at Brattonsville, York District, South Carolina, July 12, 1839. Brattonsville, S.C., 1839.
Adams, Lark Emerson, and Rosa S. Lumpkin, eds. *Journals of the House of Representatives, 1785–1786.* Columbia: Published for the South Carolina Department of Archives and History by the University of South Carolina Press, 1979.
Barnwell, Joseph W., ed. "Correspondence of Hon. Arthur Middleton, Signer of the Declaration of Independence." *South Carolina Historical and Genealogical Magazine* 26, no. 4 (1925): 183–213. Cited in notes as "Middleton Correspondence 1."

———. "Correspondence of Hon. Arthur Middleton." *South Carolina Historical and Genealogical Magazine* 27, no. 1 (1926): 1–29. Cited in notes as "Middleton Correspondence 2."

———. "Correspondence of Hon. Arthur Middleton." *South Carolina Historical and Genealogical Magazine* 27, no. 2 (1926): 51–80. Cited in notes as "Middleton Correspondence 3."

Bland, Humphrey. *A Treatise of Military Discipline; in Which Is Laid Down and Explained the Duty of an Officer and Soldier.* 4th ed. London, 1740.

Brown, Alan S. "James Simpson's Reports on the Carolina Loyalists, 1779–1780." *Journal of Southern History* 21, no. 4 (1955): 513–19.

Burke, Aedanus. *An Address to the Freemen of the State of South-Carolina.* Philadelphia, 1783.

Collins, James P. "Autobiography of a Revolutionary Soldier." In *Sixty Years in the Nueces Valley, 1870 to 1930,* edited by S. G. Miller. San Antonio, Tex.: Naylor, 1930.

Cooper, Thomas, and David J. McCord, eds. *Statutes at Large of South Carolina.* 10 vols. Columbia: Johnston, 1836–41.

Crary, Catherine S., ed. *The Price of Loyalty: Tory Writings from the Revolutionary Era.* New York: McGraw-Hill, 1973.

Cuthbertson, Bennett. *A System for the Complete Interior Management and Oeconomy of a Battalion of Infantry.* 2nd ed. London, 1779.

de Roulhac Hamilton, J. G. "King's Mountain: Letters of Colonel Isaac Shelby." *Journal of Southern History* 4, no. 3 (1938): 367–77.

Desaussure, Henry William. *An Oration, Prepared, to Be Delivered in St. Phillip's Church, before the Inhabitants of Charleston, South-Carolina, on the Fourth of July, 1798, in Commemoration of American Independence.* Charleston, S.C., 1798.

Drayton, John, and William Henry Drayton. *Memoirs of the American Revolution as Relating to the State of South Carolina.* 2 vols. New York: New York Times, 1969.

Edwards, Adele Stanton. *Journals of the Privy Council, 1783–1789.* Columbia: Published for the South Carolina Department of Archives and History by the University of South Carolina Press, 1971.

Ellet, Elizabeth. *Women of the American Revolution.* 3 vols. New York, 1856.

Fanning, David. *The Narrative of Col. David Fanning.* Edited by Lindley S. Butler. Davidson, N.C.: Briarpatch, 1981.

Garden, Alexander. *Anecdotes of the Revolutionary War in America, with Sketches of Character of Persons the Most Distinguished, in the Southern States, for Civil and Military Services.* Charleston, S.C.: Miller, 1822.

Gibbes, Robert Wilson. *Documentary History of the American Revolution.* 3 vols. New York: New York Times, 1971.

Gilbert, Felix. "Letters of Francis Kinloch to Thomas Boone 1782–1788." *Journal of Southern History* 8, no. 1 (1942): 87–105.

Gilman, Caroline, ed. *Letters of Eliza Wilkinson.* New York: Arno, 1969.

Gregg, Alexander, and John Julius Dargan. *History of the Old Cheraws; Containing an Account of the Aborigines of the Pedee, the First White Settlements, Their Subsequent Progress, Civil Changes, the Struggle of the Revolution, and Growth of the Country*

Afterward, Extending from About A.D. 1730 to 1810, with Notices of Families and Sketches of Individuals. Rpt. of the enlarged ed. of 1925 with addenda. Baltimore: Genealogical Publishing, 1967.

Hamer, Philip M., George C. Rogers, and David R. Chesnutt, eds. *The Papers of Henry Laurens.* 16 vols. Columbia: Published for the South Carolina Historical Society by the University of South Carolina Press, 1968–.

Hemphill, William Edwin, Wylma Anne Wates, and R. Nicholas Olsberg, eds. *Journals of the General Assembly and House of Representatives, 1776–1780.* Columbia: Published for the South Carolina Department of Archives and History by the University of South Carolina Press, 1970.

Hill, D. H., Col. *William Hill and the Campaign of 1780.* N.p., 1919.

Holcomb, Brent. *Edgefield County, South Carolina, Minutes of the County Court, 1785–1795.* Easley, S.C.: Southern Historical Press, 1979.

———. *Newberry County, South Carolina Minutes of the County Court, 1785–1798.* Easley, S.C.: Southern Historical Press, 1977.

———. *Probate Records of South Carolina.* Easley, S.C.: Southern Historical Press, 1977.

———. *Some South Carolina County Records.* Easley, S.C.: Southern Historical Press, 1976.

———. *Two 1787 Tax Lists: Ninety Six District, South Carolina.* Clinton, S.C.: Holcomb, 1974.

———. *York County, South Carolina Will Abstracts: 1787–1862.* Columbia, S.C.: SCMAR, 2002.

Holcomb, Brent, and Elmer O. Parker. *Camden District, S.C., Wills and Administrations, 1781–1787 (1770–1796).* Easley, S.C.: Southern Historical Press, 1978.

Hooker, Richard James, ed. *The Carolina Backcountry on the Eve of the Revolution: The Journal and Other Writings of Charles Woodmason, Anglican Itinerant.* Chapel Hill: University of North Carolina Press, 1953.

Jones, E. Alfred, and Wilbur Henry Siebert, eds. *The Journal of Alexander Chesney, a South Carolina Loyalist in the Revolution and After.* Rpt., Columbus: Ohio State University, 1921.

King, Susan L., ed. *History and Records of the Charleston Orphan House 1790–1860.* Easley, S.C., 1984.

Kolb, Wade S., III, and Robert M. Weir, eds. *Captured at Kings Mountain: The Journal of Uzal Johnson, a Loyalist Surgeon.* Columbia: University of South Carolina Press, 2011.

Krawczynski, Keith, ed. "William Drayton's Journal of a 1784 Tour of the South Carolina Backcountry." *South Carolina Historical Magazine* 97, no. 3 (1996): 182–205.

La Valiere, Chevalier de. *The Art of War.* Philadelphia, 1776.

Maxcy, Jonathan. *A Discourse, Delivered in the Chapel of the South-Carolina College, July 4th, A.D. 1819, at the Request of the Inhabitants of Columbia.* Columbia, S.C., 1819.

Meriwether, Robert Lee, William Edwin Hemphill, and Clyde Norman Wilson, eds. *The Papers of John C. Calhoun.* 28 vols. Columbia: Published by the University of South Carolina Press for the South Caroliniana Society, 1959– .

Merrens, Harry Roy. *The Colonial South Carolina Scene: Contemporary Views, 1697–1774*. Columbia: University of South Carolina Press, 1977.

Meyer, Jack Allen. *The Mount Sion Society of Charleston and Winnsboro, South Carolina, 1777–1825*. Winnsboro, S.C., 1978.

Moultrie, William. *Memoirs of the American Revolution*. 2 vols. New York: Longworth, 1802.

Oliphant, Mary C. Simms, Alfred Taylor Odell, and T. C. Duncan Eaves, eds. *The Letters of William Gilmore Simms*. 5 vols. Columbia: University of South Carolina Press, 1952– .

Preston, John S. *Celebration of the Battle of King's Mountain*. Yorkville, S.C., 1855.

Ramsay, David. *An Address Delivered on the Fourth of July, 1820*. Charleston, S.C.: W.P. Young and Son, 1820.

———. *An Address to the Freemen of South-Carolina, on the Subject of the Federal Constitution, Proposed by the Convention, Which Met in Philadelphia, May 1787*. Charleston, S.C.: Bowen, 1788.

———. *A Chronological Table of the Principal Events Which Have Taken Place in the English Colonies, Now United States, from 1607, till 1810*. Charlestown, S.C.: Hoff, 1811.

———. *History of South Carolina: From Its First Settlement in 1670 to the Year 1808*. 2 vols. Newberry, S.C.: Duffie, 1858. Rpt., Spartanburg, S.C.: Reprint Co., 1959.

———. *An Oration, Delivered on the Anniversary of American Independence, July 4, 1794, in Saint Michael's Church, to the Inhabitants of Charleston, South Carolina*. London 1795.

Ramsay, David, and Charles Colcock Jones. *The History of the American Revolution*. Philadelphia: Aitken, 1789.

Robertson, William Spence, ed. *The Diary of Francisco De Miranda, Tour of the United States, 1783–1784*. New York: [Hispanic Society of America], 1928.

Rutledge, John. *The Speech of His Excellency John Rutledge, Esquire, Governor and Commander in Chief of the State of South-Carolina, to the General Assembly, Met at Jacksonburgh, on Friday the 18th Day of January, 1782*. Jacksonborough, S.C., 1782.

Ryan, Frank. "Travelers in South Carolina in the Eighteenth Century." In *City of Charleston Year Book*. Charleston, S.C., 1945.

Salley, A. S. *Col. William Hill's Memoirs of the Revolution*. Columbia: Historical Commission of South Carolina, 1921.

Salley, A. S., ed. *Journal of the House of Representatives of South Carolina, January 8, 1782–February 26, 1782*. Columbia: State Company for the Historical Commission of South Carolina, 1916.

———, ed. *Journal of the Senate of South Carolina January 8, 1782–February 26, 1782*. Columbia: Historical Commission of South Carolina, 1941.

Showman, Richard K., ed. *The Papers of General Nathanael Greene*. 13 vols. Chapel Hill: University of North Carolina Press, 1976.

Simes, Thomas. *The Military Guide for Young Officers*. 2 vols. Philadelphia, 1776.

Simms, William Gilmore. "Biographical Sketch of the Career of Major William Cunningham of South Carolina, Part I." *Southern Literary Messenger* 12, no. 9 (1846): 513–24.

———. "Biographical Sketch of the Career of Major William Cunningham, Part II." *Southern Literary Messenger* 12, no. 10 (1846): 577–86.

———. "The Civil Warfare in the Carolinas and Georgia, Part I." *Southern Literary Messenger* 12, no. 5 (1846): 257–65.

———. "The Civil Warfare in the Carolinas and Georgia, during the Revolution, Part II." *Southern Literary Messenger* 12, no. 6 (1846): 321–36.

———. "The Civil Warfare in the Carolinas and Georgia, during the Revolution, Part III." *Southern Literary Messenger* 12, no. 7 (1846): 385–400.

———. *The Geography of South Carolina: Being a Companion to the History of That State.* Charleston, S.C.: Babcock, 1843.

———. *The History of South Carolina, from Its First European Discovery to Its Erection into a Republic.* Charleston, S.C.: Babcock, 1840.

———. *Katharine Walton, or, The Rebel of Dorchester.* Philadelphia: Hart, 1851.

———. *The Life of Francis Marion.* New York: Langley, 1844.

———. *The Life of Nathanael Greene, Major-General in the Army of the Revolution.* New York: Derby & Jackson, 1861.

———. *The Partisan.* 2 vols. New York: Harper, 1835.

———. *South-Carolina in the Revolutionary War; Being a Reply to Certain Misrepresentations and Mistakes of Recent Writers in Relation to the Course and Conduct of This State.* Charleston, S.C.: Walker & James, 1853.

———. *Woodcraft; or, Hawks about the Dovecote; a Story of the South at the Close of the Revolution.* Rpt., Ridgewood, N.J.: Gregg, 1968.

Smith, William. *An Oration, Delivered in St. Philip's Church, before the Inhabitants of Charleston, South-Carolina, on the Fourth of July, 1796, in Commemoration of American Independence.* Charleston, S.C.: Young, 1796.

Stevens, Michael E., ed. *Journals of the House of Representatives, 1792–1794.* Columbia: Published for the South Carolina Department of Archives and History by the University of South Carolina Press, 1988.

Stevens, Michael E., and Christine M. Allen, eds. *Journals of the House of Representatives, 1787–1788.* Columbia: Published for the South Carolina Department of Archives and History by the University of South Carolina Press, 1981.

———, eds. *Journals of the House of Representatives, 1789–1790.* Columbia: Published for the South Carolina Department of Archives and History by the University of South Carolina Press, 1984.

———, eds. *Journals of the House of Representatives, 1791.* Columbia: Published for the South Carolina Department of Archives and History by the University of South Carolina Press, 1985.

Stoney, Samuel Gaillard, ed. "The Memoirs of Frederick Augustus Porcher." *South Carolina Historical and Genealogical Magazine* 44, no. 2 (1943): 65–80.

Thompson, Theodora J., and Rosa S. Lumpkin, eds. *Journals of the House of Representatives, 1783–1784.* Columbia: Published for the South Carolina Department of Archives and History by the University of South Carolina Press, 1977.

Tucker, Thomas Tudor. *An Oration Delivered in St. Michael's Church, before the*

Inhabitants of Charleston, South-Carolina, on the 4th of July, 1795; in Commemoration of American Independence. Charleston, S.C., 1795.

United States Bureau of the Census. *Heads of Families at the First Census of the United States Taken in the Year 1790: South Carolina.* Baltimore: Genealogical Publishing, 1966.

Walsh, Richard, ed. *The Writings of Christopher Gadsden, 1746–1805.* Columbia: University of South Carolina Press, 1966.

Ward, George Atkinson. *The Journal and Letters of Samuel Curwen, an American in England, from 1775 to 1783.* 3rd ed. Boston: Little Brown, 1864.

Zubly, John Joachim, and Lilla Mills Hawes. *The Journal of the Reverend John Joachim Zubly, A.M., D.D., March 5, 1770 through June 22, 1781.* Savannah: Georgia Historical Society, 1989.

Secondary Sources

Anderson, Benedict R. *Imagined Communities: Reflections on the Origin and Spread of Nationalism.* Rev. ed. London: Verso, 2006.

Babits, Lawrence E. *A Devil of a Whipping: The Battle of Cowpens.* Chapel Hill: University of North Carolina Press, 1998.

Bacot, D. H. "South Carolina Middle Country at the End of the 18th Century." *South Atlantic Quarterly* 23, no. 1 (1924): 50–60.

———. "South Carolina up-Country at the End of the Eighteenth Century." *American Historical Review* 28, no. 4 (1923): 682–98.

Bailey, Raymond C. *Popular Influence upon Public Policy: Petitioning in Eighteenth-Century Virginia.* Westport, Conn.: Greenwood, 1979.

Bailyn, Bernard. *The Ordeal of Thomas Hutchinson.* Cambridge, Mass.: Belknap Press of Harvard University Press, 1974.

Ball, Edward. *Slaves in the Family.* New York: Farrar, Straus & Giroux, 1998.

Bannister, Jerry, and Liam Riordan. *The Loyal Atlantic: Remaking the British Atlantic in the Revolutionary Era.* Toronto: University of Toronto Press, 2012.

Bargar, B. D. "Charles Town Loyalism in 1775: The Secret Reports of Alexander Innes." *South Carolina Historical Magazine* 63, no. 3 (1962): 125–36.

Barnes, Timothy M. *Loyalist Newspapers of the American Revolution, 1763–1783: A Bibliography.* Worcester, Mass.: American Antiquarian Society, 1974.

Barnwell, Robert W. "Migration of Loyalists from South Carolina." *South Carolina Historical Association Proceedings* (1937): 34–42.

Bass, Robert D. *Ninety Six: The Struggle for the South Carolina Back Country.* Lexington, S.C.: Sandlapper, 1978.

Beeman, Richard R. *The Evolution of the Southern Backcountry: A Case Study of Lunenburg County, Virginia, 1746–1832.* Philadelphia: University of Pennsylvania Press, 1984.

———. *The Varieties of Political Experience in Eighteenth-Century America.* Philadelphia: University of Pennsylvania Press, 2004.

Beeman, Richard R., Stephen Botein, and Edward Carlos Carter, eds. *Beyond Confederation: Origins of the Constitution and American National Identity.* Chapel Hill: University of North Carolina Press, 1987.

Berger, Carl. *Broadsides and Bayonets: The Propaganda War of the American Revolution.* Philadelphia: University of Pennsylvania Press, 1961.

Blassingame, John W. "American Nationalism and Other Loyalties in the Southern Colonies, 1763–1775." *Journal of Southern History* 34, no. 1 (1968): 50–75.

Bloch, Ruth H. "The Gendered Meanings of Virtue in Revolutionary America." In "Women and the Political Process in the United States," special issue, *Signs* 13, no. 1 (1987): 37–58.

Bogin, Ruth. "Petitioning and the New Moral Economy of Post-Revolutionary America." *William and Mary Quarterly* 3rd ser., 45, no. 3 (1988): 391–425.

Bolton, S. Charles. *Southern Anglicanism: The Church of England in Colonial South Carolina.* Westport, Conn.: Greenwood, 1982.

Borick, Carl P. *A Gallant Defense: The Siege of Charleston, 1780.* Columbia: University of South Carolina Press, 2003.

———. *Relieve Us of This Burthen: American Prisoners of War in the Revolutionary South, 1780–1782.* Columbia: University of South Carolina Press, 2012.

Bowden, David K. *The Execution of Isaac Hayne.* Lexington, S.C.: Sandlapper, 1977.

Bragg, C. L. *Crescent Moon over Carolina: William Moultrie and American Liberty.* Columbia: University of South Carolina Press, 2013.

Brichford, Charles H. "That National Story: Conflicting Versions and Conflicting Visions of the Revolution in Kennedy's 'Horse-Shoe Robinson' and Simms's 'The Partisan.'" *Southern Literary Journal* 21, no. 1 (1988): 64–85.

Brinsfield, John Wesley. *Religion and Politics in Colonial South Carolina.* Easley, S.C.: Southern Historical Press, 1983.

Brown, Richard D. "The Confiscation and Disposition of Loyalists' Estates in Suffolk County, Massachusetts." *William and Mary Quarterly* 3rd ser., 21, no. 4 (1964): 534–50.

Brown, Richard Maxwell. *The South Carolina Regulators.* Cambridge, Mass.: Belknap Press of Harvard University Press, 1963.

———. *Strain of Violence: Historical Studies of American Violence and Vigilantism.* New York: Oxford University Press, 1975.

Brown, Wallace. *The Good Americans: The Loyalists in the American Revolution.* New York: Morrow, 1969.

———. *The King's Friends: The Composition and Motives of the American Loyalist Claimants.* Providence: Brown University Press, 1965.

———. "The View at Two Hundred Years: The Loyalists of the American Revolution." *Proceedings of the American Antiquarian Society* (1970): 25–47.

Buchanan, John. *The Road to Guilford Courthouse: The American Revolution in the Carolinas.* New York: Wiley, 1997.

Bull, Henry D. "A Note on James Stuart, Loyalist Clergyman in South Carolina." *Journal of Southern History* 12, no. 4 (1946): 570–75.

Busick, Sean R. *A Sober Desire for History: William Gilmore Simms as Historian.* Columbia: University of South Carolina Press, 2005.

Calhoon, Robert M. ———. "Aedanus Burke and Thomas Burke: Revolutionary Conservatism in the Carolinas." In *Tory Insurgency: The Loyalist Perception and Other*

Essays, edited by Robert M. Calhoon, Timothy M. Barnes, and Robert S. Davis, 334–49. Columbia: University of South Carolina Press, 2010.

————. *The Loyalists in Revolutionary America, 1760–1781.* New York: Harcourt Brace Jovanovich, 1973.

————. "The Reintegration of the Loyalists and the Disaffected." In *The American Revolution: Its Character and Limits,* edited by Jack P. Greene, 51–74. New York: New York University Press, 1987.

————. "Religion, Moderation, and Regime-Building in Post-Revolutionary America." In *Empire and Nation: The American Revolution in the Atlantic World,* edited by Eliga Gould and Peter S. Onuf, 217–36. Baltimore: Johns Hopkins University Press, 2005.

Calhoon, Robert M., Timothy M. Barnes, and George A. Rawlyck, eds. *Loyalists and Community in North America.* Westport, Conn.: Greenwood, 1994.

Carlsmith, Kevin M., Timothy D. Wilson, and Daniel T. Gilbert. "The Paradoxical Consequences of Revenge." *Journal of Personality and Social Psychology* 95, no. 6 (2008): 1316–24.

Carter, Jimmy. *The Hornet's Nest: A Novel of the Revolutionary War.* New York: Simon & Schuster, 2003.

Cashin, Edward J. *The King's Ranger: Thomas Brown and the American Revolution on the Southern Frontier.* Athens: University of Georgia Press, 1989.

————. *William Bartram and the American Revolution on the Southern Frontier.* Columbia: University of South Carolina Press, 2000.

Chambers, Thomas A. *Memories of War: Visiting Battlegrounds and Bonefields in the Early American Republic.* Ithaca, N.Y.: Cornell University Press, 2012.

Chaplin, Joyce E. *An Anxious Pursuit: Agricultural Innovation and Modernity in the Lower South, 1730–1815.* Chapel Hill: University of North Carolina Press, 1993.

Cheng, Eileen Ka-May. "American Historical Writers and the Loyalists, 1788–1856: Dissent, Consensus, and American Nationality." *Journal of the Early Republic* 23, no. 4 (2003): 491–519.

Chernow, Ron. *Alexander Hamilton.* New York: Penguin, 2004.

Chopra, Ruma. *Unnatural Rebellion: Loyalists in New York City during the Revolution.* Charlottesville: University of Virginia Press, 2011.

Clark, Jonathan. "The Problem of Allegiance in Revolutionary Poughkeepsie." In *Saints and Revolutionaries: Essays on Early American History,* edited by David D. Hall, John Murrin, and Thad W. Tate, 285–317. New York: Norton, 1984.

Clayton, J. Glenn. "South Carolina Baptist Records." *South Carolina Historical Magazine* 85, no. 4 (1984): 318–27.

Coker, Kathy Roe. "The Punishment of Revolutionary War Loyalists in South Carolina." Ph.D. diss., University of South Carolina, 1987.

Coleman, Aaron N. "Loyalists in War, Americans in Peace: The Reintegration of the Loyalists, 1775–1800." Ph.D. diss., University of Kentucky, 2008.

Côté, Richard N. *Local and Family History in South Carolina: A Bibliography.* Easley, S.C.: Southern Historical Press, 1981.

Côté, Richard N., and Patricia H. Williams. *Dictionary of South Carolina Biography*. Easley, S.C.: Southern Historical Press, 1985.

Countryman, Edward. *A People in Revolution: The American Revolution and Political Society in New York, 1760–1790*. Baltimore: Johns Hopkins University Press, 1981.

Cox, Caroline. *A Proper Sense of Honor: Service and Sacrifice in George Washington's Army*. Chapel Hill: University of North Carolina Press, 2004.

Crow, Jeffrey J. "Liberty Men and Loyalists: Disorder and Disaffection in the North Carolina Backcountry." In *An Uncivil War: The Southern Backcountry during the American Revolution*, edited by Ronald Hoffman, Thad W. Tate, and Peter J. Albert, 125–78. Charlottesville: University of Virginia Press, 1985.

———. "What Price Loyalism? The Case of John Cruden, Commissioner of Sequestered Estates." *North Carolina Historical Review* 58 (1981): 215–33.

Crow, Jeffrey J., and Larry E. Tise, eds. *The Southern Experience in the American Revolution*. Chapel Hill: University of North Carolina Press, 1978.

Dann, John C. *The Revolution Remembered: Eyewitness Accounts of the War for Independence*. Chicago: University of Chicago Press, 1980.

Davis, Robert Scott. "Loyalist Trials and Ninety Six in 1779." *South Carolina Historical Magazine* 80 (1979): 172–81.

Deas, Anne Simons. *Recollections of the Ball Family of South Carolina and the Comingtee Plantation*. Rpt., 1978 ed. Charleston: South Carolina Historical Society, 1909.

DeMond, Robert O. *The Loyalists in North Carolina during the Revolution*. Durham, N.C.: Duke University Press, 1940.

Ditz, Toby L. "Shipwrecked; or Masculinity Imperiled: Mercantile Representations of Failure and the Gendered Self in Eighteenth-Century Philadelphia." *Journal of American History* 81, no. 1 (1994): 51–80.

Draper, Lyman Copeland. *King's Mountain and Its Heroes: History of the Battle of King's Mountain, October 7th, 1780*. Cincinnati: Thompson, 1881.

Edgar, Walter. *Partisans and Redcoats: The Southern Conflict That Turned the Tide of the American Revolution*. New York: HarperCollins , 2001.

Edgar, Walter B., and N. Louise Bailey, eds. *Biographical Directory of the South Carolina House of Representatives*. 4 vols. Columbia: University of South Carolina Press, 1977.

Ekirch, A. Roger. "Whig Authority and Public Order in Backcountry North Carolina, 1776–1783." In *An Uncivil War: The Southern Backcountry during the American Revolution*, edited by Ronald Hoffman, Thad W. Tate, and Peter J. Albert, 99–124. Charlottesville: University of Virginia, 1985.

Emmerich, Roland, dir. *The Patriot*. 158 min. United States: Columbia Pictures, 2000.

Escott, Paul D., and Jeffrey J. Crow. "The Social Order and Violent Disorder: An Analysis of North Carolina in the Revolution and the Civil War." *Journal of Southern History* 52, no. 3 (1986): 373–402.

Eustace, Nicole. *1812: War and the Passions of Patriotism*. Philadelphia: University of Pennsylvania Press, 2012.

———. *Passion Is the Gale: Emotion, Power, and the Coming of the American Revolution*. Chapel Hill: University of North Carolina Press, 2008.

Fehr, Ryan, Michele J. Gelfand, and Monisha Nag. "The Road to Forgiveness: A Meta-Analytic Synthesis of Its Situational and Dispositional Correlates." *Psychological Bulletin* 136, no. 5 (2010): 894–914.

Ferguson, Clyde R. "Functions of the Partisan-Militia in the South, during the American Revolution: An Interpretation." In *The Revolutionary War in the South: Power, Conflict, and Leadership*, edited by W. Robert Higgins, 239–58. Durham, N.C.: Duke University Press, 1979.

Ferling, John E. *A Wilderness of Miseries: War and Warriors in Early America*. Westport, Conn.: Greenwood, 1980.

Fingerhut, Eugene R. "Uses and Abuses of the American Loyalists' Claims: A Critique of Quantitative Analyses." *William and Mary Quarterly* 3rd ser., 25, no. 2 (1968): 245–58.

Ford, Lacy K. *Origins of Southern Radicalism: The South Carolina Upcountry, 1800–1860*. New York: Oxford University Press, 1988.

Foster, Thomas A., ed. *New Men: Manliness in Early America*. New York: New York University Press, 2011.

Fowler, David J. "'Loyalty Is Now Bleeding in New Jersey': Motivations and Mentalities of the Disaffected." In *The Other Loyalists: Ordinary People, Royalism, and the Revolution in the Middle Colonies, 1763–1787*, edited by Joseph S. Tiedemann, Eugene R. Fingerhut, and Robert W. Venables, 45–77. Albany: State University of New York, 2009.

Frech, Laura Page. "The Wilmington Committee of Public Safety and the Loyalist Rising of February 1776." *North Carolina Historical Review* 41 (1964): 1–20.

Freeman, Joanne B. *Affairs of Honor: National Politics in the New Republic*. New Haven, Conn.: Yale University Press, 2001.

———. "Dueling as Politics: Reinterpreting the Burr-Hamilton Duel." *William and Mary Quarterly* 3rd ser., 53, no. 2 (1996): 289–96.

Frey, Sylvia. *Water from the Rock: Black Resistance in a Revolutionary Age*. Princeton, N.J.: Princeton University Press, 1991.

Fryer, Darcy R. "The Mind of Eliza Pinckney: An Eighteenth-Century Woman's Construction of Herself." *South Carolina Historical Magazine* 99, no. 3 (1998): 215–37.

Glenny, Misha. *The Fall of Yugoslavia: The Third Balkan War*. 3rd rev. ed. New York: Penguin Books, 1996.

Godbold, E. Stanley, and Robert H. Woody. *Christopher Gadsden and the American Revolution*. Knoxville: University of Tennessee Press, 1982.

Gordon, John W. *South Carolina and the American Revolution: A Battlefield History*. Columbia: University of South Carolina Press, 2003.

Gorn, Elliot J. "'Gouge and Bite, Pull Hair and Scratch': The Social Significance of Fighting in the Southern Backcountry." *American Historical Review* 90 (1985): 18–43.

Gould, Eliga. "Fears of War, Fantasies of Peace: British Politics and the Coming of the American Revolution." In *Empire and Nation: The American Revolution in the Atlantic World*, edited by Eliga Gould and Peter S. Onuf, 19–34. Baltimore: Johns Hopkins University Press, 2005.

Griswold, Charles L. "The Nature and Ethics of Vengeful Anger." In *Passions and Emotions*, edited by James E. Fleming, 77–124. New York: New York University Press, 2013.

Gross, Robert A., ed. *In Debt to Shays: The Bicentennial of an Agrarian Rebellion*. Charlottesville: University Press of Virginia, 1994.

———. *The Minutemen and Their World*. New York: Hill & Wang, 1976.

Grubb, F. W. "Growth of Literacy in Colonial America: Longitudinal Patterns, Economic Models, and the Direction of Future Research." *Social Science History* 14, no. 4 (1990): 451–82.

Guilds, John Caldwell, and T. C. Duncan Eaves, eds. *Long Years of Neglect: The Work and Reputation of William Gilmore Simms*. Fayetteville: University of Arkansas Press, 1988.

Hall, Leslie. *Land and Allegiance in Revolutionary Georgia*. Athens: University of Georgia Press, 2001.

Handler, Richard, and Eric Gable. *The New History in an Old Museum: Creating the Past at Colonial Williamsburg*. Durham, N.C.: Duke University Press, 1997.

Hargrove, Richard J. "Portrait of a Southern Patriot: The Life and Death of John Laurens." In *The Revolutionary War in the South: Power, Conflict, and Leadership*, edited by W. Robert Higgins, 182–204. Durham, N.C.: Duke University Press, 1979.

Harlow, Ralph Volney. *The History of Legislative Methods in the Period before 1825*. New Haven, Conn.: Yale University Press, 1917.

Harrell, Isaac Samuel. *Loyalism in Virginia*. Durham, N.C.: Duke University Press, 1926.

———. "North Carolina Loyalists." *North Carolina Historical Review* 3 (1926): 575–90.

Hart, Emma. *Building Charleston: Town and Society in the Eighteenth-Century British Atlantic World*. Charlottesville: University of Virginia Press, 2010.

Hast, Adele. *Loyalism in Revolutionary Virginia: The Norfolk Area and the Eastern Shore*. Ann Arbor: University of Michigan Press, 1982.

Haw, James. *John and Edward Rutledge of South Carolina*. Athens: University of Georgia Press, 1997.

Hesseltine, William B. "Lyman Draper and the South." *Journal of Southern History* 19, no. 1 (1953): 20–31.

Heyrman, Christine Leigh. *Southern Cross: The Beginnings of the Bible Belt*. New York: Knopf, 1997.

Higginbotham, Don, ed. *Reconsiderations on the Revolutionary War: Selected Essays*. Westport, Conn.: Greenwood, 1978.

———. "Reflections on the War of Independence, Modern Guerilla Warfare, and the War in Vietnam." In *Arms and Independence: The Military Character of the American Revolution*, edited by Ronald Hoffman and Peter J. Albert, 1–24. Charlottesville: Published for the United States Capitol Historical Society by the University Press of Virginia, 1984.

Higginson, Stephen A. "A Short History of the Right to Petition Government for the Redress of Grievances." *Yale Law Journal* 96, no. 1 (1986): 142–66.

Hodgekiss, Anita. "Petitioning and the Empowerment Theory of Practice." *Yale Law Journal* 96, no. 3 (1987): 569–92.

Hoffman, Ronald, Thad W. Tate, and Peter J. Albert, eds. *An Uncivil War: The Southern Backcountry during the American Revolution.* Charlottesville: Published for the U.S. Capitol Historical Society by the University Press of Virginia, 1985.

Hofstadter, Richard. *The Paranoid Style in American Politics, and Other Essays.* New York: Knopf, 1965.

Holland, Catherine A. *The Body Politic: Foundings, Citizenship, and Difference in the American Political Imagination.* New York: Routledge, 2001.

Holman, C. Hugh. "The Influence of Scott and Cooper on Simms." *American Literature* 23, no. 2 (1951): 203–18.

———. "Simms's Changing Views of Loyalists during the Revolution." *Mississippi Quarterly* 29, no. 4 (1976): 501–13.

———. "William Gilmore Simms' Picture of the Revolution as a Civil Conflict." *Journal of Southern History* 15, no. 4 (1949): 441–62.

Holton, Woody. *Forced Founders: Indians, Debtors, Slaves, and the Making of the American Revolution in Virginia.* Chapel Hill: University of North Carolina Press, 1999.

Hosmer, Charles B. *Presence of the Past: A History of the Preservationist Movement in the United States before Williamsburg.* New York: Putnam, 1965.

Howe, Barbara J. "Women in Historic Preservation: The Legacy of Ann Pamela Cunningham." *Public Historian* 12, no. 1 (1990): 31–61.

Huff, A. V. "The Eagle and the Vulture: Changing Attitudes toward Nationalism in Fourth of July Orations Delivered in Charleston, 1788–1861." *South Atlantic Quarterly* 73 (1974): 10–22.

Iggulden, Emily. "The 'Loyalist Problem' in the Early Republic: Naturalization, Navigation and the Cultural Solution, 1783–1850." Master's thesis, University of New Hampshire, 2008.

Jacobs, Roberta Tansman. "The Treaty and the Tories: The Ideological Reaction to the Return of the Loyalists, 1783–1787." Ph.D. diss., Cornell University, 1974.

Jameson, J. Franklin. *The American Revolution Considered as a Social Movement.* New York: Princeton University Press, 1926.

Jasanoff, Maya. *Liberty's Exiles: American Loyalists in the Revolutionary World.* New York: Knopf, 2011.

Johnson, George Lloyd. "The Evolution of the Welsh Tract, St. David's Parish—the Cheraws District." Ph.D. diss., University of South Carolina, 1995.

Jones, Eldon. "The British Withdrawal from the South, 1781–85." In *The Revolutionary War in the South: Power, Conflict, and Leadership,* edited by W. Robert Higgins, 259–86. Durham, N.C.: Duke University Press, 1979.

Kachun, Mitchell A. *Festivals of Freedom: Memory and Meaning in African American Emancipation Celebrations, 1808–1915.* Amherst: University of Massachusetts Press, 2003.

Kammen, Michael. *Mystic Chords of Memory: The Transformation of Tradition in American Culture.* New York: Knopf, 1991.

Kann, Mark E. *A Republic of Men: The American Founders, Gendered Language, and Patriarchal Politics*. New York: New York University Press, 1998.

Kars, Marjoleine. *Breaking Loose Together: The Regulator Rebellion in Pre-Revolutionary North Carolina*. Chapel Hill: University of North Carolina Press, 2002.

Keesey, Ruth M. "Loyalism in Bergen County, New Jersey." *William and Mary Quarterly* 18, no. 4 (1961): 558–76.

———. "Loyalty and Reprisal: The Loyalists of Bergen County, New Jersey and Their Estates." Ph.D. diss., Columbia University, 1957.

Kelly, C. Brian. "Branded as a Rebel in Scotland, Flora Macdonald Became Embroiled in Another Rebellion in America." *Military History* 14, no. 3 (1997): 82.

Kelman, Herbert C. "Reconciliation from a Social-Psychological Perspective." In *The Social Psychology of Intergroup Reconciliation*, edited by Arie Nadler, Thomas E. Malloy, and Jeffrey D. Fisher, 15–32. New York: Oxford University Press, 2008.

Kerber, Linda K. *Women of the Republic: Intellect and Ideology in Revolutionary America*. Chapel Hill: University of North Carolina Press 1980.

Kermes, Stephanie. "'I Wish for Nothing More Ardently upon Earth, Than to See My Friends and Country Again': The Return of the Massachusetts Loyalists." *Historical Journal of Massachusetts* 30, no. 1 (2002): 30–49.

Kettner, James H. *The Development of American Citizenship, 1608–1870*. Chapel Hill: University of North Carolina Press, 1978.

Klein, Rachel N. *Unification of a Slave State: The Rise of the Planter Class in the South Carolina Backcountry, 1760–1808*. Chapel Hill: University of North Carolina Press, 1990.

Klepp, Susan E. *Revolutionary Conceptions: Women, Fertility, and Family Limitation in America, 1760–1820*. Chapel Hill: University of North Carolina Press, 2009.

Knight, Betsy. "Prisoner Exchange and Parole in the American Revolution." *William and Mary Quarterly* 3rd ser., 48, no. 2 (1991): 201–22.

Knowles, Norman. *Inventing the Loyalists: The Ontario Loyalist Tradition and the Creation of Usable Pasts*. Toronto: University of Toronto Press, 1997.

Kornfeld, Eve. "From Republicanism to Liberalism: The Intellectual Journey of David Ramsay." *Journal of the Early Republic* 9, no. 3 (1989): 289–313.

Krawczynski, Keith. *William Henry Drayton: South Carolina Revolutionary Patriot*. Baton Rouge: Louisiana State University Press, 2001.

Kruman, Marc W. *Between Authority and Liberty: State Constitution Making in Revolutionary America*. Chapel Hill: University of North Carolina Press, 1997.

Lambert, Robert S. "The Confiscation of Loyalist Property in Georgia, 1782–1786." *William and Mary Quarterly* 3rd ser., 20, no. 1 (1963): 80–94.

———.*South Carolina Loyalists in the American Revolution*. Columbia: University of South Carolina Press, 1987.

Lee, Christopher F. "The Transformation of the Executive in Post-Revolutionary South Carolina." *South Carolina Historical and Genealogical Magazine* 93, no. 2 (1992): 85–100.

Lee, Wayne E. *Crowds and Soldiers in Revolutionary North Carolina: The Culture of Violence in Riot and War*. Gainesville: University Press of Florida, 2001.

Levett, Ella Pettit. "Loyalism in Charleston, 1761–1784." Master's thesis, University of South Carolina, 1934.

Lewis, Jan. "The Republican Wife: Virtue and Seduction in the Early Republic." *William and Mary Quarterly* 3rd ser., 44 (1987): 689–721.

Lewis, Kenneth E. *Camden, a Frontier Town in Eighteenth Century South Carolina.* Columbia: Institute of Archaeology and Anthropology of the University of South Carolina, 1976.

Loughran, Trish. *The Republic in Print: Print Culture in the Age of U.S. Nation Building, 1770–1870.* New York: Columbia University Press, 2007.

Lucas, Jeffery P. "Cooling by Degrees: Reintegration of Loyalists in North Carolina, 1776–1790." Master's thesis, North Carolina State University, 2007.

Lumpkin, Henry. *From Savannah to Yorktown: The American Revolution in the South.* Columbia: University of South Carolina Press, 1981.

Lynd, Staughton. "Who Should Rule at Home? Dutchess County, New York in the American Revolution." *William and Mary Quarterly* 3rd ser., 18, no. 3 (1961): 330–59.

Maas, David E. "The Massachusetts Loyalists and the Problem of Amnesty, 1775–1790." In *Loyalists and Community in North America,* edited by Robert M. Calhoon, Timothy M. Barnes, and George A. Rawlyck, 65–75. Westport, Conn.: Greenwood, 1994.

———. *The Return of the Massachusetts Loyalists.* New York: Garland, 1989.

Maier, Pauline. "Popular Uprisings and Civil Authority in Eighteenth-Century America." *William and Mary Quarterly* 3rd ser., 27, no. 1 (1970): 3–35.

Mason, Keith. "The American Loyalist Diaspora and the Reconfiguration of the British Atlantic World." In *Empire and Nation: The American Revolution in the Atlantic World,* edited by Eliga H. Gould and Peter S. Onuf, 239–59. Baltimore: Johns Hopkins University Press, 2005.

———. "Localism, Evangelicalism, and Loyalism: The Sources of Discontent in the Revolutionary Chesapeake." *Journal of Southern History* 56, no. 1 (1990): 23–54.

McCrady, Edward. *The History of South Carolina in the Revolution, 1775–1780.* New York: Macmillan, 1901.

McCrossen, Alexis. *Holy Day, Holiday: The American Sunday.* Ithaca, N.Y.: Cornell University Press, 2000.

McCurry, Stephanie. *Masters of Small Worlds: Yeoman Households, Gender Relations, and the Political Culture of the Antebellum South Carolina Low Country.* New York: Oxford University Press, 1995.

McDonnell, Michael A. *The Politics of War: Race, Class, and Conflict in Revolutionary Virginia.* Chapel Hill: University of North Carolina Press, 2007.

McDonnell, Michael A., Clare Corbould, Frances M. Clarke, and W. Fitzhugh Brundage. *Remembering the Revolution: Memory, History, and Nation Making from Independence to the Civil War.* Amherst: University of Massachusetts Press, 2013.

McDonough, Daniel J. *Christopher Gadsden and Henry Laurens: The Parallel Lives of Two American Patriots.* Sellinsgrove, Penn.: Susquehanna University Press, 2000.

Meleney, John C. *The Public Life of Aedanus Burke: Revolutionary Republican in Post-Revolutionary South Carolina.* Columbia: University of South Carolina Press, 1989.

Messer, Peter C. "From a Revolutionary History to a History of Revolution: David Ramsay and the American Revolution." *Journal of the Early Republic* 22, no. 2 (2002): 205–33.

Moltke-Hansen, David. "Why History Mattered: The Background of Ann Pamela Cunningham's Interest in the Preservation of Mt. Vernon." *Furman Studies* 26 (December 1980): 34–42.

Moore, John Hammond. *South Carolina Newspapers.* Columbia: University of South Carolina Press, 1988.

Morgan, Philip D. *Slave Counterpoint: Black Culture in the Eighteenth-Century Chesapeake and Lowcountry.* Chapel Hill: University of North Carolina Press, 1998.

Morgan, Robert. *Brave Enemies.* Chapel Hill, N.C.: Algonquin, 2003.

Morris, Richard B. "Ending the American Revolution: Lessons for Our Time." In "Peace Research in History," special issue, *Journal of Peace Research* 6, no. 4 (1969): 349–57.

Mount Vernon Ladies Association. *Historical Sketch of Ann Pamela Cunningham, "the Southern Matron."* New York: Printed for the Mount Vernon Ladies Association by Marion Press, 1911.

Murray, John E. "Family, Literacy, and Skill Training in the Antebellum South: Historical-Longitudinal Evidence from Charleston." *Journal of Economic History* 64, no. 3 (2004): 773–99.

Murrin, John M. "The Great Inversion, or Court versus Country: A Comparison of the Revolution Settlements in England (1688–1721) and America (1776–1816)." In *Three British Revolutions: 1641, 1688, 1776,* edited by J. G. A. Pocock, 368–453. Princeton, N.J.: Princeton University Press, 1980.

———. "A Roof without Walls: The Dilemma of American National Identity." In *Beyond Confederation: Origins of the Constitution and American National Identity,* edited by Richard R. Beeman, 333–48. Chapel Hill: University of North Carolina Press, 1987.

Nadelhaft, Jerome J. *The Disorders of War: The Revolution in South Carolina.* Orono: University of Maine at Orono Press, 1981.

———. "'The Snarls of Invidious Animals': The Democratization of Revolutionary South Carolina." In *Sovereign States in an Age of Uncertainty,* edited by Ronald Hoffman and Peter J. Albert, 62–94. Charlottesville: University of Virginia Press, 1981.

New, M. Christopher. *Maryland Loyalists in the American Revolution.* Centreville, Md.: Tidewater, 1996.

Newman, Simon P. *Parades and the Politics of the Street: Festive Culture in the Early American Republic.* Philadelphia: University of Pennsylvania Press, 1997.

Newton, Craig A. "Three Patterns of Local History: South Carolina Historians, 1779–1830." *South Carolina Historical and Genealogical Magazine* 65 (1964): 145–57.

Nobles, Gregory H. "Breaking into the Backcountry: New Approaches to the Early American Frontier, 1750–1800." *William and Mary Quarterly* 3rd ser., 46, no. 4 (1989): 641–70.

Norton, Mary Beth. *The British-Americans: The Loyalist Exiles in England, 1774–1789.* Boston: Little, Brown, 1972.

———. "Eighteenth-Century American Women in Peace and War: The Case of the Loyalists." *William and Mary Quarterly* 3rd ser., 33, no. 3 (1976): 386–409.

———. *Liberty's Daughters: The Revolutionary Experience of American Women, 1750–1800.* Boston: Little, Brown, 1980.

———. "The Problem of the Loyalists—and the Problems of Loyalist Historians." *Reviews in American History* 2, no. 2 (1974): 226–31.

Olwell, Robert. *Masters, Slaves, and Subjects: The Culture of Power in the South Carolina Low Country 1740–1790.* Ithaca, N.Y.: Cornell University Press, 1998.

O'Neall, John Belton. *Biographical Sketches of the Bench and Bar of South Carolina.* Charleston, S.C., 1859.

Ousterhout, Anne M. *A State Divided: Opposition in Pennsylvania to the American Revolution.* New York: Praeger, 1987.

Palfreyman, Brett. "Peace Process: The Reintegration of the Loyalists in Post-Revolutionary America." Ph.D. diss., Binghamton University, 2014.

Palmer, Gregory. *Biographical Sketches of Loyalists of the American Revolution.* Westport, Conn.: Meckler, 1984.

Pancake, John S. *This Destructive War: The British Campaign in the Carolinas, 1780–1782.* University: University of Alabama Press, 1985.

Papas, Phillip. "'That Ever Loyal Island': Loyalism and the Coming of the American Revolution on Staten Island, New York." Ph.D. diss., City University of New York, 2003.

Pasley, Jeffrey L. "Conspiracy Theory and American Exceptionalism from the Revolution to Roswell." Paper presented at "Sometimes an Art": A Symposium in Celebration of Bernard Bailyn's Fifty Years of Teaching and Beyond, Harvard University, Cambridge, Mass., May 13, 2000.

———. *"The Tyranny of Printers": Newspaper Politics in the Early American Republic.* Charlottesville: University Press of Virginia, 2001.

Pearsall, Sarah M. S. *Atlantic Families: Lives and Letters in the Later Eighteenth Century.* New York: Oxford University Press, 2008.

Peckham, Howard H., ed. *The Toll of Independence: Engagements and Battle Casualties of the American Revolution.* Chicago: University of Chicago Press, 1974.

Perry, Benjamin F. "The Revolutionary History of South-Carolina, Reviewed." *Southern Quarterly Review* 11, no. 22 (April 1847): 468–85.

Piecuch, Jim. *Three Peoples One King: Loyalists, Indians, and Slaves in the Revolutionary South, 1775–1782.* Columbia: University of South Carolina Press, 2008.

Porter, Darwin, and Danforth Prince. *Frommer's Portable Charleston.* New York: Wiley, 2003.

Potter, Janice. *The Liberty We Seek: Loyalist Ideology in Colonial New York and Massachusetts.* Cambridge, Mass.: Harvard University Press, 1983.

Power, J. Tracy. "'The Virtue of Humanity Was Totally Forgot': Buford's Massacre, May 29, 1780." *South Carolina Historical and Genealogical Magazine* 93, no. 1 (1992): 5–14.

Purcell, Sarah J. *Sealed with Blood: War, Sacrifice, and Memory in Revolutionary America.* Philadelphia: University of Pennsylvania Press, 2002.

Randall, Willard Sterne. *Alexander Hamilton: A Life.* New York: Harper, 2003.

Rankin, Hugh F. "The Moore's Creek Bridge Campaign, 1776." *North Carolina Historical Review* 30, no. 1 (1953): 33–60.

Rankin, Richard. "'Musqueto' Bites: Caricatures of Lower Cape Fear Whigs and Tories on the Eve of the American Revolution." *North Carolina Historical Review* 65 (1988): 173–207.

Reilly, John Thomas. "The Confiscation and Sale of the Loyalist Estates and Its Effect upon the Democratization of Landholding in New York State: 1799–1800." Ph.D. diss., Fordham University, 1974.

Resch, John Phillips. *Suffering Soldiers: Revolutionary War Veterans, Moral Sentiment, and Political Culture in the Early Republic.* Amherst: University of Massachusetts Press, 1999.

Rogers, George C., Jr. *Charleston in the Age of the Pinckneys.* Norman: University of Oklahoma Press, 1969.

Rosenbaum, Thane. *Payback: The Case for Revenge.* Chicago: University of Chicago Press, 2013.

Rotundo, E. Anthony. *American Manhood: Transformations in Masculinity from the Revolution to the Modern Era.* New York: BasicBooks, 1993.

Royster, Charles. "Founding a Nation in Blood: Military Conflict and American Nationality." In *Arms and Independence: The Military Character of the American Revolution,* edited by Ronald Hoffman and Peter J. Albert, 25–49. Charlottesville: Published for the United States Capitol Historical Society by the University Press of Virginia, 1984.

———. *A Revolutionary People at War: The Continental Army and American Character, 1775–1783.* New York: Norton, 1981.

———. Russell, David Lee. *The American Revolution in the Southern Colonies.* Jefferson, N.C.: McFarland, 2000.

Sabine, Lorenzo. *The American Loyalists, or Biographical Sketches of Adherents to the British Crown in the War of the Revolution.* Boston: Little & Brown, 1847.

Salmon, Marylynn. *Women and the Law of Property in Early America.* Chapel Hill: University of North Carolina Press, 1986.

Sarris, Jonathan Dean. *A Separate Civil War: Communities in Conflict in the Mountain South.* Charlottesville: University of Virginia Press, 2006.

Savage, Kirk. *Standing Soldiers, Kneeling Slaves: Race, War, and Monument in Nineteenth-Century America.* Princeton, N.J.: Princeton University Press, 1997.

Scoggins, Michael C. *The Day It Rained Militia: Huck's Defeat and the Revolution in the South Carolina Backcountry May–July 1780.* Charleston, S.C.: History Press, 2005.

Scott, Anthony J. *Brutal Virtue: The Myth and Reality of Banastre Tarleton.* Bowie, Md.: Heritage Books, 2002.

Sears, John F. *Sacred Places: American Tourist Attractions in the Nineteenth Century.* New York: Oxford University Press, 1989.

Selesky, Harold E. "Colonial America." In *The Laws of War: Constraints on Warfare in the Western World,* edited by Michael Howard, George J. Andrepoulous, and Mark R. Shulman, 59–85. New Haven, Conn.: Yale University Press, 1994.

Shy, John W. *A People Numerous and Armed: Reflections on the Military Struggle for American Independence.* Rev. ed. Ann Arbor: University of Michigan Press, 1990.

Siebert, Wilbur H. "The Dispersion of the American Tories." *Mississippi Valley Historical Review* 1, no. 2 (1914): 185–97.

———. *The Loyalists of Pennsylvania.* Columbus: Ohio State University, 1920.

Singer, Charles Gregg. *South Carolina in the Confederation.* Philadelphia: Porcupine, 1976.

Sirmans, Marion Eugene. *Colonial South Carolina: A Political History, 1663–1763.* Chapel Hill: University of North Carolina Press, 1966.

Slauter, Eric Thomas. *The State as a Work of Art: The Cultural Origins of the Constitution.* Chicago: University of Chicago Press, 2009.

Smith, Don L. "The Right to Petition for Redress of Grievances: Constitutional Development and Interpretations." Ph.D. diss., Texas Tech University, 1971.

Smith, Paul H. "The American Loyalists: Notes on Their Organization and Numerical Strength." *William and Mary Quarterly* 3rd ser., 25, no. 2 (1968): 259–77.

Smith, Rogers S. *Civic Ideals: Conflicting Visions of Citizenship in U.S. History.* New Haven, Conn.: Yale University Press, 1997.

Snipes, Christy. *Rosemont Plantation, Laurens County, South Carolina: A History of the Cunningham Family and Its Life on the Land.* Laurens, S.C.: Laurens County Historical Society, 1992.

Sparshott, Christopher James Macintosh. "The Popular Politics of Loyalism during the American Revolution, 1774–1790." Ph.D. diss., Northwestern University, 2007.

Starr, Raymond Gale. "The Conservative Revolution: South Carolina Public Affairs, 1775–1790." Ph.D. diss., University of Texas at Austin, 1964.

Stauffer, Michael E. *The Formation of Counties in South Carolina.* Columbia: South Carolina Department of Archives and History, 1994.

Stearns, Carol Zisowitz, and Peter N. Stearns. *Anger: The Struggle for Emotional Control in America's History.* Chicago: University of Chicago Press, 1986.

Stock, Catherine McNicol. *Rural Radicals: Righteous Rage in the American Grain.* Ithaca, N.Y.: Cornell University Press, 1996.

Stout, Harry S. *Upon the Altar of the Nation: A Moral History of the American Civil War.* New York: Viking, 2006.

Tiedemann, Joseph S. "Patriots, Loyalists, and Conflict Resolution in New York, 1783–1787." In *Loyalists and Community in North America,* edited by Robert M. Calhoon, Timothy M. Barnes, and George A. Rawlyk, 75–88. Westport, Conn.: Praeger, 1994.

Tillman, Kacy Dowd. "Eliza Lucas Pinckney as Cultural Broker: Reconsidering a South Carolinian Legacy." *Southern Studies: An Interdisciplinary Journal of the South* 18, no. 2 (2011): 49–65.

———. "The Epistolary Salon: Examining Eighteenth-Century American Letter-Writing as a Vehicle for Female Political Engagement." *Literature in the Early American Republic* 3 (2011): 62–80.

Tillson, Albert H., Jr. "The Localist Roots of Backcountry Loyalism: An Examination of Popular Political Culture in Virginia's New River Valley." *Journal of Southern History* 54, no. 3 (1988): 387–404.

———. "The Southern Backcountry: A Survey of Recent Research." *Virginia Magazine of History and Biography* 98 (1990): 387–422.

Townsend, Leah. *South Carolina Baptists 1670–1805.* Florence, S.C.: Genealogical Publishing, 1935.

Travers, Len. *Celebrating the Fourth: Independence Day and the Rites of Nationalism in the Early Republic.* Amherst: University of Massachusetts Press, 1997.

Troxler, Carole Watterson. "Refuge, Resistance, and Reward: The Southern Loyalists' Claim on East Florida." *Journal of Southern History* 55, no. 4 (1989): 563–96.

Ulrich, Laurel Thatcher. "Hannah Barnard's Cupboard: Female Property and Identity in Eighteenth-Century New England." In *Through a Glass Darkly: Reflections on Personal Identity in Early America,* edited by Ronald Hoffman, Mechal Sobel, and Fredericka J. Teute, 238–73. Chapel Hill: University of North Carolina Press, 1997.

United States Senate, Committee on Interior and Insular Affairs. *Ninety-Six and Star Fort National Historic Site Report to Accompany S. 2642.* Washington, D.C.: U.S. Government Printing Office, 1976.

Van Buskirk, Judith L. *Generous Enemies: Patriots and Loyalists in Revolutionary New York.* Philadelphia: University of Pennsylvania Press, 2002.

Varg, Paul A. "The Advent of Nationalism, 1758–1776." *American Quarterly* 16, no. 2, pt. 1 (1964): 169–81.

Waldstreicher, David. *In the Midst of Perpetual Fetes: The Making of American Nationalism, 1776–1820.* Chapel Hill: University of North Carolina Press, 1997.

Walsh, Richard. *Charleston's Sons of Liberty: A Study of the Artisans 1763–1789.* Columbia: University of South Carolina Press, 1959.

Weigley, Russell Frank. *The Partisan War: The South Carolina Campaign of 1780–1782.* Columbia: University of South Carolina Press, 1970.

Weir, Robert M. "'The Harmony We Were Famous For': An Interpretation of Pre-Revolutionary South Carolina Politics." *William and Mary Quarterly* 3d. ser., 26, no. 4 (1969): 473–501.

———. *"A Most Important Epocha": The Coming of the Revolution in South Carolina.* Columbia: University of South Carolina Press, 1970.

———. "The Violent Spirit, the Reestablishment of Order, and the Continuity of Leadership in Post-Revolutionary South Carolina." In *An Uncivil War: The Southern Backcountry during the American Revolution,* edited by Ronald Hoffman, Thad W. Tate, and Peter J. Albert, 70–98. Charlottesville: University of Virginia Press, 1985.

———. "Who Shall Rule at Home: The American Revolution as a Crisis of Legitimacy for the Colonial Elite." *Journal of Interdisciplinary History* 6, no. 4 (1976): 679–700.

West, Patricia. *Domesticating History: The Political Origins of America's House Museums.* Washington, D.C.: Smithsonian Institution Press, 1999.

Wilson, David K. *The Southern Strategy: Britain's Conquest of South Carolina and Georgia, 1775–1780.* Columbia: University of South Carolina Press, 2005.

Wilson, Lisa. *Ye Heart of a Man: The Domestic Life of Men in Colonial New England.* New Haven, Conn.: Yale University Press, 1999.

Wilson, Timothy James. "'Old Offenders': Loyalists in the Lower Delmarva Peninsula, 1775–1800." Ph.D. diss., University of Toronto, 1998.

Wimsatt, Mary Ann. *The Major Fiction of William Gilmore Simms: Cultural Traditions and Literary Forms.* Baton Rouge: Louisiana State University Press, 1989.

Wingfield, Nancy M. *Flag Wars and Stone Saints: How the Bohemian Lands Became Czech.* Cambridge, Mass.: Harvard University Press, 2007.

Wood, Gordon S. "Conspiracy and the Paranoid Style: Causality and Deceit in the Eighteenth Century." *William and Mary Quarterly* 3rd ser., 39, no. 3 (1982): 401–41.

Worden, Blair. *Roundhead Reputations: The English Civil Wars and the Passions of Posterity.* London: Lane, 2001.

Wyatt-Brown, Bertram. *Honor and Violence in the Old South.* New York: Oxford University Press, 1986.

Yoshpe, Harry Beller. *The Disposition of Loyalist Estates in the Southern District of the State of New York.* New York: Columbia University Press, 1939.

Young, Alfred Fabian. *The Democratic Republicans of New York: The Origins, 1763–1797.* Chapel Hill: University of North Carolina Press, 1967.

Zagarri, Rosemarie. *Revolutionary Backlash: Women and Politics in the Early American Republic.* Philadelphia: University of Pennsylvania Press, 2007.

Zeichner, Oscar. "The Loyalist Problem in New York after the Revolution." *New York History* 21, no. 3 (1940): 284–302.

———. "The Rehabilitation of Loyalists in Connecticut." *New England Quarterly* 11, no. 2 (1938): 308–30.

Index

Page references given in *italics* indicate illustrations or their captions.

Lexington and Concord, Battles of (1775), 12
literacy, 107
local communities: character witnesses from, 116–17; citizenship and, 88–90; epistolary campaigns from, 91; Loyalist militias subverted by, 85–86; Loyalist reconciliation and, 6, 68, 73–74, 76, 128–29; petitions and, 64; print culture in, 183n7; support from, and Loyalist reconciliation, 8–9, 90–96
Loocock, Aaron, 79
Lord, Ann Gadsden, 134
Love, Matthew, 59
lowcountry South Carolina: black majority in, 13, 15, 130, 137; British estate sequestration in, 35; British occupation of, after surrender, 36; Loyalist punishment in, 133; Loyalist reconciliation in, 47; post-Yorktown skirmishes in, 43; pre-Revolution political geography of, 13
Lowndes, Rawlins, 19
Loyalist diaspora: black Loyalists and, 5–6, 63, 112; from Charleston, 112, 128; Confiscation Act and, 62–63; extent of, 175n6 (Intro.), 184n23; Loyalist reconciliation and, 116; Patriot efforts to stoke fears about, 42; in public historical memory, 143–45, *144*; scholarship on, 5; slavery and, 1–2
Loyalist militias: commanders of, and Confiscation Act, 52, 55, 59, 83, 98, 105, 116–18; community collusion against, 85–86; plunder/destruction by, 3–4, 25–27, 86, 116–17; recruitment attempts for, 18; reputation of, 18–19; service in, and citizenship, 86–87
Loyalist press, 62, 112
Loyalist punishment: civil war legacy and, 34; confiscation opponents and end of, 102–3; democratization of, 56–59; emotional logic of, 36–41; intent of, 36; legislative deliberations over, 7–8, 41–51, 62; Loyalist reconciliation

vs., 52; Patriot mildness in application of, 4–5. *See also* Amercement Act (1782); Confiscation Act (1782)
Loyalist reconciliation/reintegration: apologies as essential to, 73–76; character defenses for, 82–90, *89*, 116; character witness testimony for, 116–17; civil suits and, 8, 58; class solidarity and, 125–26; clemency and, 120–25; economics and, 131–33; elite favoritism and, 133–34; excuses given for Loyalist affiliation and, 76–82; legacy of, 173; local support as essential to, 6, 8–9, 90–96, 128–29; Loyalist punishment vs., 52; Loyalist strategies toward, 9, 111–19; mob violence incidents and, 114–15, 123–24; multigenerational, 189n24; partisan politics and, 129–30; Patriot reasons for pursuing, 42–45, 131–34; personal negotiations over, 51; petitions as avenue for, 9, 63–66, 76–82, *77*; post-1784 improvements, 9–10, 134–39; public advocacy for, 99–111; public historical memory and, 141, 170–71; in South Carolina vs. other states, 125–34; timing of, 126–28; women's petitions, 64–65, 66–72. *See also* clemency; petitions/petitioning
Loyalists: anti-Patriot retribution by, 25–26, 37; casualties suffered by, 32; Confiscation Act and, 35; female, petitions of, 64–65, 66–72; female, status of, 181n18; ideological, 123–24; literary portrayals of, 164–67; pragmatic reasons for becoming, 1, 15–22, 81–82, 90, 97–99, 167; scholarship on, 5; social diversity of, 5–6, 15; use of term, xiii; violence against, 10, 104, 107, 123–24; voting rights of, 60–61; wartime persecution of, 23–25, 37. *See also* black Loyalists; Loyalist militias; Loyalist punishment; Loyalist reconciliation/reintegration; white Loyalists
Lynah, James, 87

Maas, David E., 130, 186n44
MacDonald, Flora, 23
Machiavelli, Niccolò, 105
Mackey, Eleanor, 71
Mackey, James, 70–71, 117
Madison, James, 88, 148
Marion, Francis, 154; as Confiscation
    Act opponent, 100–102, 103; corre-
    spondence of, 1, 41–42, 103, 178n12;
    descendants of, 155; Jacksonborough
    Assembly location choice and, 43,
    46; as Patriot militia commander, 25,
    29; Simms biography of, 165; spies
    reporting to, 62–63; testimony of, in
    clemency hearings, 117–18
Maryland, Loyalist reintegration in,
    155–56
Massachusetts, Loyalist reconciliation in,
    113, 126, 186n44
Massachusetts Historical Society, 162
Massachusetts Loyalists, 126
Mathews, John, 58–59
Mazyck, Stephen, 97
McGillivray, Ann, 70
Mellichampe (Simms), 166–67
Methodists, 138
Middleton, Arthur, 38, 42, 69, 179n25
military passes, 9, 102
militia warfare, 8, 27–32, 36, 37. *See also*
    Loyalist militias; Patriot militias
mob violence, 10, 91, 104, 114–15, 138
Moore's Creek Bridge, Battle of (1776), 23
motherhood, Republican view of in new
    nation, 71
Moultrie, Alexander, 72
Moultrie, William, 138
Mount Vernon (Fairfax County, Va.), 7,
    140, 161–62
Mount Vernon Ladies Association, 140,
    162
Murray, Patrick Muckle, 86–87
Murrell, Robert, Jr., 136
Murrin, John, 90

Nash, Gary, 20

national identity, 90
nationalism, 171–72. *See also* southern
    nationalism
Native Americans, xiii, 13, 15, 21–22, 137;
    American Revolution fueled by, 100;
    petitioning rights of, 64
naturalizations, 87–88
natural law, 100
neighborliness, 82, 96
New England Loyalists, 15, 126, 159
New Orleans, Battle of (1815), 148–49
newspapers, 62, 94, 100, 107–9, 115, 183n7
New York: anti-Loyalist legislation in,
    36, 125; civil war in, 13, 127; Loyalist
    reconciliation advocacy in, 104, 109;
    Loyalist reconciliation in, 125, 127,
    186n42
New York City, 43, 129
Ninety Six district, 15, 27, *93*, 114, 156
North Carolina: anti-Loyalist legislation
    in, 23, 36, 56, 179n35; Loyalist recon-
    ciliation in, 108, 126, 186n49; post-
    Yorktown skirmishes in, 43
North Carolina Loyalists, 23, 58, 128
Norton, Mary Beth, 181n18
Nova Scotia, 5, 42, 109, 112
nullification controversy (1830), 158

oaths of allegiance, 24–25, 53, 82, 84–85
office-holding, ban on, 122
"O Fly, Cries Peace" (illustration; Sto-
    thard), *110*
orphans, 84, 111, 137, 184n22
Osterhaut, Anne, 130

Paine, Thomas, 100
Paine, William, 162–63
Palmetto Day, 23, 146, 149–50
"paranoid style," 80
Pardon Act (1782), 45, 58, 60
Paris, Treaty of (1783), 59, 108, 131
Park, George, 26
Parliament (British), 87
paroles, 17–18
Partisan, The (Simms), 165, 166

women: Confiscation Act and, 55–56, 57, 67, 68, 113; Loyalist, 181n18; petitioning rights of, 64–65, 66–72, 113, 124; political roles of, 66

Wood, Gordon, 80

Woodcraft (Simms), 166, 189n40

Wragg, John, 48–49, 134

Yorktown, Battle of (1781), 3–4, 12, 13, 17, 35–36, 43, 150

Young, Alfred Fabian, 186n47

Zeichner, Oscar, 130, 186n48

Zubly, John Joachim, 74–75